D1707097

Community Impact
Creating Grassroots Change
in Hard Times

HN
90
C6
B47

Community Impact
Creating Grassroots Change in Hard Times

by
William R. Berkowitz

12/12/83 mu

CALIFORNIA SCHOOL OF PROFESSIONAL PSYCHOLOGY LOS ANGELES

SCHENKMAN PUBLISHING COMPANY, INC.
Cambridge, Massachusetts

Copyright © 1982

Schenkman Publishing Company, Inc.
3 Mount Auburn Place
Cambridge, MA 02138

Library of Congress Cataloging in Publication Data

Berkowitz, William R., 1939–
  Community Impact

  Bibliography: p.
  Includes index.
  1. Community organization – United States. 2. United
States – Social conditions. I. Title.
HN90.C6B47   973   81-14617
ISBN 0-87073-447-4   AACR2
ISBN 0-87073-448-2 (pbk.)

Printed in the United States of America.

All rights reserved. This book, or parts thereof, may not be reproduced
in any form without written permission from the publisher.

*In a world where there is so much
to be done, I felt strongly impressed that
there must be something for me to do.*

— Dorothea Dix

A Word to the Reader

This book is about creating social change in your own community setting. It emphasizes small-scale changes, within the average person's grasp. It aims to strengthen your ability and your desire to create those changes, and therefore the type of community you want.

The underlying rationale is simple: An era of government leadership in implementing social programs is over. Publicly funded professional helping agencies and services will be caught in a progressively worsening dollar crunch. In the future, people will be forced to rely more and more upon their own neighborhoods and communities for social and economic support. They will have to build new community supports for themselves. To do so, they will have to change things from the way they are now.

What will this take? Community-building skills, to begin with. All of us ought to be as proficient as we can in assessing needs, in planning, in program execution, and in evaluation. And all of us ought to appreciate the value of carrying out the simple, cut-and-dried, day-to-day tasks which make things happen. But skill has to be combined with the willingness to use it—with motivation, and with confidence in the skills we already have. This book hopes to strengthen both skill and will.

The writing here is intended as a guide for people who are currently involved in a community activity, or who may become involved later on. This includes community leaders (present or aspiring), club and church group members, volunteers, any person with concern. It includes students in psychology, sociology, social work, any of the helping professions. And it includes professionals in service agencies—they have a special role to play, as we will see shortly.

Most social commentators of the day forecast hard times of one degree or another. Many of these same commentators also argue that hard times will actually be better times, that a lowered material standard of living will mark a return to more enduring values and a richer personal and social life. I subscribe to the first forecast, but am less certain about the second. Up to a point, economic hard times can bring people closer together and enrich the quality of their lives. But it's only a possibility, by no means a given; hard times can also drive people apart. To take advantage of the possibility will require us to make our communities more supportive places to live, and, more generally, to increase our community impact.

If these ideas make sense to you, then let's begin.

Contents

1
Introduction

DIGGING IN

The mood is one of digging in. No single word or image can describe the American social climate in full. But the image that recurs most often for me is a homestead on a chilly November afternoon, the householders bringing things in from the yard, chopping the rest of the wood, tightening up the inside of the house, getting ready for winter.

Retrenchment tightens its hold. A familiar litany: American society in decline, the best of times a memory, social programs as failures, inflation as a way of life, energy shortages, stagnating productivity, resource depletion, foreign competition, global confrontation, second-rate power, diminished expectations, doing with less. The litany is worn by now. Whether true or not, repetition grinds it into the hearts of its hearers, feeding the spirit of retrenchment, hastening the rate of digging in.

On a national scale, retrenchment manifests itself statistically and in vignettes. It's not hard to document that social welfare expenditures have peaked; that charitable contributions appear to be levelling off; that a large and increasing majority feels overtaxed; that the percentage of self-identified conservatives is on the rise; that real spendable incomes are falling; and that national expectations are falling along with them.[1]

This list is incomplete, for we are not attempting a complete problem statement. The items noted in it are selective, fluctuating, at a distance from daily life. You can draw your own statistical portrait; or perhaps better, simply look into your everyday exper-

1

ience, read the newspaper, watch the titles at your local bookstore, talk to your friends. Check your evidence against mine.

For me, the most significant single indicator of national retrenchment is the lack of a national social vision, a clearly articulated statement of where we want to go and how we can get there. The New Deal and the Great Society, whatever their flaws in conception and execution, provided a focus for collective social aspiration, a social growing edge. But this time we lack both focus and edge. If there is a vision at all, it is a vision in absentia, in the sense of government uncoupling itself from many of its prior social functions, encouraging citizens and corporations to pursue private concerns as best they can. The social planner, not to mention the utopian dreamer, is regarded with suspicion, or as a bit of a fool, or both. The social visionary is a frisbee player in a hardball world.

National government, having played out its inning, hands the ball back to the individual. State and local governments follow in turn. With less government intervention and taxation, the individual should simultaneously become freer to shape life and take more responsibility for it. Whether or not this is desirable public policy is not the issue here; the point is that it appears to be the actual policy of our time. This is the policy we have to reckon with, and there is no turnaround in view.

One problem with this policy is that in difficult times individuals act like nations. They retrench. When nations feel their security threatened, they increase their appropriations for defense and cut back on other spending. So do individuals, in their way. Individual defense expenditures do not result in missiles and bombers, but in barricades between the self and the outside world. People under economic stress pull closer into themselves, guard against attack, engage in personal energy conservation.[2]

And as nations cut back on social expenditures, individuals do too. They narrow their vision, reduce their contacts, deal mainly with those they have to help or who can help them. To believe that, under economic pressure, either individuals or the combined private sector will automatically assume full responsibility for the benefits previously conferred by governments – that is genuinely utopian. On the contrary, unless there is visible and compelling incentive, individuals and groups give less when they have less to give. Forces for self-preservation are stronger than forces prompting sacrifice for others. Moreover, personal fortification and constriction stimulate distrust, cynicism, bitterness, and despair – each of them toxins to collective social organization. Social problems intensify, and digging in accelerates; each fuels the other. The spirit of retrenchment grows stronger.

This diagnosis is abbreviated, since diagnosis is not our purpose here. In any case, the symptoms are clear and bright. The time at our disposal is not unlimited. The question is what is to be done?

AN IDEAL SOCIETY

I believe that an ideal society is still possible, that utopian dreams are still worth dreaming. If we cannot fully achieve the ideal, we can at least achieve a high-order approximation. The loss of government leadership in social programs does not doom us, and should the national economy move from wobble to slide, that is not the end of the road. This is because the requirements for the good life are simple at the core. Food on the table, good health, a roof, a sense of physical security, people to love and like, meaningful work, peace of mind – these are still the basics, and there is solid evidence that these basics are still most highly valued, seen as sufficient conditions for a happy and meaningful existence.[3] Most everything else is postponable.

The ideal society ensures these basics, then moves beyond them, from happiness to joy, and from meaningfulness to fulfillment. My ideal is unelaborated here, and yours may differ. To approximate your ideal or mine, even to maintain what we have now, will take a substantial amount of personal commitment and organizational skill. It will certainly require a powerful incentive, largely self-induced. But I believe that most parts of the society that most of us want can be brought about without excessive time investment; without high reliance on money; without great dependence on material resources, energy supplies, or the gross national product; without specialized knowledge beyond the grasp of the average person; without close attachment to governments or formal institutions; and without political struggle or violent confrontation. I believe too that this society can come about through the actions of ordinary people, spiritually untransformed if need be, complete with flaws.

One key to the ideal is the planning and implementation of small-scale social change activities on a community level, by community people, with professional encouragement when necessary. Cooperatives, exchanges, communication networks, self-help groups, training programs, citizen associations are some broad-brush examples. These activities can be formal or informal, structured or not. But their common goal is the strengthening of helping relationships and community support systems. The concept of a community support system in particular is at the heart of this book and needs some further expansion.

COMMUNITY SUPPORT SYSTEMS

The community.

The emphasis in scale here is on the community and neighborhood levels. "Community" has no rigidly defined size, but the modal figure I have in mind is about 10,000; neighborhoods may be several degrees smaller. If national social vision fades, if state and local governments tighten their purses and lower their sights, it makes sense to pay more attention to the next level down the organizational ladder. And there are distinct advantages to working at the community level. The community is large enough to hold a diversity of human resources, including technical specialists. It's large enough to be economically self-sufficient. But it is small enough so that each member can know many, or most, of the other people within it. On a community level, it's simpler to get people involved.

Involvement may come easier because peer pressures are harder to avoid. Yet it's also easier to feel that one is getting things done, and to get things done in fact. Local involvement occurs because its rewards are quicker, more perceptible, more tangible. Rhetorical flourishes like "shared control over shared destiny" can take on real meaning. Finally, when things do get done well, social bonds among the participants are tightened, providing additional satisfaction, maintaining the focus of life energy within the community, and reinforcing the disposition to stay involved in the future.

We can cite historical evidence to back up the choice of community scale. The first small communities have been associated with the beginnings of morality and of the neighborhood relationship, with promoting order, stability, decentralized power, and responsibility.[4] One recent study of community life notes that ancient and medieval urban centers tended to stabilize at populations of 5,000 – 10,000; that organization into relatively small communities appears to be one of the very few cultural universals; and that ". . . the oldest institution is not the family, as is popularly thought, but the community."[5] The early dominance of small-community life in America and its contributions to our culture are of course well known.[6]

We can also make two fairly confident future projections: (a) should the economic climate get worse, the extent and impact of publicly funded social services will decline; and (b) should energy become more expensive and scarce, travel for both business and pleasure will decrease. Now, combine the two: people will then be spending more time in their own communities and neighborhoods. And, as institutional support systems weaken, they will have to create new supports for themselves right there. We discuss both these projections at greater length in the last chapter. The point for now is that people will need to rely more and more on those living close by them – as once they did – out of necessity if not also out of choice.

A few disclaimers. Community life is not the only level of social organization deserving of attention. It's vitally important to forge a world order, to work out appropriate roles for any level of government, and to find ways of living more harmoniously in families. And it's not our intent to sugar-coat community life, nor to regard it as a cure for social ills. It's rather that anyone wanting to make the world better, private citizen or public servant, has to decide where to invest the bulk of one's world-bettering assets. Where is the point of greatest impact? Where can one get the highest rate of return? Though each of us starts with different assets and objectives, there's good reason to think that, especially now, community enterprises are a timely investment choice.

Support systems.

If two basic structural concepts in pursuing the ideal are the community and neighborhood, their functional counterparts are mutual helping relationships and support systems. Structure and function are related, since in many (most?) cases help and support can more easily, more economically, and more effectively be given by the community rather than by higher-level organizations. There are significant exceptions: for example, the community may be less able than the state to provide extended dollar assistance or highly specialized care. And mutual help and support are of course not the only components of an ideal society – they will be shaped by (and also help to shape) a physical and economic base. But the social base, and the helping/supportive relationships forming it, will be our primary concern here. While "helping" is well understood, "support systems" are less so, and a few explanatory paragraphs are in order.[7]

A social support system in general terms is an array of individuals, groups, and organizations which maintains order and gives meaning to a person's social existence. The family unit, nuclear or otherwise, is frequently but not always the primary source of support. Other sources: extended family members, housemates, friends, and neighbors; the work organization, including bosses, subordinates, and coworkers; membership groups, such as churches, clubs, unions, professional associations; acquaintances, even people you know by face only; social institutions, including local government, schools, mass media, and particularly social service agencies, whose specific function is often to provide support not available elsewhere.

Collectively, a support system is the stage set – or the "supporting cast" – through which one plays out a life. The exact cast members and their relative importance will vary from person to person and for the same person over time. But taken together, social supports perform several distinct and far-reaching functions.

Think about your own support system, and what it does for you. It sustains you, both passively and actively. To start with, it gives you *security*, just by being there, like money in the bank you never touch. More actively, it provides *recognition*; you are known, as a person. It confers *affirmation*; you are worthwhile, a valuable person. People in your support system can extend *task-oriented assistance*, ranging from watering the plants when you are away, to providing information on your legal rights, to offering cash payments when you are dead broke. They can give *emotional comfort* when you need a sympathetic ear, or someone to guide you through a personal crisis. Your support system stimulates your *participation* in community life, by allowing you to express your competence, and by supplying you with chances to reciprocate the support you have received. And finally, your supports promote *personal growth,* by making it easier to take risks; you have the backing to try, the encouragement along the way, the approval if you succeed, the cushioning should you fall.

All of this would be so much literary footwork were it not for research findings, many of them recent, which confirm our starting beliefs about the importance of supports:

1. The presence of an effective support system protects against emotional illness and contributes strongly to feelings of psychological well-being. Acquisition of appropriate new supports tends toward the same general result.

2. The absence of an effective support system is a major determinant of emotional illness. Analogously, the loss of existing social supports can cause both emotional and physical disruption.

3. Stress normally leads to an increase in support-seeking behavior within the prevailing support system, and to a corresponding decrease in other social contacts.

4. Repeated failures to secure adequate support increase tendencies toward personal and social disorganization.[8]

What do these findings mean for our own lives?

STRONGER SUPPORTS: NOT EASILY FOUND

Most of us have operating support systems of one kind or another.

Some of us live in loving families, in warm and tight-knit neighbor-hoods, among close friends, with secure and fulfilling work, and with as many social connections as we can handle. Some others are single, transient, friendless, jobless, and alone. The bulk of us fall somewhere in the middle; our support systems function tolerably, but are imperfect. Whether because of time or money pressures, shyness or other personal flaws, bad luck or poor timing, we feel a vague (or not-so-vague) unease about our lives, that we are missing something in our dealings with others, that we are neither as sus-tained by them, nor as sustaining of them, as we would like to be.[9]

There is plenty of room for most of us to broaden and deepen our personal support systems. We may choose to ration intimacy carefully, but contact, warmth, and caring are easier to divide and harder to exhaust. There is room especially to build supports out-side our immediate households, in our community settings, the next ring out from the core. The benefits are clear: tangible assist-ance when it's needed, good will around the clock, a safety net, an inflation hedge, shared values, shared meaning in life, a bonding to the community, a kind of social security that could never be delivered through a check in the mail.

I'll step up the argument here and suggest that the strengthening of personal supports in the community is not only theoretically desirable, but will become close to practically necessary. The need for local supports should increase markedly, for reasons soon to fol-low. And new types of supports will be called for, often depending on group as well as individual initiative. We will be obliged to create new opportunities for involvement and participation, speci-fic pathways for maintaining or improving the quality of commu-nity life. In the future, we are likely to see more home-spun but carefully woven supports such as block associations, parent cooper-atives, skills exchanges, mediation centers, youth service projects, community gardens, anticrime patrols, after-school programs, pot-luck suppers, home sharing, car pools, ad hoc action committees, and barter economies. None of these is new to the loom, but all con-tain the fiber from which lasting community supports are made.

The problem is that while a smile or a caring personal gesture can be easily managed, more complex supportive activities like those above are something else again. They can't be plucked from the air, or bought off the shelf; they have to be *created*, though not necessarily from scratch. They require resisting the tendency to pull back in. They take work, sometimes collective work. To build new supports means to *change* something, and success will then depend on: (a) an active commitment to change, and (b) an ability to make change happen, to get what you want. The chances are slim that someone else will create the change you want for you, and slimmer still that the change will happen entirely by itself. Anyone seeking change must become a change agent. The intent of this book is to help you become a better one.

If you've followed the flow of the discussion so far, and if you're sympathetic to the main points made, you might ask why community support systems are not nearly as strong as they could be. We've all experienced the emotional highs that come from people pulling together. But why don't we experience them more often? Why don't more of us share feelings of close community? And why do so many of us feel fragmented, isolated, split into little compartments?

We can offer several plausible reasons why. First, we may lack the concrete knowledge, the organizational skills, to create the needed supports. (There's some truth to this, but less than meets the eye.) Second, we may lack the requisite confidence – we see ourselves as being powerless, inadequate, less competent than we really are. Third, we may lack sufficient motivation to spend the time; there's no overpowering incentive, no apparent crisis, no immediate necessity. Fourth, we may lack the basic physical and/or emotional energy to take on something new and probably unpaid, for making a living is tough enough, and when the sun sets we are more than ready to pitch our tents for the night.

All these reasons are close on target, but don't quite cover the bull's-eye. We need an understanding that goes beyond the citation of personal deficits. This understanding is social, not individual; it would explain why on the one hand people are *capable* of magnificent community efforts, yet why on the other citizen-initiated community supports may be no more developed now than they were several generations ago, and possibly less.

I think part of this understanding may emerge from examining how helping and support systems have evolved in Western society, in America in particular, and how helping power has moved steadily from individuals to institutions. This is only one vantage point, but an important one, and one not very often highlighted in writings on community change. We'll take the space to highlight it here and to develop it as a chapter theme. In doing so, our hope will be to appreciate better why institutional helping services can inhibit natural support development; why many existing supports are presently threatened; and why professional helping agencies must realign their services and work more closely with community people to build new community supports together.

THE INSTITUTIONALIZATION OF HELPING SERVICES

As a society develops, the diversity of the helping relationships within it expands and the concentration of those relationships shifts.[10] The outer edge of social organization moves historically from the individual within a clan or kinship group to the village, the town, the city, the nation-state. Social support systems follow along in parallel. So does social vision, and the range of social concerns; they move progressively outward, like the date-rings of a tree. The United Nations, the concepts of "world citizen" and "Spaceship Earth," are twentieth-century visions, even if internalized by only a small minority.

The basis for the expansion of helping relationships is largely economic. Brecht put it well: "Grub first, then ethics." When necessities of life are scarce, competition for them is keen. Sharing is limited to a tight circle of people, immediate blood ties. Sharing beyond the circle may then conflict with the biological drive for individual survival; in any case, it requires a well-developed moral consciousness.

With economic development, with societal growth, there are more resources to share. Technology increases the physical assets which one can give to another. Pressure to give to others increases too, partly because resources become more unequally distributed, partly because there is more actual time for outside social and moral concerns. The society can now afford to subsidize people whose function is to extend the boundaries of those concerns—spiritual leaders, for example. In other words, the message to help becomes centralized. In Western civilization, the major early central force for helping was the church.

But as the helping message is centralized, the form of help given begins to change. In a preindustrial society, helping and support are more personal. Family members are numerous and close by. The setting of daily life is small in diameter. Mobility is low. The one needing help may have nowhere else to turn. The one able to give is likely to know both the needy person and the circumstances. Mutual aid may be seen as necessary to maintain the local social structure, the only social structure there is. These conditions bring out feelings of personal responsibility.

The same sense of responsibility cannot be maintained with industrialization. Industrialization stimulates mobility and transiency, drawing people to where wealth is stored. Industrialization concentrates people in dense urban environments. Early industrialization spurred population growth. All industrialization loosens people from their traditional support systems. A new migrant to the city may have left family and friends at home. Extra support is needed to cope with the unfamiliar and competitive demands of city life. But less may be received. The migrant knows fewer people now, is known by fewer as well. The potential helper, whose own life demands are increased, in turn sees that people needing help are beyond personal capacity to assist. They may be worse off than before, but there are simply too many of them. And the helper does not know who they are. The same sense of responsibility cannot exist. A personal bond has been broken.

The last paragraph describes nineteenth-century America. The American solution to the problem was to institutionalize it. What was institutionalized was not just the message to help, but helping resources themselves. Money, credits, information, guidance, economic and social supports of all descriptions were funneled through centralized sources designed to dispense help in much the same way as retail stores dispense goods.[11] The sponsoring organizations were at first private associations and charities. But as the country grew wealthier, publicly funded assistance became more feasible and more prevalent. Substantial state and then federal involvement in "human services" – a twentieth-century term – was a natural outcome. It was mostly a twentieth-century outcome; the relative recency of government intervention is easily forgotten. Such interventions tend to be taken for granted in a country where the median age is about thirty.

In the generation after World War II, government-funded helping resources expanded at a rate which had never been seen before and which will probably never be seen again. Between 1950 and 1975, public social welfare expenditures rose from 8.9 percent to 19.9 percent of GNP, and from 37.4 percent to 57.9 percent of all government outlays. Parallel figures for the federal government alone rose even more sharply.[12] Other illustrations: the number of programs in the former Department of Health, Education, and Welfare tripled between 1961 and 1973.[13] Real-dollar federal contributions to the poor on a per capita basis quadrupled between 1964 and 1980.[14] Most other federal social programs not specifically targeted toward the poor continued to grow, or at least hold their own, through the end of the Carter administration.[15]

These resources were typically made available through human service agencies, often newly minted for the purpose. You can verify this through your own experience by noting what percentage of the service agencies in your own community were present fifty, twenty-five, or even ten years ago. The formation of new agencies created millions of new public service jobs, many of which could only be filled by persons with specialized training – by "helping professionals." The new professionals were quick to identify social problems that called on their expertise and required continued government funding. The net result was an accelerated institution-alization of economic and social supports. As late as the mid-1970s, a former secretary of Health, Education, and Welfare could write:

> To enhance the well-being of individuals in the present-day environment and the immediate years ahead will require, it seems to me, that human service organizations play a more diversified and increased role in the lives of more people. . . . Despite temporary setbacks, it seems inevitable that public funding of human services organizations will continue to increase in the future.[16]

The institutionalized helping system has definite advantages. A person desiring help and knowing where to look can choose from a variety of organizations available, and occasionally competing, to serve. The range of services in most mid-sized communities or larger appears in theory to encompass every significant human need. For certain problems, some agencies can provide direct financial aid, surely stretching beyond the capacity of single benevolent individuals. The nonmonetary helping skills of agency professionals are frequently superior to those found elsewhere. Agency staff, knowing the other helping resources in the community (often, other agencies), can make useful referrals and give sound practical advice. They can sometimes pull strings. And more often than not they can give assistance for as long as is needed – once engaged in the system, the client becomes an organizational responsibility, not easily tossed aside. Despite their faults, we could do much worse as a society than to preserve if not expand the institutional supports now in place.

INSTITUTIONAL PROBLEMS

But there is a darker side.

1. When support systems are institutionalized, help becomes less personal. The helpers generally do not know the people they are helping before they meet, by the very fact that the helping organization is public, open to all who are eligible. Helping is a job; helpers are workers, even if their work is social work. Most helpers work 9-to-5. Most get paid. Many live outside the community, di-vorced from community life. All are accountable to higher-level bureaucracies – funding sources, or boards of directors, or central offices, or all three – often still further removed from those being served. Help may be given more from job-role than from moral

obligation, more from supervisory requirement than from personal concern.

2. Helping may be used as a means of social control (cf. footnote 11). The helping agency holds the cards. To get help, the recipient has to play by its rules. The rules are established to ensure that the recipient acts in ways the agency finds acceptable. If the recipient deviates, the agency may threaten to withhold help, and sometimes carry out its threat. By controlling rewards, the agency shapes behavior – for an undoubted good, if one agrees with agency standards and goals; for a questionable good, if one observes that to get help the recipient must stifle individuality and conform to an alien value system.

3. The person needing help usually must reach out and ask the helping organization for it. Most such organizations, seeing themselves already buried with work, do not seek out new clients. The paradox is that those most in need are often precisely those least able or willing to make a first approach. They are isolated, uninformed, perhaps incompetent. They do not know what to do or where to go; or if they do, they hold onto their dignity by rejecting outside assistance. Family or friends could direct them to services, but again the most needy are the least likely to have such sources of support to begin with. Getting help requires knowledge and motivation, and many needing help may lack one or both. They then go unserved.

4. The helping process may be accompanied by suspicion and derogation. The helpers, who tend to come from (or settle into) more affluent circumstances than recipients, may not comprehend the lifestyle or the motivations of the people they are helping. (Helpers recently up from below are frequently the harshest critics.) There is social distance, as well as impersonality. But helpers are trained professionals – they know what to do. If advice is not followed or benefit is not derived, the problem cannot be with the helper, nor with the system which pays the helper, but rather with the stupidity and ingratitude of the recipient. To mock and blame one's clients, in small groups and behind their backs, is daily bread; blaming is easy shop talk, a source of humor, an outlet for frustrations, a projection of deficiencies.

5. The recipients of help may also be suspicious and derogatory, especially if they don't like the help they get. Most people feel anxiety in asking anyone for help, but especially in asking an organization. Some feel reduced. Almost all are unsure of what they can realistically and legitimately expect. But having made the move, they want real help, personal help, not the kind of bureaucratized help they may receive from an organization which doesn't under-

stand them as individuals, and certainly not help tinged with condescension or intimidation, intentional or not. Recipients may turn their frustrations and negative feelings back upon their helpers covertly, just as their helpers do to them. Ironically, both sides may feel power through blaming the other; but insofar as bad feelings will find ways of leaking out, estrangement between helper and recipient in the longer run will only increase.

6. The help given may be inadequate. This is not the place to review the literature on the effectiveness of professional helping services, but it's no revelation that for a combination of reasons institutional assistance often comes up short. We do know, in the mental health field for example, that seeking professional help leads to more subsequent help-seeking.[17] Sometimes the agency cooperates, by subtly or not-so-subtly fostering dependence among its clients. The agency *needs* its clients, to satisfy its staff, to pay its bills, to justify its existence. The annual report goals may be to strengthen and empower; the day-to-day goals, almost never stated openly, may be to calm daily crises and keep client flow at steady, manageable levels.

7. From the viewpoint of the ordinary citizen, helping organizations can relieve personal responsibility. If my neighbor needs help, I can give directions to this or that social agency. If someone I don't know needs assistance, I can assume it will be found. I do not have to get personally involved in a situation which may not only be sticky and time-consuming, but which may also go well beyond my ability or willingness to help. I wish neighbor and stranger well, but I am less personally responsible for them, because society has established an institutional support system to solve their problems.

8. Helping agencies also attract power away from individuals and local supportive networks, absorbing it into the larger organization. If I as an individual no longer feel as responsible for helping, I suppress much of my own capacity to help; I give it over to the helping agency, as the legitimate authority on the matter. In this sense, my own helping power diminishes, strained though it might have been by continuous demands. If those around me think the same, the mutual dependencies in our community – a source of community strength – weaken, for we have transferred our dependency from ourselves to an institution. We are that much more separate from each other.

These arguments all point to a carefully constructed barrier between helping agencies and the people they are mandated to serve – a psychological rather than a physical barrier, but no less imposing. The barrier has been built up by both sides, and is maintained by both through tacit consent. It is a semipermeable barrier, in that some people needing help can pass through it and return, often in better condition than before. But basically, the two sides keep to themselves.

Helping agencies try to do good, and frequently succeed. But they operate in their own world, by their own regulations. Having expropriated much helping power—legally, openly, with encouragement all around—they now hoard it carefully and release it guardedly. They become insulated, self-perpetuating, and often elitist. They respond imperfectly to community needs or not at all, for they are out of touch with what the community is thinking and feeling. They are as corporations of another country, set down on foreign soil, busy and powerful, rich and paternalistic, willing to dictate what is best for their hosts, responsible to some other headquarters far away.[18]

People in the community, on the other hand, are generally oblivious to the helping agencies around them. They know little about what services are provided, and the knowledge they do have is frequently false. Nor do they especially care to know, except when they may need some service themselves. They have traded away responsibility and power in return for not having to worry about someone else's misfortune. They have made donations or paid tax dollars for agencies to worry, and they will tolerate gross defects as long as agencies stay pretty much out of sight and do not impinge upon their own lives. Helping organizations are strangers in their midst, entitled to deference and a kind of diplomatic immunity, but not to be approached unless all else fails, and then with caution.

I'm writing these words as a community psychologist and as a member of a professional helping organization. In my own history, I left college teaching to take a job in a community mental health center in a city of about 90,000, not far from Boston. For six years there I was involved in developing and directing a variety of community-based outreach programs, geared mostly toward preventing mental illness, promoting mental health, and enhancing the quality of community life. My work brought me into near-daily contact with both helping agencies and community people. My experiences taught me something about how agencies operate and about how people relate to them. One experience in particular is still vivid.

I was invited to speak at a lunchtime meeting of personnel directors in our area. We had been talking at work about beginning some modest programs for the business community, so this invitation was more than usually welcome. Over dessert and coffee, I gave a more or less stump speech about our mental health center, what its mission was, what services it provided, and how people in the community could use existing services and work together with the center to develop new ones. I'd given this kind of talk several times before, and thought I had it down pretty well. Since my audience seemed moderately attentive (eyes remained open), I was pleased enough with myself when I stopped and asked for questions.

A hand waved: "Where did you say you were from?"

"It's the Solomon Mental Health Center."

"What was that?"

"Solomon Mental Health Center."

"Is that in town? Do you mean there's a mental health center right here in town?"

"Yes, there sure is."

"Good grief, where is it?"

"Well, it's about a few hundred yards down the road from here. . . ."

I wasn't so much struck by these questions as such. True, the center occupied a city block on a main thoroughfare, had foot-high identifying letters facing the street, and had been there for about ten years at the time. What registered more, though, was that the questioner's ignorance turned out to be shared by the rest of the group. Yet these were personnel directors, people often among the first to come in contact with a troubled employee in their company, people who needed to know how to give help themselves and when, where, and how to look outside for it. Of course, we were at least as ignorant of them as they were of us. We were planets in space, destined to brush near each other every so often, then to spin apart.

Not all encounters are this sobering, nor are all agencies as unattractive as depicted in the pages above. We have stressed the negatives, largely in order to provide an agenda for correction. Some more sensitive agencies are an unmixed blessing to the communities they serve. Most existing agency faults are correctable, and those which are not may be less faults of the system than of the human beings working within it.

Though agencies have drained off too much individual helping power, they are not solely responsible for deficits in community supports. Let us grant that the agency system is at least partly responsible for improving minimum levels of individual and community welfare. Were there no agencies, we would surely not be better off. Individuals acting by themselves are capable of great benevolence, but also of great cruelty, and, more often than either, of great indifference. And that leads to a main thesis of this chapter.

A TURNING POINT, AND A GRIM SCENARIO

Most formal helping organizations are on the edge or in the process of cutting back their services. The cuts are sharp in many cases, with no reversal of the trend in sight. This is very simply because agencies need money to pay their staff and overhead – another "disadvantage." Most helping agencies cannot be self-supporting, because those most needing help are among those least able to pay for it. Public funding has been necessary, but public money now appears to be drying up. In hard economic times, in times of social stress and personal loss, more people seek out agency supports. But the same economic forces which draw people toward agencies imperil agencies themselves. Social problems will remain, or get worse. Yet, having signed away much of our personal helping power and responsibility, if agency supports begin to disappear, what will take their place?

Official statistics lag behind reality. But at this point it is clear that government contributions to social welfare programs are declining, either as percentages of total budgets or of GNP.[19] Helping agencies in particular are under the gun. The prevailing federal philosophy is that "the taxing power of government . . . must not be used to regulate the economy or to bring about social change."[20] "Social change" appears to take in "social support"; at any rate, public service programs of all kinds are being cut back, and programs specifically designed to help people help themselves have been among the first candidates for extinction.[21]

Lowered commitments by governments are matched by lowered expectations people have for themselves. Surveys indicate that views of one's personal future were more pessimistic at the end of the 1970s than on any of seven previous polling occasions. The same finding, in stronger form, was obtained for perceptions of the national future. In both cases, the gap between present and future perceptions has narrowed over time; we are less likely to think that the future will be better than the past.[22]

But we do not need a complete socioeconomic analysis in order to understand two basic themes:

1. When people feel a genuine threat to their accustomed lifestyles, they move to protect what they have and put pressure on government to act. Their range of social concerns narrows; personal security needs come first. If the threat is economic, but if one is not yet in personal crisis, the governmental action most typically advocated is reduced spending, which translates into lower taxes

and more apparent disposable income, but also less government revenue and fewer institutional supports. Elected officials must listen, or risk losing their jobs.

2. When public helping organizations feel similarly threatened, they too act self-protectively. They too retreat further inside themselves; they scrap new program ideas, shut off peripheral services, focus increasingly on serving only those who are most desperate. And they put heavy pressure on their funding sources to hold the line. However, to spend resources defending one's position, scrambling with equally frightened competitors for the same-size slice of a shrinking dollar pie, can be a massive organizational energy drain. At the least, the money chase takes time away from providing supportive services to people.

You, the reader, may see the economic threat to helping organizations as unfortunate and regrettable, but not as making that much difference to you personally, not as especially meaningful to you in your own life. Perhaps this scenario will bring the situation closer to home:

In the last years of the twentieth century, economic hard times continue. Inflation and unemployment both increase. Productivity declines. Living standards gradually erode. To respond to an aroused citizenry, governments on all levels cut spending. Less public money is available for all public needs, including social services. Helping organizations cut back substantially. In any organization, there is some redundancy, some fat; but eventually the cuts strike muscle and bone. The more vulnerable organizations do not survive.

Many of those cut off from services experience severe hardship. New segments of society feel true hardship for the first time, as everyone moves several notches down the economic scale. The hardship is acute for some, chronic for others, but cumulating for all over time. Private voluntary organizations, their own contributions reduced, cannot come close to meeting demands placed upon them. The corporate sector, in a declining economy, is limited in its own response. Governments make sporadic gestures to reduce suffering, but their new programs operate sluggishly and are no match for need.

People dig in, make do, go without. They dim their lights. They insulate themselves in their houses. They dull their senses with chemicals or television. They look to whatever can ease them through the day. When able to get beyond apathy and fear, they search for targets to blame – government, minorities, those who are weaker. Or they burst into violence.

Almost everyone needs help, yet few sources are left to provide the helping. Public support systems are crippled or dead. Many traditional community patterns of helping behavior have faded away—if they ever existed at all. Individuals will not or cannot pick up the slack. The human service professionals who remain cannot go out and strengthen communities, for their present clients are overwhelmed by life-threatening crises. Grass-roots attempts to establish mutual aid falter through lack of internal commitment, technical know-how, or follow-through.

Instead, the needs of others are increasingly seen as threats to one's self. Attraction for authoritarian forms of leadership grows. Authorities prepare to maintain order by repression. The stage is set for a purge of the scapegoats, the defenseless, and their more advantaged advocates. Unless, that is, those most threatened rise up in successful mass revolt against prevailing authority, abetted by old-line liberals and others whose socioeconomic or moral disaffection outweighs their distrust of the masses.

This is a stark scenario. It lacks shades of gray, and it may be overblown. Helping behavior is grounded in thousands of years of civilization, if not also in our genes. Personal helping is not going to disappear at a stroke. But it can die a bumpy and lingering death. Like any other behavior, the motivation and then the ability to help will diminish if not practiced and then rewarded. The first scene in the scenario has already begun. I fear that under continued stress our capacity to support each other will wither away unless we take preventive action.

CORRECTIVE STEPS

But what kind of action to take?

I visualize action on two basic levels, corresponding to those in our previous discussion—the individual and the helping agency.[23] Actions on both fronts should center around the creation and maintenance of community-based social and economic supports—those small-scale activities, programs, and interventions involving existing and prospective members of the community support system that will increase the ability to cope with and take pleasure from life. Specific examples, in addition to those mentioned earlier, are embedded throughout the rest of this book. The range of supportive actions is limitless, though even pushing hard and in all directions will not yield limitless success. Concentrating on community supports is not an all-encompassing solution to social problems, but more like a big step down the right path.

The individual.

Despite our pointed criticisms of social agencies, they are not the villians of the piece. Ultimately, the individual – the ordinary person – must take responsibility for providing required help and support. Opportunity will not be lacking. The same economic system that pulls people out of their communities and neighborhoods, can, when it deteriorates, push people back in. If the community will in fact be the locus of increasing amounts of social, economic, and political activity, then it's reasonable to believe that people will see their self-interest to lie in developing a solid network of community supports, through both individual and organized group action. The motivation to do so should be rekindled. Confidence in one's ability to do so should increase with practice. More physical and emotional energy should be available for the task. And people may discover that they already possess many necessary skills to plan and implement mutually desired social changes, just as they did before social agencies came upon the scene. In short, many of the previous obstacles to community support-building may be significantly weakened.

Not to romanticize any throwback to community self-dependence. Personal and organizational realignments will have to be made; they won't all be made without struggle. It won't be easy to keep turning outward while larger social institutions keep turning in. And even when mutual benefits are an arm's reach away, community organization and community action are sooner said than done. But the first step starts with awareness; awareness can be built up right now. The crucial awareness here is that individuals will in practice become more responsible for their own supportive needs, whether or not that matches one's social philosophy. An individual cannot control all life events, but can and will have to extend control as far as possible.

The agency.

As for helping agencies, they again deserve special attention, because they are usually more powerful than individuals or community groups, richer and better organized, with more community clout. Since much of their power has been co-opted from people at large, they have a special obligation to use it to build the supports people will need. And if their helping power is about to weaken, their obligation is all the more pressing.

What agencies must do is to right the balance of helping power, to intentionally shift it away from themselves. (By "power" here I mean the ability and willingness to help and support one another.)

They must begin a process of divestiture, of "deinstitutionalization," where they confer much of their power back upon its original source, upon the people who gave it to them. You as reader may be among those people, in which case you may wish to finish this chapter so conferred.

The way for agencies to transfer power is not for them to stop dead in their tracks, nor to abandon the direct services which are so essential for people in urgent need. Instead, the way is to provide a greater percentage of services in which actual helping and supportive *skills*—not just help and support—are overtly shared, and through which larger numbers of people are empowered. These "indirect" services go by different names—consultation, education, training, prevention, outreach, technical assistance, community development, community organization—but at bottom each is designed to get people to help both themselves *and* others, to make people transmitters as well as receivers. Here, I believe, is where the greatest long-run agency impact can come about.

These ideas aren't new. They were stated with particular force at the end of the 1960s by the psychologist George Miller. In this presidential address to the American Psychological Association, Miller was referring to other psychologists, but the words "social scientist" or "helping professional" can easily substitute:

> Psychology must be practiced by non-psychologists. . . . There simply are not enough psychologists, even including nonprofessionals, to meet every need for psychological services. The people at large will have to be their own psychologists, and make their own applications of the principles that we establish . . . .

> Our responsibility is less to assume the role of experts and try to apply psychology ourselves than to give it away to the people who really need it—and that includes everyone. The practice of valid psychology by nonpsychologists will inevitably change people's conception of themselves and what they can do. When we have accomplished that, we will really have caused a psychological revolution.[24]

Miller literally wants to give psychology away, and so labels the next section of his talk. In theory, the gift should be easy, because:

> The techniques involved are not some esoteric branch of witchcraft that must be reserved for those with PhD degrees in psychology. When the ideas are made sufficiently concrete and explicit, the scientific foundations of psychology can be grasped by sixth-grade children.[25]

Giving skills away sounds simple enough, but the experienced professional knows it is not. For one thing, education and related activities bring in less money than direct counseling or casework, in either public or private settings. Giving skills away may really mean giving them away, and professionals and their host organizations have mouths to feed too. For another, professional helpers are not necessarily trained to teach, nor even to value teaching; teaching others to help themselves – as contrasted with just helping them – goes with a somewhat different training and professional ethic. A third point is that ordinary people may show no consuming need to learn helping and supportive skills – either for themselves or others – at least not openly and not at first. Skill-sharing activities will often have to be *marketed*, another ability helpers don't always have. Finally, helping professionals may not *want* to give their skills away. For in their view, their skills *define* them as professionals, and if everyone is a counselor, then who will hold the "real" counselor in high regard, or give out a job?

There's no sidestepping the fact that giving helping skills away will require wholesale professional adjustments, and that some of these adjustments may hurt. To share our power makes others more powerful (we applaud) and also releases our power over them (we hesitate). But there's no other way; one goes with the other, and to hesitate reinforces the current system.

I'd like to see power transferred so that there is more of a partnership between the individual and the helping agency. I'd like to see the partners do more touch-dancing and less freestyle. In this partnership, the agency would stress the development of self-help and community support-building skills and programs. The individual would seek out those skills and also help keep the agency accountable. Power would be seen as infinitely expandable, available to all. And the agency and the individual would work together to leverage their power. For example, they would jointly put pressure on other institutions – governments, businesses, churches, schools, mass media – to follow their lead and stimulate community self-empowerment. Even if the analyses and forecasts in this chapter are hopelessly wrong, would the partnership proposed here still be a good idea? I think so.

Mindset.

There's one fundamental point left to make in this section: community support-building is more than a matter of technical skill. That realization inevitably comes from getting involved in community work, but if you can grasp it beforehand, so much the better. Whatever your social role, effective community work is also a matter of *mindset*, and particularly of the feeling that you can, should, and will use the skills you already own to help others, to build supports, and to create desired change. You must not only be conferred with power: you must also feel that you *are* powerful, and that with your power you can do social good, and should, and will.

This mindset is no delusion. On a fundamental level, we already know how to nurture someone in distress, how to work cooperatively in a small group, or how to get someone excited about our cause. We may not do these things often, we may not be perfect at them – few of us are – but life experience, as a fringe benefit, gives us a rough idea of where and how to start. Most of the desired responses are lodged in the repertoire. In perhaps the majority of cases, the task is less one of learning new skills than of shaking loose latent skills that are already there. The same applies to inner attitudes: it's a task of freeing up, of taking away, not just of adding on. Just as the furniture stripper gets down to natural wood, the meditator to clear mind – the therapist to authentic person – so it can be for people set upon community change. Put more directly, success involves clearing out the junk inside ourselves which keeps us from acting as we would like.

The concerned individual will eventually learn this through experience. The community group will too, once it gets a taste of its own power. The agency can speed up the process. The agency can point to the right skill, ideally also to the right mindset, to the right set of attitudes for getting things done. But this requires more a personal sort of communication. In this sense, Miller's gift is incomplete. Skill must be accompanied by will. The gift must be not just of "psychology," but also of one's self.

I hope it's clear by now that this book is intended for people who want to make their communities better, whether they are concerned citizens, community leaders, agency professionals, or students whose major involvement is yet to come. And I hope too it's apparent that its purpose is to strengthen the ability and the desire of people to help and support each other, and to create the social changes they seek in their own community settings. Some limitations are built in: I can't offer specific guidance for all possible situations you may come across; and I can't rise off this page and make you use the power you have. But if you can accept these limitations, we can move on to describe in more detail what this book is and is not, and then to mention the major topics on the agenda.

THE REST OF THIS BOOK

What this book is not is a textbook on social programming, social change, community psychology, or anything else – it's neither comprehensive enough, nor dispassionate enough. It doesn't present new theory, nor does it advocate one theory over another. It's not a review of the scholarly literature, a presentation of research data, or a commentary on the writings of others. It doesn't offer much in the way of brand-new knowledge or facts. It's not a how-to-do-it manual, in the sense of giving line-by-line instructions on how to make things happen. It's not a rule book. It doesn't treat fully all situational variables which might be present and might help to determine the success of a particular intervention. And it doesn't teach directly how to manage other people, or run a rummage sale, or lead discussion groups.

Instead, this book is a guidebook for those who want to carry out small-scale social change activities in a neighborhood or community. It's a companion for the practitioner of change, or potential practitioner, with or without formal affiliation. It discusses day-to-day problems and concerns that a community worker will face, not worrying too much about providing definitive answers, but rather with the intent of raising key issues so that the reader may become fully conscious of them and move toward resolution. It does set down some general principles, guidelines, and thought-starters. It aims to cut across situations, to relate to most social change activities and settings—though it focuses on the local level, where more potential change agents are and where I think the most positive changes are going to occur. It's a book based upon six intensive years of full-time community work, plus twelve years of teaching social and community psychology. Finally, it describes a philosophy and approach which fit with my own value system and which may have the greatest chance of bringing about necessary changes in society.

The next chapter sets out a rather detailed case history of one successful support-building change activity, successful at least for a while and in conventional terms. It will be good to remind ourselves of what change looks like in the flesh. From that example, we want to extract some of the major components involved in creating community change, and return to them at greater length later on.

The four chapters following deal with issues of technique common to most social interventions, roughly in the order they arise. Chapter 3 considers the initial choice of activity—assessing needs, benefits, and resources, and using the assessment to figure out what to do. Chapter 4 concentrates on planning for the action chosen; it outlines some principles and obstacles, and compares alternative sample plans. Chapter 5 dissects program action itself—

getting into the situation, executing the actual program, and then getting out. Chapter 6 examines program evaluation, methods for determining whether your program really had the effects you intended. The goals of these chapters taken together are to add to or refine your own skill, to sharpen appreciation of technique, and to stimulate thought on how it might best be applied in specific situations you might encounter.

The next two chapters focus more on personal and philosophical issues in doing community change work. Chapter 7 analyzes the role of personal qualities, or personal style, in the success of any social intervention. Chapter 8 raises the general issue of limits of change and the specific questions of how much social change can and should one person aim to accomplish. Finally, chapter 9 surveys some of the social and economic realities that the change agent is likely to face in the near future, and suggests a number of specific support-building initiatives for turning them to best advantage. This chapter is followed by an annotated list of books and pamphlets which discuss social change skills and techniques in more detail than is possible here.

Some terms used throughout the text deserve clarification. "Community" is used loosely and broadly here, taking in "neighborhood" and smaller units as well. A "social program" refers to a planned and organized service designed to strengthen community supports and more generally to improve the quality of community life; it usually affects more than a few people for more than a little while, but it can be quite simple. A "social activity" means almost the same thing, but may be smaller in scale, less structured, and less enduring. A "social intervention" is simply a way of summarizing the actions taken to establish a social program or activity. And a "community worker" or "change agent" is anyone who, through even the humblest program or activity, attempts to change the community for the better. These shorthand terms should not obscure the fact that the change agent is (or could be) you.

And I think it will help to read this book as it does apply (or could apply) to you. That is, keep your own experiences and plans in the forefront; compare your notes with mine. Whatever fails to register here, you can pass by or set aside for another time; but whatever you find useful, I hope you will use. Using what we know is the key. A viable society, and certainly an ideal society, will depend upon many more of us actively striving to transform what we know and what we hope for into a matching social reality. Success is never certain. But it's possible; the effort enriches us; and if you are not ready to head for shelter, what better option is there?

2
A Success Story, for a While

THE STORY

The saying goes that if the sun shines once, then not all days are cloudy. This is a story about a sunny day.

I first met Laurie in late May of 1974. She was about to start graduate work in sociology in the Boston area. I was directing community-based programs in Lowell. Laurie needed to do a one-year field placement; would I be interested in being her supervisor?

How we came to meet in the first place was quirky and coincidental, as so many things are. Laurie's advisor at school was Don; Don's wife had previously worked at our mental health center as an occupational therapist. So he knew our place. Perhaps because of that – or was there some other reason? – Don expressed an interest in training sociologists to work in centers like ours. He called and asked if he could bring a prospective student out. It was fine with me, for I was always looking for new resources to help improve the mental health of the Lowell community. (In those days, I could voice those kinds of aspirations without self-consciousness or second thoughts.)

At our first meeting, we all agreed on the ground rules for field placement and supervision. Laurie would work full-time during the summer, two days a week during the coming academic year. The content of her field work would be a project that we would pick out together. The specifics were up to us. Laurie spoke of wanting to define clear goals for herself, and also of desiring to start something which she could finish up in a year. That made sense to me.

25

Laurie herself was twenty-two at the time. She had come from the San Francisco area to go to school in the East. In her background was experience working in juvenile court, in evaluating neighborhood social programs—nothing that leaped out at you, though her service activities went back through high school. She liked to wear scarves over her dark hair, which lent her a gypsylike quality; she had a big laugh and eyes that shined intently at you when you talked. Those were my first impressions.

So the next step was to pick out a task. No lack of opportunity here. From a well-stocked folder, I laid out a list of possibilities ranging from food cooperatives to block associations to ethnic research to demonstration projects in a specific neighborhood. Laurie's assignment for next time was to narrow the range of alternatives.

At our next meeting, early in June, Laurie said she was interested in focusing on adult education. She had done some tutoring and counseling in high school and college, and was thinking about teaching after she finished graduate school, so there was a natural fit. Her basic idea was to set up a cooperative community learning center. The center would provide education geared toward everyday living problems; it would be targeted toward lower-income people; it would have a preventive function, dealing with problems before they developed into crises; it would offer an alternative to traditional adult education programs given through community centers or public schools.

It was true that if you lived in Lowell at the time, not much in the way of continuing education was open to you. You could finish up a high school diploma or enroll in a college degree program. But if you wanted to take an informal or recreational course, meet people and learn things in a no-pressure environment, you more than likely had to look toward Boston or Cambridge, forty-five minutes away. Laurie's idea accordingly filled a gap.

Laurie had previously gone out and talked to some community people, especially people living in housing projects. What did they think about a learning center? A good idea. What courses would they like to see offered? They gave examples. Would they sign up for a course themselves? Maybe. What other thoughts did they have? "Everyone makes promises." "I'll believe it when I see it." Despite skepticism, and the lack of a formal survey, there was some evidence that the learning center also filled a perceived need.

The idea was ambitious: to provide some educational programs for adults was one thing; to put together a "learning center" was quite another. But shouldn't students (or community workers, or ourselves) be allowed a healthy share of rope? Don't we as trainers want to encourage ambition? When you really want to do something, isn't that a first and essential step toward doing it? So in my role I said okay, see what you can do.

In developing most new social program ideas, a standard set of questions applies. Essentially, these are the news-reporter's questions of who, what, where, when, why, and how, to which we as good resource managers add questions of evaluation, coordination, and cost. These questions applied here: translated into language for this program, somewhat amplified, and rearranged, they were:

> Why undertake a learning center?
> > What would be the benefits?
> > Would the benefits outweigh the costs?
> > Is the idea feasible?
>
> What would be taught?
> > What course content?
> > How determined? (What criteria?)
>
> Who would teach the courses?
> > With what qualifications?
> > How would teachers be recruited?
>
> Who would be taught?
> > Concentration on specific target groups?
> > > If so, which? And how determined?
> > How to customize publicity to reach designated
> > > groups?
>
> Where would the courses be held?
> > One or more locations?
> > What criteria for choice of location(s)? What physical
> > > facilities, equipment, and supplies needed?
>
> When would courses start?
> > What month of year? What day of week? What time
> > > of day?
> > Would courses be repeated later? Which ones?
> > > When?
>
> How would courses be taught?
> > How many courses?
> > Format? Length? (per period and per course)
> > How would courses in general be publicized?
>
> How would courses be evaluated?
> > And by whom?
>
> Who would coordinate the operations of the program?
> > Who would have responsibility and authority?

What would be the mechanism for transfer of
responsibility and authority to others?

How much would all this cost?
Where would the money come from?
Where would it go?

In general form, these questions adapt readily to all social interventions: they can also expand or compress to suit your desired
level of specificity. With very little practice, it becomes easy to sit
at your desk and rattle them off. You can learn to enlarge upon
them, and to sound very wise in doing so. This is not to deny that
these questions are both real and fundamental. They are. Laurie
and I agreed on their validity and usefulness. A few weeks after we
began, by the end of June, she had sketched out some tentative
answers to them, together with a rough timetable.

The "Why?"—the essential opening question—we had already
answered to our satisfaction. Course content would aim toward life
issues, toward strengthening competence, though we would take
pretty much what we could get the first time around. The teachers
would be recruited largely from social service agencies, since they
could then work on agency time; other teacher contacts would be
followed up, too. We'd push for about twenty courses in all. They
would be open to anyone, without restriction, but with an
emphasis on appeal to lower-income groups, who had more problems of living and less educational opportunity. Downtown Lowell,
being accessible by foot or public transportation to most of the
target group, would serve as the course location. Courses would
run for about six weeks, for an hour or two at a time, some during
the day and some at night. They would be small and informal.
Teachers and students would both give back course evaluations.
Laurie would coordinate activities for the time being. And, a key
point, the courses would be entirely free; no money should change
hands. We would hustle any dollars needed for basic operating
expenses. Opening day was planned for the end of September.

Coming up with paper answers is not too difficult, either. The
logic is by-the-numbers: take the first question, make your best
judgment, move on to the next one. What's more, all kinds of
answers can be dressed up to look plausible, especially if they don't
have to step outside the door. In many cases, several different
answers may really *be* plausible, and workable in practice. We
judged what we had so far as being "reasonable" (a good word for
hedging bets), and passed ourselves on the logic and plausibility
tests.

Our answers defined our objectives. Now all that remained was to bring about a learning center. This would be Laurie's job. We would meet together once a week to review what had just happened and what needed to happen next.

The courses came first. Laurie compiled a potential course list, a second list of agencies and contact people (prospective teachers), and then started making phone calls and visits to marry the lists to each other. Making programs grow is a selling job, no less in community work than in private industry. You need an attractive product to sell, and someone skilled to sell it. None of Laurie's contacts could deny the need for more adult education. The proposal for a learning center was idealistic, but not outlandish; it might work; it had appeal. For those without formal teaching background, teaching a course would be a new experience as well as a professional credential. Teaching was particularly attractive if it could be done on work time, and in an area of special interest. The personal time and energy cost was relatively small. It was also summer, a good season to plan, since fall times were not yet booked. For all of these reasons, the product took on some glamour.

As a salesperson, Laurie was absolutely superb. She would approach you as if what she was doing was the most important thing in the world. Her radiant energy filled the room. She would flatter you so outrageously that you could only laugh. She would listen and respond to you with her full being. She always left you feeling special. All of this in pure sincerity, untinged by guile, as far as I could ever tell. How could anyone say no?

Inside of three weeks, Laurie had about ten courses lined up, with a few others as tentative. She had also acquired a small cadre of volunteers, including several outpatient clients of the mental health center looking for meaningful work, plus an expanding list of contacts. One contact she made steered her toward a community center downtown, where she charmed her way into temporary headquarters. The Chamber of Commerce found some turn-of-the-century office furniture and added some supplies. The Lowell City Library had a room it could lend out a few hours a week, as did the local Council on Aging. Then, the principal of a nearby elementary school agreed to have his custodians keep a couple of rooms open one night a week. So three centrally located classroom locations and an office fell into place, all within five minutes' walk of each other.

Laurie understood the importance of close agency connections, but knew it was just as important to stay independent. The prospects in this case would have been bleaker with agency sponsorship. The learning center, for one thing, did not fit neatly into a single agency's jurisdiction. No agency would have taken the risk to sponsor it officially. Moreover, people in general kept their distance from agencies, just as agencies did from each other. And formal mental health center backing, even had it been possible, would surely have been the kiss of death. Accordingly, a separate identity and a separate location were both called for. The trick was (and is) to use agency resources without being used by them.

Education at its core requires only teachers, students, and a place for them to meet. Having arranged for the first and the last, the next task was to attract some people to learn. To attract them would involve publicity, and this, for the first time, meant money. Who was the most logical supporter for an educational program slanted toward promoting mental health? Clearly, it was the local Mental Health Association, whose executive director found a way to come up with $250 in seed money, plus the use of a bulk mailing permit, in exchange for some discreet publicity credits. The money bought a phone for the office, together with paper for catalogs and posters. A bank balance in turn freed up the energy to work out a publicity plan. Two months into the project, Laurie was ready to advertise. One more step: the program needed a name. After several spins of the wheel, the Lowell Cooperative Learning Center (or L.C.L.C.) came out the winner.

Laurie had 3,000 eight-page catalogs and 250 posters printed up in fall colors. The publicity theme was "Broaden Your Horizons," featuring a logo of sun, moon, and stars in a celestial landscape. In the first days of September, Laurie and her friend Anne sat with maps, planned their routes to concentrate on downtown Lowell, then distributed most of the catalogs and posters themselves—covering, among other places, social service agencies, housing projects, clubs, pharmacies, churches, cleaners, grocers, hardware stores, and pizza shops.

Over 200 packets were mailed at the same time to agencies, clubs, clergy, and selected businesses. Each packet had an introductory letter, a summary sheet describing the center, a catalog, and five registration cards. Press releases went out to local newspapers and radio stations, courtesy of the public relations director of Lowell General Hospital. Public service spots for radio and short announcements for community calendars were sent as well. Laurie got herself invited on a local radio program to talk about the center in person—the station was always ready to boost the community. None of these publicity techniques was in any way unorthodox or

BROADEN YOUR HORIZONS

DAYTIME

AND EVENINGS

FRee! REGISTER NOW

INFORMAL CLASSES FOR TEENS AND ADULTS OF ALL AGES

SEPT. 30 TO NOV. 7

OFFICE AT 400 MERRIMACK ST. OPPOSITE PUBLIC LIBRARY

FOR INFORMATION CONTACT:

LOWELL COOPERATIVE LEARNING CENTER

PHONE NOW 458 7812

OR COME SEE US

exceptional; but all of them were executed thoughtfully, thoroughly, and on time.

It was the second week of September. Volunteers had been recruited to staff the office, process registrations, and keep records. Registrations started to flow in, by mail or phone. Some people stopped by. All phone or in-person registrants were asked how they had heard of L.C.L.C., for future publicity purposes. (Mailed coupons had been precoded by location.) Evening child care at fifty cents per class was arranged for through the Lowell Girls Club. Two weeks before opening day, Laurie met with all teachers to give them an idea of what to expect, to go over course policies, and to build esprit de corps. Things were about ready to go.

On September 30, the Lowell Cooperative Learning Center officially opened its doors, with 290 students enrolled in eighteen free courses. Course offerings included "Tenants' Rights," "Separation and Divorce," "Where to Turn for Help," "Human Sexuality," "Job Dynamics," "Tips on Tots," "Diet Together," and "Making the Most of Your Money," plus some purely recreational courses, such as "Patchwork Quilting" and "Flowers for Fun." There were miscalculations—two courses did not draw. There were student dropouts—about one-third over the duration. And there were minor catastrophes—one art teacher decided at the last minute that he wouldn't work without pay, and left fifteen students waiting outside a locked door. But on the whole, the six-week semester went off cleanly.

In three and one-half months, Laurie had created a social service agency. Many others had helped out; but the creation was essentially her own, accomplished with no prior knowledge of Lowell, and from absolute ground zero. Looking at it one way, setting up the center was just a question of figuring out what you needed to do, and then doing it, one step at a time. Really. It all seemed easy, so easy that any halfway perceptive and motivated person with sufficient time could have done the same thing. But if this was so, why was Laurie's achievement unparalleled in my experience, before or since? We need to return to this question later, after learning more about what happened during the rest of the year.

Once the semester was under way, there was much more work to be done. A second semester had to be planned; more money had to be raised to cover basic expenses; the office had to be kept staffed and open. Laurie's time for L.C.L.C. was now down to two days a week, as she had returned to school. Others had to pick up some of the slack.

Over the summer, Laurie had sounded out agency and community people about being on an advisory board. The same combination of appealing prospect, minimal time investment, and compelling salesmanship yielded eighteen persons who said they would serve, or at least come to a first meeting. In mid-October, the board met for the first time. The energy level was high, high enough so that a loose collection of acquaintances and strangers decided to transform itself into a formal Board of Directors. There was an election of officers, a division into committees, and the beginning of broadly based planning and decision making for the center's future.

The most pressing need was for money, since the phone company and the post office could not be cajoled into donating their services. Somewhere around Thanksgiving, Laurie thought of putting on Dickens's *A Christmas Carol* as a fund-raiser, which would also get L.C.L.C. some added exposure. A few days later she had lined up a cast, assembled a stage crew, arranged for an auditorium, found a director, blocked out publicity, and started rehearsals. Laurie played Mrs. Cratchit. On a Friday night, three weeks from the gleam, the show played to a full house – a hit, judging by audience reaction. Together with an accompanying bake sale, L.C.L.C cleared about $300. A little later on, a minister on the board got his church to donate a few hundred dollars more. These funds and donations, plus a few private contributions, brought total center revenues to around $1500. That was the working budget for the first year.

A second semester in the winter sped by, and a third semester in the spring. Each time, operating procedures went a little more smoothly. Course selection could now be based more accurately on community response to courses previously given. The curriculum, publicity, finance, and planning committees began to pull some weight. Fund-raising and publicity policies were drawn up and approved. Board members visited classes to talk about L.C.L.C. and generate community support. A new and larger rent-free office-classroom was found in a downtown church. Each semester offered a few more courses and drew in a few more students than the one before. Word of mouth was a valuable ally. The center now had momentum.

Recruiting teachers turned out to be (nearly) as easy as putting your line in the water and waiting for the fish to bite. As a Curriculum Committee member (I'd been persuaded to join the board), I remember walking into a local health food store and walking out with a course on nutrition. The same experience with stamps and coins. Once, the fish bit almost literally. I recall in particular getting a call at work from a fellow who had heard about L.C.L.C. and wanted to teach a tropical fish course. When I wondered out loud if there was enough local interest to fill it, I got in return a long discourse on the half-dozen or so tropical fish stores and clubs in the Lowell area alone, etc. (File under "knowing your community.") That course went over pretty well.

Since even the best professional human service agencies do not always execute properly, it's no surprise that all-volunteer organizations should also make mistakes. Laurie herself was fallible, was known to miss a beat here and there. And L.C.L.C. had its slippage problems. Occasionally, a volunteer scheduled to staff the office did not show up; too many people would sign up for courses and not attend them; office record-keeping left something to be desired; child care turned out not to be a major need; the modest amount of course evaluation data collected never really got put to full use. This is a partial list, which possibly screens out the most memorable foul-ups.

But in retrospect, I remember L.C.L.C.'s first year as a success beyond any "reasonable" expectation. Students and teachers kept coming back and looked happy. People had a chance to meet and to talk to each other across social, ethnic, and neighborhood lines. The Board of Directors hung together, with a highly motivated core group putting in the necessary hard work. By-laws were written; incorporation papers, for nonprofit status, were filed. There was even some money in the bank. As spring 1975 drew to a close, the one big question mark was what would happen when Laurie's time at L.C.L.C. ended in June.

What happened was that Laurie found three volunteers to replace her. Sue and Renee were local; one would handle publicity and outreach, the other fund raising. Linda, a Boston-area graduate student like Laurie herself, this time in continuing education, would monitor day-to-day center operations. At the last board meeting in the spring the three were installed as co-coordinators. L.C.L.C. looked like it was set to go for a second year.

There was a spirited thank-you and goodbye party for Laurie and Anne, who had also put in a lot of supportive time throughout the year. Then, almost exactly a year from the day she arrived, Laurie left L.C.L.C. She was headed for Maine, to continue graduate school long-distance, and to take on another placement in public television.

THE INGREDIENTS

Most dreams do not come true. Most ideas for social programs do not reach the seedling stage, and there are those who would change "most" to "almost all." In any case, very few program ideas in my experience turned out as well as the Lowell Cooperative Learning Center. Why was this so? As social scientists or as social activists, or simply as socially concerned persons, we want to capture and bottle the magic ingredients.

But as social scientists, we are not (yet) quite certain what those ingredients are. (As laymen, we may be more inclined to make an offhand judgment.) Laboratory knowledge may be of limited transferability. Nor can we easily do naturalistic experiments in the field to check out our assumptions. If we still want to get past the limits of our own experience, we turn to the case history as a source of general principles. The case history is not the only method open to us, and by no means the only desirable one, but neither is it to be dismissed solely for lacking methodological rigor. Freud, among others, built a psychology on case observations. As students of social change, we too are clinicians, here of the social order.

In our case history, what ingredients contributed most to success? Suppose we offer these for a beginning analysis:

1. There was the *vision* to start the center in the first place. The starting idea could have been considerably more modest, and/or it could have been less attuned to what was happening in Lowell at the time. The vision, the conceptual leap, was Laurie's, tempered by her external perceptions then. But the reasons for coming up with *that* vision, instead of some other worthwhile but commonplace idea, must have been internal. They must have gone back through Laurie's own history, back to her own learning experiences and reinforcement patterns.

2. There was the *ambition* to create the center – not just the idea, but the motivation to implement it. The ambition showed; it bubbled to the surface like a hot spring. The sources of this ambition were deep-down, internal, and historical as well.

3. The center met a *need*. The need started out as Laurie's, yet it turned out to be no less a need of the community. The vision, when brought up close and into focus, was shared. The center was publicized attractively enough to lure participants, but it was actual educational benefits that kept them coming back for more. The community need had been suspected by noting the scarcity of local adult education resources. Some confirmation had come from informal conversations and feedback along the way. But there were no test runs before opening, no other prior research to determine whether people in Lowell in fact had any interest in L.C.L.C. Laurie began with what she wanted: to a large extent, she played a hunch and won.

4. There was enough *time* to start the center in motion, time to convert idea and intent into specific action steps. The time was decks-cleared time, free from other demands or impingements. In that first summer, Laurie had no other work commitments and comparatively few other personal obligations. (Living in New Hampshire then, she was driving 130 round-trip miles five days a week, sometimes six and seven.) She was free to devote her full and focused attention to the project, to nurture the vision and sustain the ambition.

5. The center was well *planned*. The plan was an early sequel to the vision, and took up a good amount of the time available. The organization of the plan itself was simple, rational, totally devoid of magic or even subtlety. To review: it was only a matter of identifying the tasks that needed to be done, putting them in sequential order, blocking out a rough time frame for each, and assigning responsibility for them. (The last part was straightforward, in that Laurie initially assigned almost all responsibilities to herself.) Having done that much, the next step was to figure out how best to implement the first task on the list, and then to go ahead and execute. The same process was repeated for each task in order, making modifications as needed along the way. In terms of the planning *concepts* involved, organizing the L.C.L.C. was on an approximate par with doing one's Christmas shopping or painting the porch: the same conceptual steps are followed in sequence. True, in this case task identification and layout took some extended thought, and task execution was more complex, but there was sufficient time for both planning and action.

6. The center gained the *support* of others, who gradually assumed responsibility for its operation. A community project, such as a learning center, requires community involvement. One person cannot and should not sustain the operation alone indefinitely. To gain support, the learning center had not only to meet a community need; supporters also had to recognize that it did, spot benefits for themselves, and then see their way clear to participating, and eventually to taking responsibility in limited though specific ways. This meant recruitment, and it meant salesmanship, both dependent in good measure upon the internal vision and ambition of the recruiter and seller.

Certainly, other contributors might compile longer or shorter lists, or assign different verbal labels. But I think that the six factors listed here come fairly close to explaining success in this case, as well as in many other social interventions. To the extent this is so, it's important to consider some implications.

Vision, ambition, time, need, planning, support – a collection of highly conventional concepts. No surprises here. If anything distinguishes them as a group, it is their simplicity, their downright ordinariness. And that is precisely the point: successful program execution does not involve mysterious or swashbuckling technique, nor does it demand knowledge very far removed from everyday living situations. What it does require is a sensitively chosen idea, coupled with the sustained application of relatively simple skills of planning and persuasion, plus the strongest possible desire to make the program work. These attributes do not guarantee success, for no one can completely control the outside environment. But with them, success is within the reach of anyone.

To highlight a point, and to anticipate chapter 7, successful community change depends greatly upon the personal qualities of the change agent. This is not to discount the importance of knowledge or technique. Knowledge and technique almost always help; novice and master are not equals. When working in highly specialized settings, or with specialized target groups, knowledge and technique can be indispensable. But personal qualities too are vital; this is the point that has been neglected in the literature of social change, and accordingly the one to stress here. Vision and ambition are found within the personality of the change agent; so is the ability to rally support. Laurie had the requisite personal qualities in abundance. The learning center succeeded because she knew how to operate in the world, but no less because of the force of her own being.

THE AFTERMATH

With Laurie gone, the learning center wobbled. Sue and Renee, two of the three coordinators, had a falling out. Sue quickly left to take a paying job; Renee quit shortly thereafter. Linda was overwhelmed, but stuck it out for six months, when a new coordinator arrived, paid for through the CETA program. Board membership turned over rapidly. Finances were never too much better than precarious. Still, the center kept alive. Community fund-raisers and open houses were moderately successful. A Sunday square dance drew 200 people. The city manager took a fancy to the program and taught backgammon. Quality of instruction apparently held. The number of courses and students somehow continued to inch upward.

L.C.L.C. hung on through the fall of 1979. During a five-year period, it offered more than 400 free courses to more than 4,000 people. Representatives of several groups outside Lowell came to observe it, with an eye toward importing the idea to their own communities. At one point, courses branched out into a suburban town.

But growth eventually did level off. More recreational courses began to be offered, fewer dealing with problems of living. A long list of people, CETA-funded and pure volunteer, moved into and out of the coordinator role. The original core group on the board went their separate ways. The same organizational and planning issues came up over and over again in meetings. The doorbell outside the office, which never worked from the start, remained faithfully inoperative.

And then, five years after it began, L.C.L.C. pulled to the side of the road. It had multiple maladies. A major, first-time grant application had failed, while government funding had continued to dry up. Board involvement, never as forceful as during the first year, had become even spottier than usual. The leadership had scattered without finding adequate replacements. Other educational opportunities had meanwhile increased, with the expansion of adult education programs at local high schools and junior colleges, the opening of a new vocational school, and the creation of a university in Lowell itself. The need was very possibly not as strong as at the beginning. But in addition, the L.C.L.C. had evolved from a fresh and exciting idea to an institution approaching middle age. The pride of ownership wasn't the same. Few people were left to love the center, and they did not love it quite enough.

As I write, L.C.L.C. is dormant, but not entirely dead. Some people still talk about reviving it, getting some others together, starting over again. Maybe this will happen, maybe not. I hope that it will: but I can also accept death as an eventual part of organizational as well as personal life, and realize that sometimes with the passage of months or years an organization or group or social program may have served its purpose.

Whatever the outcome, Laurie and the Lowell Cooperative Learning Center taught me in personal terms, and indelibly, that positive social change is possible and that one person can bring it about. This book is dedicated toward stimulating more change like it. To that end, we will revisit several of the concepts referred to in this account – needs, planning, support, personal qualities – in upcoming chapters. There's one other concept we won't revisit separately, but which leads into a fitting close.

We tend to view social change as an either-or proposition. Either you work within the system, or you fight against it. In one case, you are limited by the system itself; it will only bend so far. In the other, you are limited by lack of power; the system has more. The system, any system in fact, needs change from both inside and outside. Of course this is oversimplified: either way, change is possible; but either way, it is hard.

However, there's a third option, and that is to create your own system. You work neither within nor against, but alongside. If you can create your own system, you don't have to play by the bigger system's rules, and you don't have to beat yourself into the ground fighting it. If you are attractive and nonthreatening, you can draw resources from the bigger system, and if you are steadfast, you won't be co-opted by it. The learning center is an example of this third kind of change. Creating your own system, even a tiny one, is not necessarily easier, or more effective, or always advisable. But the less capable bigger systems are of meeting present-day needs, the more this option is worth thinking about.

3

Assessment

FIGURING OUT WHAT TO DO

Imagine your own community setting: the people, the places, the total environment. Give the images some time to sink in. Imagine yourself now entering a social change role, a role where you will help make community life better in some way. You are no longer a passive reader, but a willing actor. The possibility is there for you to do something truly outstanding.

Where do you begin?

In addressing any task, from fishing in a stream to damming up a river, we can identify four basic task components:

1. Figuring out what to do
2. Figuring out how to do it
3. Doing it
4. Checking to see how well it was done.

These four components are the topics of our next four chapters. They represent different phases of the same overall process of doing community work. Note right away that the actual "doing" takes up but one of the four phases, and that the first two involve preparation, or "figuring out." In practice, the "doing" phase can be the easiest, especially if preparation has been sound. Preparation, on the other hand, requires the deepest thought and possibly the most time. And it goes against the grain. That is why there will be much emphasis on preparation here.

So a good place to begin in community work is with figuring out what you are going to do. Would you agree, and agree too that we ought to go about this in the most orderly and logical way? Of

41

course, we "figure out what to do" all the time in everyday living situations, where even the most scatter-brained among us manage to muddle through with some success. Is it possible, then, to add anything here to what we know already? I believe so, for we want to do more than muddle.

HOW MOST PEOPLE GET STARTED

But on thinking a little more carefully, it becomes clearer that most people who get involved in community work hardly figure out what to do at all. Perhaps these situations strike a chord:

• You get involved because of a personal life circumstance or event. You have a deaf child, so you work for the hearing-impaired. You can't get a loan, so you try to change bank policy. You react to adversity. Some people who live with handicaps, who suffer outrage, who feel singled out for unjust treatment, become lifetime crusaders. But at least at the start, they act because acting meets *their* needs as much as anyone else's.

• You act because you think you have a good idea. Your gut feeling tells you so. Your idea may satisfy some of your own needs, maybe some community needs as well. In any event, you're convinced enough it will work that you don't bother to check it out.

• You pick up the first activity that comes along. You have some time and are looking for something to do. You see a notice on the bulletin board; it looks interesting. You go to a meeting and things flow from there.

• You join up because you are asked. A friend calls you up and wonders if you could help out on _____ . You have no special interest in _____ , but you'd like to oblige (and maybe you owe a favor). You feel some pressure, you have some spare moments, and so you agree. It's the path of least resistance.

• You follow a group decision. A club or organization you belong to is deciding on its agenda for the year. The majority favors one thing; you lean toward another, but don't really oppose the first. The group means something to you, so you go along.

• You need a job. Your background and interests are in guidance counseling, but the job that opens up is in youth employment. If you get hired, youth employment work is what you'll be doing.

• Once on the job, your boss tells you what to do. You don't make the decision. You have an assignment, and you don't have much choice but to do it. In fact, your boss may be responding to mandates and priorities set from above and afar; bosses too may have little choice.

I think these situations cover the majority of cases. We get involved out of personal issues, hunches, social pressures, commands, or twists of fate. There are constraints, internal or external. The issue of "figuring out what to do" does not arise, because one way or another things are already figured. But community work goes on, and under these conditions excellent work, even distinguished work, can be done. If this were universally so, we could sigh with relief, abandon the topic, quit this chapter early, and move on to the next.

STARTING WITH A CLEAN SLATE

It's not universally so, and community work suffers as a result. Suppose instead we shift gears and treat the issue of "figuring out" with full seriousness. Try this argument on:

Before beginning new community work, any project likely to take up a sizeable chunk of time, you should carry out a thorough and thoughtful assessment of potential activities. A formal assessment is most desirable, a semiformal assessment is okay, and even an informal assessment will be better than none at all. In this assessment, you should gather hard data on at least the following factors for each activity option:

1. *Your needs* — what you want
2. *Community needs* — what your target group (the group you plan to serve) wants
3. *Benefits* — projected net benefits to the user, over and above stated costs
4. *Resources available* — to undertake a given project
5. *Resources required* — to undertake it successfully

When all factors have been assessed, the data should be combined. The activity you choose should be the one with the highest overall value. The process should be repeated periodically, as a matter of course, to review choices made.

Perhaps I can anticipate some of your reactions. The argument is brilliantly stated. It's a fine idea. It makes a lot of sense. It's well-intentioned. It may not work in practice. It's not the way people do things. It's a frill we can do without. It's one more bureaucratic hurdle. It's divorced from reality. It wastes time and delays action. You wind up assessing people to death. It's naive, irrelevant, and plain dumb.

And perhaps some of your reactions conflict with each other. The basic conflict in my experience is between theory and practice. The theory sounds good; the actual practice is too difficult, too disconnected, too uncertain, or otherwise off-putting. As a result, assessments are rarely done, not by individuals, nor groups, nor public service agencies. If one statement in the above paragraph is false, it's that "people are assessed to death." (When was the last time anyone asked you what you wanted?) The fact is that helpers go their own way. The percentage of community actions that follow from any assessment at all is minute. Yet assessment has untapped value; our task is to place it more within reach, to bring the percentage up. Toward this end, we first want to make a case for it, and then to suggest how you might do it.

A case for assessment.

As a community worker, you begin with the assumptions that you can't do everything, but that you can do something. Further, the something you choose should be satisfying for you, produce measurable community benefits, and be feasible under your particular circumstances. Further, the activity chosen should also respond to a need in the community, should be expressly valued by the people you are attempting to serve. To stay with community need for a moment, you may know what's needed, or think you know, but maybe you don't.

As we've suggested, most community work goes on without reference to expressed community need. Individuals in particular are likely to act for personal satisfaction; they're not out to change the world. Service agencies in particular are likely to assume (rather grandly) that they know what community needs are (without checking), and many, preoccupied with their own survival, do not appear very interested in community needs at all. Sometimes, action and need collide; other times, not. Most times, there's a mismatch between the helper and the one being helped. On an agency level, failure to assess perpetuates the separation and distrust between agency and community we spoke of in chapter 1. This is tradition by now, difficult to break. Except that in hard times, we can't afford mismatch and distrust. The limited helping resources we have must be used at peak efficiency, with minimum waste.

So far, this is ideology. Let's move to more down-to-earth reasons for starting out with a full-blooded assessment. If well-executed:

- Assessment can give you information you didn't know before. A group of community people, even if not entirely representative, will collectively be more in touch with what is needed than you alone.
- Assessment can verify (or disconfirm) what you thought you knew.
- Assessment can help you prioritize the tasks that are most important to do.
- Assessment can provide a data base for you or others to use later, for lobbying, explaining actions, writing proposals, evaluating, whatever your purpose.

- Assessment can put you in touch with people you didn't know previously, and so extend your own contact network.
- Assessment can sometimes bring different groups of people together, thus extending their own networks.
- Assessment can supply you with feedback on what people think about activities already going on.
- Assessment can offer people the hope that something will be done.
- Assessment can build awareness, trust, and support for you, through participation in the assessment itself. When others express an opinion, the very act of expression may bond them to it and to you.

For all these reasons, assessment should increase community impact. Success depends largely upon whether people want what you have to offer. Community assessment is your market research, your testing to see what is in demand, your insurance that your eventual offer will be accepted. Though we've focused mostly on community need, similar reasoning could be directed at personal need, benefits, and resources. Assessment there too should pay off and justify the time spent.

A case against.

There are points on the other side, arguments for swooping down instead of circling around:

- Assessment may tell you no more than you knew already. You may be absolutely sure what is needed; needs may be grabbing you by the throat. When you're gasping for air, you know without assessment that you need to breathe.
- Assessment may be time away from action. Instead of figuring out what to do, you could be doing it. It may make more sense to head where the squeaking is loudest, and take things from there.
- Assessment may lead to additional delay or near-paralysis when several options emerge with equal values.
- Assessment may deal in hazy generalities far removed from daily routines.
- Assessment may corner you into something you have no interest in doing (or no intent of doing).
- Assessment may be a high-sounding and/or politically expedient tactic for justifying what you already planned to do.
- Assessment may uncover needs you are incapable of meeting.
- Assessment may raise people's hopes falsely and damage your credibility if you don't follow through.
- Assessment may be wasteful and misleading, since (especially in a paying job situation) you may have no choice but to continue on your present course.

There's some merit in these claims, and there are times when assessment will not help you very much. When you have an indisputable, throat-grabbing case; when you must respond to a crisis; when a careful assessment has already been done; when you are acting for a higher cause, even if the cause is yours alone; when you will do what you want to do anyway; when you have no freedom of choice. In these instances, whether existing for good reason or not, there's less value in analysis before action.

But most of the time these counterarguments are outweighed, and it's better to assess. I push hard at this point largely because real-life assessment is unfamiliar and often intellectually challenging, though not necessarily difficult. It's easier to duck the challenge and glide along with whatever takes the least effort. Few of us have the natural inclination to investigate, to resist, or to strike out on our own as freelancers. But prior assessment is important because it's ideologically correct and because, in the long run, it's more effective. Or think of it this way: how would you proceed if you had total freedom to choose? Having felt that freedom, you should strive toward it, and toward removing the constraints that prevent you from doing what has the most social value.

The rest of this chapter is based on the premise that prior assessment pays off. There's a second premise, which is that assessment can best be accomplished by rational, linear, one-step-at-a-time thinking. Our aim will be to propose how you could do an assessment yourself and make a decision based on it. Our strategy will be to take up the components of assessment—your needs, community needs, benefits, resources—in order. The most time by far—about half the chapter—will be spent on community needs, on the assumption that you know much more about your own needs and resources, your own circumstances, than about the needs of those you plan to serve. At the end, you should be able to carry out and utilize an assessment that will help you in your own situation.

DOING AN ASSESSMENT

Your Needs

Assessment starts with you (and with your task group if you're working in one). You may not know yourself perfectly, so chalk up an added gain from self-exploration. But you can probably identify your values and preferences, and both properly shape choice of action. Community action should be something you believe in, something that comes from the heart, something that meets your own needs. When it does, your energy will flow freely and mingle easily with others'. But if you don't believe in it, if it's alien to you, it can hardly work. Do something else if you can. Your work should be fun, not just self-sacrifice, and maybe without sacrifice at all. It's true that there has to be some match between your needs and what is needed out there. But start first with yourself; give your needs free play. Later on, the range can be narrowed further.

Community Needs

When it comes to community needs, though, that's another story. Others are less accessible than you, and there are more of them. To find out what other people want can take more than self-exploration and trust in feelings. It can take skill.

Sometimes, assessing community needs is easy.[1] Someone may hand you a thesis-quality assessment just back from the printer; all you have to do is execute. Or the need may literally be outside the door; if a tornado hits town, and you are the Red Cross, survey forms are unnecessary. And sometimes your target group will be quite small; if your concerns are limited to a dozen or so people, you can learn what they want just by getting them together to talk.

But as the size and diversity of your target group increases, assessing needs becomes more difficult. What if you are a member of a service club looking for a new project? What if your group wonders about sponsoring some kind of discussion series? What if you are sounding out possible activities for a new neighborhood association? What if your agency wishes to learn more about the needs of its clients? There are too many target people to talk to. You probably don't know who all of them are. And even if you do, you're not sure how best to approach them to get the information you desire. Your procedure in this and similar cases is not immediately obvious. Here is where social science may add something to what you already know.

There's a healthy literature on community "needs assessment" (finding out what other people want), and there's a parade ground full of assessment techniques to choose from. We'll inspect them here; it will take a while. Imagine that you're able to do the best community needs assessment you can, free from all preconceptions and limitations. Put yourself up on an imaginary reviewing stand, and see how you react to each of the possibilities as they come into view.

Basically, you find out about community needs the same way you find out about most anything else. You read what's available, you listen, and you ask around. "Reading" applies in particular to projects with large target groups, where written material is more likely to exist. "Listening" and "asking" apply anyplace and anytime. That's the short course; an intermediate course follows:

Reading

Previous assessments.

Someone else might already have conducted a needs assessment which speaks directly or even partially to your concerns. While you may doubt this, maybe rightfully so, it's usually worth a little digging around to see if anything similar has been done before. Since written assessments are typically circulated narrowly and forgotten quickly, it's not inconceivable that you might uncover someone else's masterpiece molding away on a dusty shelf. A few hours of research here could save you many more hours of duplicated effort. Even an out-of-date or out-of-town assessment can help determine your own approach. Good places to look: local libraries, community planning agencies, town halls, universities, and any agencies or groups relating to your general interests. You can also ask each person you contact where else you might check.

Newspapers.

A newspaper usually provides the most current overview of community needs, even though they're not neatly summarized, and you may have to sift through a lot of extraneous material to find them. It's a plus to read your local newspaper regularly, and, since memory is short, a bigger plus to clip, date, and file those articles dealing with your concerns. A good clip file can also provide ammunition for convincing others, documentation for any formal applications or proposals you might write, and rainy-day value when you want to look over your own press notices.

Reports.

Written reports about your community may not be assessments as such, but they may allude to community needs and contain other supporting information not found elsewhere. These reports can be tracked down in the same locations where you looked for previous assessments. References cited in the reports may give some further leads.

Demographic data.

The decennial United States census releases voluminous data on, for example, household composition, employment, income, education, mobility, ethnicity, and housing for each census tract (areas of about 4,000 to 5,000 people). More limited, and less widely distributed, data are available for each block or group of blocks. State and town censuses and public surveys often provide more recent or supplementary information. If you know, for just one instance, that the percentage of divorced persons is highest in one particular section of town (or that it increased sharply from a previous census), that suggests a potential need for a support group or for family counseling services keyed to that section. Your regional United States census office, state census office, town hall, or local library can provide you with additional details.

User data.

Other statistics are derived from users of services themselves. It may be possible to learn, for instance, how many people used the legal clinic or consumer hotline last year, how many who requested the service could not be accommodated, how both figures compared to the year before, who the users were, what they were concerned about, and what they thought of the service received. These user data, sometimes available from sponsoring agencies (when they are not, they should be), can point to a need for a new service, more or less service, or some other adjustment in the service delivery pattern.

Listening

No special technique here, just the ability to keep your thoughts to yourself and take in what's being said. Listening can be the easiest and most informal method of all; it's how many community organizers get started. You can put more structure on listening by going to places where issues that concern you are likely to be talked about. It's also possible to take notes, during or after the fact. But you are not intervening yet, not asking any questions. If and when you do (of course you will have to listen then as well), you cross over into another category.

Asking

When you read, you are collecting information that already exists. When you ask others, you are collecting information that never existed before. It's wise, then, before setting out to think through whom you are going to ask, what asking context you will choose, what your questions will be, how many questions will be chosen, how your questions will be presented, and how many people will be involved.

Whom you ask.

People you know. Friends, acquaintances, or other personal contacts you have. One problem with asking people you know (and any other grouping except a random sample) is that they probably do not constitute a representative cross-section of the people you want to serve. Another problem is that people you know, not wishing to offend, may be more likely than strangers to tell you what they think you want to hear. (See "pitfalls" later on.) But this can cut both ways: good friends and some acquaintances may be more honest with you, spend more time with you, and give you more information than you could get from other sources. (They may also be able to help in other parts of the assessment.) There's value in asking people you know, as long as you don't rely on them exclusively – unless, of course, you know and ask everyone in the target group.

Previous users. If user data (see above) do not exist, you may find it helpful to collect them yourself. Previous users of the service, even if at another time or place, are in a unique position to comment on need. You may have to do a bit of legwork to locate past users, and you will have to locate a representative sample of them, but you may turn up significant findings no one else has unearthed.

Community leaders. Here meaning agency directors, club presidents, corporate executives, clergymen, politicians, town officials, educators, newspaper editors, radio and TV station managers, neighborhood organizers, and influential others with no particular name tag. These are the people who know more about what is happening and what is needed in the community than the average person, and who are also in a superior position to help you directly or indirectly once your project begins. On a political level, their opinions may swing weight and as such may be worth knowing; but you also ought to remember that community leaders are not representative of your target group as a whole, may not themselves be the people you want to serve, and may have their own particular axes to grind.

Prospective leaders. Current community leaders may not be able to get heavily involved in any new programs themselves. But if you need or prefer to have others working with you or providing a service, you should assess their interest in advance. If the most logical leaders or helpers jump right on the wagon, that's telling you one thing. If they shuffle their feet and look right through you, that's telling you something else.

Selected sample of target group. Community needs assessment should concentrate on potential users, and since people in the four categories above may fall outside your target group, other samples may be called for. You can select a target group sample in endless ways: by knocking on doors; by stopping people on the street; by choosing people ("habitués") at gathering places related to your concerns (bus stops, bingo games, beauty parlors, as the case may be); by seeking out people believed to feel the greatest need (e.g., corporate executives for employee health programs); or by focusing on people thought to be at the greatest risk (e.g., teen-age parents for parent education programs). Habitués, high-need, and high-risk people will presumably be higher-probability users.

A very different selected-sample approach would be to put a note in the newspaper or club bulletin about community needs and ask for response, or to convey the same message via specifically targeted flyer, poster, or other impersonal publicity device. In theory, this approach can reach many target group people and yield a potentially large return with minimum effort; in practice, response rates tend to be low and feedback tends to come from a highly unrepresentative subgroup of well-motivated individuals. But these may be the higher-probability users identifying themselves.

Random sample of target group. In all random samples – there are several methods of choosing them – each person in the target group has an equal likelihood of being assessed. For instance, if you know your target group has 1000 members and if you know who they are, you can select and assess 50 of them by some sort of lottery, here giving you a 5 percent random sample. Selecting a random sample and getting feedback from each person within it assures you, by definition, that your results will be representative. All nonrandom samples are subject to bias. Unfortunately, random samples are often technically hard to construct, and it's often harder still to reach each person chosen; the larger your target group, the truer this is.

While the mechanics and variations of random sampling procedures are beyond the scope of this book, you can approach randomness by utilizing such aids as membership lists, town censuses, or street address directories. By carefully doing so, you can make a reasonably good approximation, especially if you can obtain professional consultation when you need it. The bigger question is whether attempting to draw a random sample constitutes the best use of your time. (More on this later.)

The context of asking.

"Context" here means that you can ask people about needs individually or in a group. Each way has variations. The advantages and disadvantages of the two basic approaches are easy to fathom. By talking to people individually, you can go into more detail; you can make sure that each person sampled has a full say, apart from group pressures; and you will be more likely to get the direct and honest feedback that stems from a personal relationship. Assessing needs from an assembled group can yield you the same quantity of information in much less time; group members can be made more aware of each other's needs from listening to the discussion; members can pick up some new ideas themselves; and, as an often-unanticipated result, group solidarity may be increased when group members hear others express the same feelings.

If you ask individuals, you need to choose again among face-to-face, telephone, or mail contact. The more personal the contact, the greater percent of compliance, but the longer a given contact takes. How much longer depends on where the contact occurs: their place, your place, or neutral territory. Normally, you, if anyone, will be doing the traveling, and that runs into more time still. As for the other two options, mail contact – possibly a form letter with a short questionnaire – can extend to many hundreds of people very quickly if you can absorb printing and mailing costs; but for a nonprofessional survey, a return rate of 50 percent or better is impressive, and rates of 10 percent or even lower have been rumored to exist. Telephone contact lies somewhere in the middle; you can reach more people in the same time as face-to-face contact if you are willing to sacrifice some intimacy and detail, but your percentage of respondents, while exceeding the percentage mailing back replies, will probably not be as high. Some people don't open up over the phone, and some are never at home.

Similarly, there are alternative ways of assessing group needs. In unstructured natural group settings – youth groups on street corners, for instance – you can listen, and maybe stimulate a discussion after a while. For more structured naturally assembling groups, such as club or board meetings, school classes, and some social get-togethers, you have the additional options of passing out a short survey form, having the group brainstorm for needs, breaking it up into smaller discussion units, or asking group members to write down their thoughts individually before coming together to discuss them.[2] In planning an assessment, it could be helpful to inventory the relevant natural groups (both public and private) in your own setting and to determine which ones you might contact. Doing this can also pay off when it comes time to publicize your new activities or plans.

Sometimes, you may want to create an ad hoc or "artificial" group, one which comes together only for a special and usually short-term purpose – such as assessing needs. You can invite people of your choice together privately, to meet at home, office, or corner cafe; you can have someone organize some friends and neighbors to meet with you, Tupperware-style; or you can advertise a public meeting and make it open to all. Many public organizations routinely hold public hearings, or sponsor community forums, with varying degrees of formality. Most of the feedback techniques applicable to natural groups also apply to transient ones. Ad hoc meetings are nonrepresentative by definition, but their compensating advantage is that you can be pretty sure the people who are present are among those with the largest potential interest in what you are doing or planning.

Let's pause to review our progress so far. You've been attentive if you've realized that there are multiple methods of assessing needs. And you've been insightful if you've also grasped that the methods described to date fall into a matrix which even in abbreviated form looks something like this:

Table 1
Some Methods for Assessing Needs

CONTEXT OF ASKING

Whom You Ask	Individual			Group natural			Group "artificial" (ad hoc)	
	in person	*by phone*	*by mail*	*pub.*	*priv.*	*priv. invtd.*	*pub. hrg.*	*comm. forum*
People you know • friends • acquaintances • other contacts								
Previous users of services								
Community leaders								
Prospective leaders								
Selected sample of target group • door-to-door • street-corner • habitués • high-need • high-risk • self-selected (via publicity)								
Random sample of target group								

If we were to put ruled lines on this matrix, many of the boxes would designate legitimate assessment methods. Other classifications may serve as well or better. Some form of classification is important, but it's equally important to appreciate the range of open options. The options don't end here, for we've only considered two main dimensions of choice. Once you've decided whom you will ask and in what context you will ask them, you must still compose questions. These questions can vary with respect to content, number, and format.

What questions to ask?

As for content, stacking the deck is legal, accepted, and desired practice. Why? *The questions you ask help limit the range of needs assessed.* For instance, if you've decided to work in the area of housing, or if that's your job assignment, it's unwise to ask many questions about education or energy conservation, unless they are directly connected with your interests or unless someone you know will use the data. Focus instead on housing. You're not assessing *all* possible needs, just the ones you could do something about. That's really fair enough: you don't have to be all things to all people, and it's right to set some limiting conditions. You can insert your own pet questions, too, as long as you're aware that asking *only* those questions may obscure the bigger picture and bias your assessment unduly. *Within* your chosen area, diversity of content does make sense – and it's a good idea to ask others near the scene what questions they feel should be included.

How many questions?

Once you've settled on an area, you should cover as much of the territory as time allows. Put differently, once you've gotten attention, you might as well ask all the questions that genuinely interest you. The number of questions is bounded only by the tolerance of your audience and your willingness to process the data. In practice, though, both are bounded. Your informant may be willing to talk for a moment, but not to be interrogated for an hour. And it's wasteful to gather pages full of numbers if you're not committed to analyzing each one. There's no single ideal; by keeping your assessment in perspective, you can find the middle ground that's right for your situation.

What format to use?

Question format can be general or specific, open-ended or closed. Suppose you were in fact assessing the needs of tenants in a housing development. You could ask:

• "What is the biggest need you have as a tenant living here right now?" (A general and open-ended question – possibly too general unless the underlying reason for questioning has been established. Otherwise, you might get answers like "to shoot my next door neighbor," "to get my TV fixed," or "to move out of here.")

• "How would you feel about putting in playground equipment on the south side of the property?" (Specific, and open-ended, in that the question does not limit the form of response; this question could be part of a series of similar specific questions on different topic areas.)

• "On a scale of 1 to 10, where 10 is the most favorable rating and 1 is the least, how would you feel about putting in playground equipment . . . ?" (Specific and closed-ended, as response choices are limited to ten; possibly too formal a question for some target groups.)

• "This list has a number of different ideas on it. Could you check off those which have the most appeal to you?" (A general question incorporating many specific ones; closed-ended, since each item can only be checked or not checked. Alternatives: rank-ordering instead of checking; limiting responses to top three choices, or top five, etc.)[3]

More general and open-ended questions may tap deeper needs, but responses are more likely to be vague, irrelevant, rambling, and harder to categorize. More specific and closed-ended questions elicit more precise and scorable responses, but run the risks of superficiality, excessive formality, and limitation of content. The positive attributes of the different question types complement each other, and it's certainly possible, often desirable, to combine both in the same overall assessment.

In addition, any one of these formats, or virtually any other format you might choose, could be oral or written. That is, you could converse with the respondent personally, or hand out a written form. Briefly, oral questioning is often (not always) easier to initiate, more informal, and more subject to the usually unwanted influences of tone of voice, body language, and other nonverbal cues. Written questions are often (not always) more formal, more exact, more time-consuming (in typing and duplicating), and more efficient (in potentially reaching many people at once). And there are wheels within wheels here too. Oral questions may or may not be read from a previously written text; oral questions may ask for either oral or written responses; written questions may be responded to now, or returned later; oral and written modes can both be used; and so on.

To say the least, potentially useful question formats are in plentiful supply. Soon we will have to decide how to choose among them.

How many people?

If you can contact everyone in your target group, that is excellent. However, when the group edges past 50 people (very roughly speaking, with wide variations), you may opt for a representative sample, as close to random as possible. The size and percentage of your sample will depend upon the overall size of your target group, in addition to your personal resources. With a target group of 500, assessing 50 representative people (a 10 percent sample), possibly even fewer, may be sufficient for your purposes. With a target group as large as 5000, or even larger, a 2 percent sample (here, 100 people) may be perfectly adequate if the sample is chosen carefully. Remember that national polling organizations – using highly refined techniques – sample a much smaller percentage of the national population (.00001 percent or less) in deriving their often remarkably accurate conclusions.

Further reading (see bibliography) can instruct you on the finer points of how many people to assess. But unless you are doing professional survey research, there are few fixed rules and wide boundaries of acceptability. From the standpoint of sampling alone, the basic rules come down to these: (1) The more people you can assess, the better; (2) Even more important, the people you assess should be representative of the people you want to work with. A smaller representative sample will prove more accurate than a larger unrepresentative one.[4]

Criteria

Where do we go from here? There are about as many ways to assess community needs as pebbles on the beach. We don't want to reach for every pebble, for we would grow stooped and gray – and community needs would go unmet – before we finished. Clearly, we need some selection process, one that will give the best reading of need consistent with interests, target population, and resources available. Here are some criteria that can help in making your own selection:

Table 2
Some Criteria for Choosing Assessment Methods

1. *The depth and breadth of relevant assessment that has been done before.*

2. *The extent of your assessment skill.* It's fine to learn by doing, but you may not want to bite off too much more than you can chew.

3. *The purpose behind the assessment* – that is, the manner in which the

data will be used. Are you required to produce quantitative data before you start? Will the amount of service be perfectly matched to the amount of need expressed? Or do you just want to get some preliminary ideas, or to make sure you won't be laughed at if you go ahead with some existing plans? Or are you someplace in the middle?

4. *The amount of time you can make available for the assessment.*

5. *The number of people available.* Is it only you who will be assessing, or are there others who are assigned, or who could be called upon, to help you? Unless the target group is very small, it's usually better to work with others if you have a choice; the contributions of others can strengthen the assessment plan, and make the assessment itself more comprehensive and easier to conduct.

6. *The amount of money available.* Talking to your friends is free, but a full-scale community survey costs money for paper, printing, duplicating, and possibly for mailing and data processing.

7. *The size of your target population.*

8. *The characteristics of your target population.* Are they all located in one place, or isolated and spread out? Are they accepting of being questioned, or suspicious and resentful? Are they used to written survey forms, or threatened and confused by them?

9. *The type of connection you have with the target population.* Is it close, casual, or previously nonexistent?

10. *The scale of the activity you may initiate as a result of the assessment.* A one-day open house needs less prior checking out than a year-round community service. The energy invested in your assessment should be in proportion to the energy investment in your program.

What these criteria suggest is that if a fairly broad choice of activities is open to you, if no one has ever formally studied the needs in your setting, if no critical issue leaps out, if you envision a long-term activity serving a large and heterogeneous community, and if you have plenty of time, experience, money, and people at your disposal, then community needs assessment may merit a major commitment. You might spend considerable time talking to people informally, arranging for small-group dialogues, possibly accompanying them with a fairly extensive survey of representative target group members and eventually a larger community meeting. These are options, not necessarily specific recommendations.

On the other hand, if your alternatives are fixed from the start; if your setting has been well-researched; if there is an immediate burning issue; if you are planning a short-term intervention with a small, tight-knit group; and if you have very limited resources, then your investment need not be as extensive. You may be able to complete an adequate assessment in a single meeting or in a one-night stand of phone calls. And if you fall somewhere in between on the dimensions listed above, as is likely, you can gauge your assessment requirements and formulate your plan accordingly.

Whatever your plan, you don't have to limit yourself to just one assessment technique. Different subgroups can be approached differently, and each respondent can be assessed in more than one way. The options cited are not mutually exclusive. Resources permitting, it's better to employ several techniques together, for doing so will strengthen the overall reliability of your conclusions.

Finally, the human dimension in your choice deserves special mention. Ideally, a needs assessment should generate interest, even excitement, among the people you are assessing, and—unless you are an outside surveyor—a bond between you. Methods involving long questionnaires or numerical judgments are indisputably useful and maybe preferable, but not if they create too much interpersonal distance. Excessive formality and precision can block communication, while honest concern, even if clumsily expressed, can open it up. The most desirable approach is one which will gain you the precision you want while keeping both you and your respondents at ease.

Examples

Two actual examples may help illustrate. The first involves needs assessment within a local church. This church was a big one—parishioners numbered over 2500—and its size alone made it difficult to keep track of whether parishioners' needs were being met. The church was flexible and strong enough to move in any of several conceivable directions; it had members who saw assessment itself as a need and who were willing to help out; the question was what assessment strategy to choose.

The solution here was straightforward. Given the target group's size, a written questionnaire seemed most appropriate. Since not all the parishioners came to church regularly, the questionnaire would be mailed. There was money enough to mail a form to every person on the rolls. A lay committee, with some outside consultation, put together a draft. Like most surveys, this one went through several revisions before a final version emerged several months later. Part of that version is reproduced in Fig. 2.[5]

The questionnaire was mailed to 2,700 people together with a cover letter signed by the church ministers. Seven hundred and eight responses, about 26 percent, came back—probably not too bad under the circumstances. The closed-ended questions turned out to be clear enough and easy to tabulate. The five most frequent-

Figure 2
St. Mary's Parish Needs Survey

This survey has been prepared to review whether our present parish organizations and activities are fulfilling the needs of you, the parishioners; to find out what your honest opinions are; and to permit you to express your ideas about activities you would like to see St. Mary's provide.

Would you take a few minutes to complete this survey? Please respond to each item, following the instructions given. Write in any additional comments in the spaces provided. You need not sign your name.

Please mail the completed survey using the envelope provided or drop it in the receptacles which will be located at the doors to the church during the next two weeks. Thank you for your concern about the needs of St. Mary's parish.

. . .

3. *Listed below are suggested activities that St. Mary's might provide if enough parishioners indicate a sufficient need. Please indicate how strongly you feel that these activities should be provided, by circling one number for each activity.*

	no opinion	not at all	some	much	very much
a) Explanation of Mass, Sacraments, changes, etc., during the Sunday sermon.	1	2	3	4	5
b) Same as above, except on a weekday evening, at regular intervals.	1	2	3	4	5
c) Traditional services (rosary, novena, etc.) on a regular basis.	1	2	3	4	5
d) Adult, spiritually-oriented organizations (such as Holy Name, Sodality, Prayer Group).	1	2	3	4	5
e) Marriage counseling services.	1	2	3	4	5
f) Parish newsletter.	1	2	3	4	5
g) Annual parish calendar, including events for each parish organization.	1	2	3	4	5
h) Parish needs coordinating committee.	1	2	3	4	5
i) Parish council.	1	2	3	4	5
j) Foster grandparents' program.	1	2	3	4	5
k) Committee to visit elderly, sick, nursing homes, etc.	1	2	3	4	5
l) Social action committee.	1	2	3	4	5
m) Men's club.	1	2	3	4	5
n) Adult's club.	1	2	3	4	5

Please list below any activities we may have forgotten, which you feel should be provided. Also, add any comments you may have about any of the suggested activities.

ly expressed needs, all with "very much" scores of 35 percent or better, were (a) explanation of Mass, (e) marriage counseling, (f) parish newsletter, (g) parish calendar, and (k) visitation committee. It wasn't entirely certain whether needs expressed were *personal* needs, or nonpersonal needs the respondent thought the church should nevertheless address. And it was decidedly true that the needs of some 2,000 parishoners remained unknown.[6] But it was also quite clear that the church now had some hard information to go on, where it had none before.

That information was used, and is still used now. Five years after the assessment, explanation of Mass is ongoing in youth education classes. A parish newsletter is distributed weekly, a parish calendar monthly. Marriage encounter groups have begun, as has a visitation group which works in cooperation with a minister who distributes the Holy Eucharist to the homebound. Were the changes due to the survey? Members of the original assessment committee thought so. Plain and uncomplicated as it was, this assessment took hold; needs were really responded to and translated into clear group benefits.[7]

The second example involves a broader-scale assessment of neighborhood needs. Several years ago, my own work group became interested in neighborhood outreach, and after some deliberation came to focus on a section of Lowell called Centralville. We had talked about doing a small demonstration project there, had come up with several possible ideas of our own, but needed to check these against community thinking before progressing further.

Our assessment here had four overlapping parts. In part one, we collected local reports and statistics about Centralville and started a clip file of relevant articles from the daily paper. In part two, we put out a mailing to about 100 local agencies, asking if they provided any services directly in Centralville, what they saw as primary needs there, and if they might be interested in working with us if we got something going. The feedback here was essentially modest and noncommital.

We knew personally a dozen or so people who lived in Centralville and knew of a dozen or so more. In part three, we went out to talk to them, still gathering preliminary information. We arrived by appointment with a fairly long printed interview form on perceptions of the neighborhood and its needs, from which we read questions and recorded responses; we followed it with a shorter checklist which we gave people to fill out. The first page of the shorter form appears here.

Figure 3
Project Ideas for Centralville

The following is a list of activities which might be possible to initiate and develop in Centralville. Would you please let us know what you think of these projects by checking the appropriate category, and by adding notes and comments of your own if you wish. Thank You for your time and thought.

	Wouldn't Work	*Not Useful*	*Good Idea*	*I would like to be involved in this.*	*I would be interested in taking some leadership to make this happen.*
1. Teaching/Training Programs for Residents (Courses, workshops, demonstrations) Specific areas/topics _____					
2. Skills Exchange (A way for people to trade skills they have, e.g., car or home repair, gardening, sewing, etc. for skills they need. Free of charge.) Comments:_____					
3. Teen Activities Night (Sports, Rap Groups, etc.) Comments:_____					
4. Community Bulletin Board (A central location where people or groups could post items of neighborhood interest.) Comments:_____					
5. Community Newsletter (Similar to 4, but in written form) Comments:_____					
6. Hassle Center (A place where objective, third parties could help people resolve disputes.) Comments:_____					
7. Parent Groups (A chance for parents to share ideas, skills, etc.) Comments:_____					
8. Babysitting Co-ops or Play Groups (A way for mothers to get some free time without spending money.) Comments:_____					

I like this kind of form as an assessment tool.[8] As in the church-needs assessment, it gives people the chance to make specific judgments on a wide range of specific ideas. It allows for expression of more open-ended thoughts (page two of the form presented ten more program ideas and solicited general comments). This particular version is also written in comfortable language, is relatively painless to fill out, and yields considerable data in a short time (about five minutes). But, in addition, this form separates out "good ideas" from those that people might want to follow up on personally. And it identifies potential leaders and organizers as well, even if there might not be very many of them. The form worked nicely in practice; it was well matched to its community setting.

In part four, a few months after we started, we scheduled a community meeting in Centralville. We invited everyone (letter plus phone call) on our expanding contact list. Our plan was to introduce ourselves, our goals, and our starting ideas, to describe what we had done so far, to elicit some ideas from residents, and to work together with them from there. I wish I could report that our meeting was a historic event, but that wasn't to be.

The meeting was poorly attended. Support for our ideas, any ideas at all, was lukewarm. This might not have deterred someone with more resolve than ourselves, but we had other responsibilities and other projects to take care of. We needed a minimum level of community support to keep us going, but it wasn't there, not then. Perhaps we weren't forceful enough, or directive enough. Perhaps we were blind to the obstacles facing an unfamiliar outside agency coming in cold to a neighborhood. Perhaps we didn't give our ideas enough time to take root. But we didn't have (we chose not to give) more time. Eventually, we decided to cut our losses and pull out.

Most of the time you will uncover something you can do, but I give this last example as a cautionary tale. Not every needs assessment turns up a need; and even if there is a need, you may not be the person to address it.[9] No regrets: I think our effort was worth a try. But we must return to our chapter theme and critique the assessment procedures themselves.

How would you rate the assessment procedures in each of the above examples? I'd rate them both as reasonably good. (Although the assessment in the second example was incomplete and no need emerged, this does not mean the assessment itself was defective up to the time it stopped.) Were the procedures the best ones possible? Should all large-scale assessments imitate them? No, and not necessarily. The approaches used here were two of many which could have been justified under each circumstance. Different assessors in different settings (especially smaller ones), with different resources and under different pressures, might correctly have employed assessments varying in form, content, and extent. "Justifiability" is the main criterion here. A community needs assessment is justifiable if it meets the following standards, which summarize our discussion to date.

1. Prior consultation with others to determine what form the assessment should take
2. Formation of an assessment plan, based in part on such consultation
3. Verification of the appropriateness of the assessment plan methods for your target group
4. Verification that the assessment is within your ability to perform
5. Prior testing of assessment techniques, especially when they are new or unfamiliar
6. Utilization of more than one assessment technique when resources permit
7. Assessment of a sufficient percentage of your target group
8. Assessment of a representative sample of your target group
9. Allocation of time and energy for the assessment on an appropriate scale with the time and energy to be devoted to any subsequent activity
10. Avoidance of the pitfalls noted below

I feel the assessments in our examples met or exceeded most of these standards, and that explains "reasonably good." Both could have been better; neither was perfect; but in these cases it might not have been worth it to shoot for technical perfection. (With smaller target groups, "perfection" is more within reach.) In any event, there is no one universally "perfect" assessment, but rather a range of choices appropriate for the situation. The primary tasks are to find the range and to choose within it. This is definitely not to excuse casualness or sloppiness, for standards have to be met. But once you have met them, or exceeded them if you can, it may be best to get on with it. Your own standards may be tougher, and if so, more power to you. Yet beyond a certain point—admittedly not often reached—preoccupation with assessment can block you and get in the way of community work itself.

Pitfalls

We have one more topic to cover before leaving community needs, and that is the "pitfalls" mentioned within the standards noted above. Pitfalls crop up in community work, as in life; and, as in life, the best way of avoiding them is to watch out for them in advance.

Some pitfalls in assessing community needs are implicit in the guidelines given, are simply their flip sides. Here is a brief review of some others:

• People may not understand what you are talking about. This means your questions have to be as clear and unambiguous as possible and that you should be able to define your terms if asked. Pretesting questions helps; sometimes it's also desirable to ask the same question in more than one way. (See also footnote 3.)

• People may not know right away what they need, or what the community needs. They may require a little time to think; you may have to be patient enough to wait, or to draw them out.

• People may confuse a personally felt need with a community need, one they see others as having. It's easy for the surveyor to be confused here, too. You should be clear which kind of need you are asking about (cf. the church-needs example). Most assessments focus on personal need, but it's possible to assess on both.

• People may express a need that is being met by some other resource in the community, even by your own group. In those cases, it's a matter of hooking people up with the right resources. Community needs assessment looks for *unmet* needs, those not being addressed by anyone. To verify that a need is unmet, you must know what the available resources are. (If high percentages of people don't know what resources exist, as is common, that may reflect a need in itself.)

• People may not want to tell you about their needs. Strangers especially may distrust your motives, or balk at justifying themselves to you, or feel that you have no business asking them, or fear future invasions of their privacy, or simply guard their time more carefully. Resistance can sometimes be minimized by contacting respondents prior to data collection and explaining your purpose. But some people will not respond no matter what, and you will have to abide by their decisions.

• People may avoid stating preferences they view as "socially undesirable." Someone may be reluctant, for example, to volunteer a need for gay health services or for a support group for families of prisoners. Ensuring anonymity and confidentiality can counter these tendencies, as can specifically assessing the need for such "undesirable" programs.

• Conversely, people may feel obliged to give "socially desirable" responses. One such response pattern is to agree with whatever is being asked. "Do you think there ought to be more recreational programs for teenagers?" It feels almost unpatriotic to say "no." Alternative phrasings, however, are possible. (See also "loaded questions" below, and in accompanying footnotes.)

• A related point: people may tell you what they think you want to hear. If people know you or your preexisting biases, or if they can make out what those biases are, or think they can, they may respond so as to support them. We all want to please; this dynamic operates all the time in social life, and it's no less important here. You can minimize its impact by creating a supportive assessment environment, by specifically encouraging honesty, by using written materials, and by making a conscious attempt to disguise your biases, sometimes even to the extent of having another person do the assessment for you.

• The questions you ask may be loaded toward getting you the answers you hope for. We're all aware of how nonverbal cues can influence response, but question content can be just as biasing. In one type of loading, questions encourage positive responses, sometimes not very subtly. (Example: "Do you think we ought to give kids the chance to take music lessons in elementary school?") In another type, the questions permit only a very narrow range of responses. (Example: "Do you think our agency ought to be open one evening a week, or are our daytime hours sufficient?")[10] In neither case can an objective picture of community needs be obtained.[11]

• People may identify needs you are not equipped to respond to. Your primary concern may be library services, but people may tell you that *their* primary concern is trash collection or (in one assessment I led) mosquitoes. These "extraneous" responses can be reduced by a more careful introduction and phrasing of the survey questions; at the least, such responses can be communicated to groups with designated responsibility or greater capacity to provide the appropriate service.

All these pitfalls can be minimized by awareness and by careful advance planning. You may not be able to fend off all of them entirely. If not, you are in good company. But you will be able to avoid enough of them enough of the time to collect meaningful information that can make a difference. You will be able to state what the most important needs are in your target group, to cluster them in rough priority order (or rank them exactly), and to back up your claims.

If you've come this far, you are a serious reader. You are probably serious enough also to realize that the data you've collected must be put to use. Not to *use* the data would invalidate all your efforts, would render a disservice to your target group, would be the biggest pitfall of all. What point is there in determining a need and then failing to act?[12] On the other hand, and this may be not as apparent, action should not be determined only by stated need, yours or others'. The figuring-out process depends also upon estimated benefits and resources, and to these topics we now turn.

Benefits

Let me describe to you a community program that would bring specific positive benefits to everyone in your target group starting tomorrow. These benefits would be frequent, possibly even continuous. They would last indefinitely. The benefits would be intense, changing both attitudes and behaviors profoundly, in ways that would make people more competent, self-confident, and supportive of each other. The program would spin off other related programs of positive benefit, thus multiplying its impact. The cost would be zero, or negligible at worst. No strings attached. Let me now offer this program to you, on behalf of your community. Will you accept?

I think you would. (I hope you would.) But suppose no one in your community, yourself included, has expressed any particular need for that program. Will you now give it back?

This example illustrates the limitations of need as a determinant of community action. Stated needs, when addressed, may not yield benefits; and, conversely, benefits can occur without previously stated needs. This is because people are not all-seeing—they can't project every possible outcome; and sometimes, for reasons beyond us, they show no desire for benefits which to us seem bright as day. You are not all-seeing either; but on the other hand, you are the decision maker. If *you* project benefits—regardless of whether anyone else does—then you must factor them into your decision equation.

Thin ice here. Am I suggesting that you may know better than others in the community what is good for them? Well, maybe some times you do. Isn't this an arrogant, elitist attitude, precisely the kind we are trying to avoid? It can be, but you needn't feel or act superior just because you see benefits others do not. Would you actually choose an activity that your target group opposes? No; there's a big difference between active opposition and lack of awareness. A community worker won't get far by flying in the face of active opposition; but if there's simple lack of awareness, and if you feel that publicizing benefits would arouse need, you can state your case, give people the option, and try to drum up support.[13] Are projected benefits a more important determinant than stated needs? I wouldn't go that far. However, decisions should not be determined by either one alone. Both make separate contributions, and both should count.

More thin ice. Are there objective measures of "benefit" for community programs, independent of the community worker? Won't the community worker's needs and values distort the benefits projected? I think there are objective measures, which are (or can be) relatively distortion-free. They are embedded in the opening paragraph of this section, and they include:

1. number of people affected (how many?)
2. frequency of effect (how often?)
3. length of effect (how long?)
4. intensity of effect (how much?)
5. type of effect (what kind?)
6. program spin-offs and sequels (how many? each one also rated on the five variables above)

These criteria can sometimes be divided further by different target group subsections (for example, opinion leaders versus ordinary members; newcomers versus old-timers, etc.). The first four can be measured numerically, the first three with relative ease, the fourth easily enough if you have set clear standards for "intensity" in advance. The fifth and sixth are harder to measure, since type of effect involves value judgments, and since spin-offs (and sequels) may be harder to forecast and trace. But even here, if our starting values are competence, confidence, supportiveness, we can define these precisely and estimate the expected degree of benefit for each one.

We've ignored costs so far – that is, costs to the target group member; we'll take up costs to the program developer shortly. The program user may be required to spend time or money or to perform some other tasks in order to gain program benefits. User costs aren't inevitable; some programs are genuinely free, in all that a participant has to do is to show up, sign up, or turn on a dial. But when specific costs do exist, they must be added up and figured in. We are really talking about "net benefits," total user benefits minus total user costs.

If you're not used to measuring program benefits this way, test yourself with this example. Suppose your general concern is with physical conditioning in the community, and you make a preliminary decision to focus on jogging programs. How would you rank the following programs in order of potential community benefit? Assume the target group is the entire community, and, for purposes of example, assume costs are equal.

- constructing a jogging trail through the central park
- sponsoring weekly races open to all comers
- offering jogging instruction through the recreation department
- awarding certificates to those jogging 500 or more miles a year
- doubling the size of the track program in the schools
- writing a series of columns in the local paper on health effects of jogging

I'll leave this solution (if there is a single solution) up to you. Rank-ordering is possible, and I suspect that different raters would be in fairly close agreement on most problems. Granted, any estimate is risky; there's no easy rule for combining criterion estimates into a single "benefit quotient" (it's harder still if costs are added or if programs are not all of the same general type); this example, any example, brings out subtleties we haven't room to account for here; and the whole process of projecting the future may just be more than you want to handle.

No one is telling you that estimating net benefits is a cup of tea. Still, such estimates can be made, and they should be tried. They needn't be time-consuming or back-breaking. Complete accuracy is not required. Any considered estimate will probably be better than none at all.

Resources and Resource Costs

No matter how compelling the need or how impressive the net benefits, a project won't happen by itself. You will have to spend some resources, and a major component of the figuring-out process is calculating how much or how many. The figure that counts most is the gap between what you have and what you need.

We've alluded to resources before. They break down easily into (1) people, (2) time, (3) money, (4) space, and (5) climate. "People" divides into (a) the number of persons working on the task and (b) the characteristics of the persons involved—their talents and skills, personal qualities, influencing power. "Time" means the total amount of person-hours for the project. "Money" is self-explanatory. "Space" refers to a separate location that may be essential for a given task. "Climate," a less tangible resource, denotes the surrounding community atmosphere and can include community receptiveness to social interventions (as distinguished from stated need), your own reputation, pressures from outside groups or institutions, time-limited conditions, and any special features in your own setting likely to help or hinder project operation.

The first step in analyzing resources is to take stock of those already on hand. You always have more than zero, for you always can start with yourself. You are one person with definite skills and interests, with a certain amount of time to spend, and possibly with a few dollars to back these up. If you are part of a work group, whether professional or amateur, your current resources multiply. The surrounding climate may augment them further—you may have an important political ally, an established track record, or a natural tie-in with National (name your cause) Month. When you have a good idea of what you or your group can bring to a project, the next step is to figure out what you will need to carry it off. This will often, though not always, call for more resources than those you have now.

Some examples: you can start a playgroup for preschool children with no more than four or five parents willing to open up their houses one afternoon a week. In this case, everything might already be in place. But if you want to set up a structured after-school program for the elementary grades, you may need parents to plan, supervise, and/or recruit, one or more paid staff, a separate space with adequate facilities, plus close cooperation with, if not also permission from, the public school administration. And if you want to establish a program for gifted students within the school system itself, that may well take specialized teaching talent, public money, several layers of administrative approval outside your direct control, a forceful collection of people to do some forceful lobbying, and the possible overcoming of opposition both to new spending and to the singling out of the gifted as specially deserving. With each of these successive activities, obstacles mount; so do resource expenses. The resources required to overcome the obstacles should be itemized in advance. If you will need to spend resources on a continuous basis rather than for a limited time only, that too should be figured into the bill.

The difference between what you now have and what you will need represents the costs of the project. More specifically, it represents additional resource costs to you (not to the user), which are the ones concerning us here.[14] The greater the new costs, the less feasible the project tends to become. Costs and feasibility are not quite synonymous, for sometimes you may be in a position to command needed resources with a snap of the fingers or twist of the arm. But most of us are not this powerful most of the time. And if the new costs are too great, the project is unlikely to work. You may simply not have the organizational strength, the dollars, or the raw power to pull it off.

It's best in community work to seek some sensible match

between what's on hand and what you must come up with.[15] Some gap is likely to exist, for few projects are cost-free; and frequently, the more ambitious the project, the more added resources it will take. Sometimes you may deliberately choose a high-cost project, believing that the benefits will be worth both the expense and the risk of failure. Such a choice may be well-justified; but before making it, you should be sure that you are able to bear the expense, that the gap is not too wide. Are you really ready to tangle with the school committee, or its institutional equivalent, and are you really prepared to slay every dragon in your path? Even if you are, would you be better off with a project less likely to take so much out of you? Maybe so, but now turn the argument around: little ventured, little gained. It may take some reflection to define a "sensible match" for you.

This completes the data-gathering phase of our assessment; the next step is to make an activity decision. Before we do, there's one important footnote to add. In discussing resources, we used the image of "stock-taking," and that image should be broadened. Just as a businessperson takes inventory every so often, so should the community worker. The ingredients which affect decision are subject to change. Your needs change; community needs change; so do benefits and the resources available to you. They may not vary on a day-to-day basis, or even week-to-week, but they are likely to vary over months, and certainly over years. Assessment should be an ongoing process, not static and once-is-forever. Needs, benefits, resources, and decisions that follow from them should be open to revision, carefully reviewed from time to time, formally reviewed — especially for long-term projects and in ongoing organizations — perhaps once a year or so. Once you have embarked, it's important to keep full speed ahead, but also important to come up on occasion from the boiler room to make sure that your ship is going in the right direction and that your passengers are still on board.

MAKING A DECISION

When you have finished collecting data, the task of figuring out is still not over. The information you have obtained must now be combined to yield the most useful activity choice. We shift our attention to the combining process now. Ideally, this process should be no less rational than the one we've described so far.

In 1772, Benjamin Franklin wrote to a friend on how to make a decision:

. . . My Way is, to divide half a Sheet of Paper by a Line into two Columns; writing over the one *Pro*, and over the other *Con*. Then during three or four Days Consideration, I put down under the different Heads short Hints of the different Motives, that at different Times occur to me, *for* or *against* the Measure. When I have thus got them all together in one View, I endeavor to estimate their respective Weights . . .[16]

More than two centuries later, can we improve on Franklin's procedure? We can try. Logic tells us to devise some sort of formula, to plug in the information we have, to compute an overall value for a given option, to repeat the process for each option, and to choose the highest overall value computed. Suppose we follow this logic through a hypothetical example.

In this example, you have completed data collection, and, to keep things simple, there are only six possible choices: *A* through *F*. Assume that for each component of assessment you can and do assign a scale value of 1 through 10, 10 being highest. And assume further that overall value for an option can be computed simply by adding your own attraction to it, community need for it, projected net benefits, and estimated feasibility. (The smaller the "needed" minus "current" resource difference, the greater the feasibility.) We then have:

Table 3
Hypothetical Needs Assessment Results[17]

Components of Assessment

Option	(1) Your need	(2) Community need	(3) Net benefits	(4) Current	(5) Needed	(6) Feasibility	Total value
A	2	2	2	2	6	6	12
B	2	4	8	8	8	10	24
C	8	4	6	4	6	8	26
D	4	8	6	4	6	8	26
E	10	10	4	4	10	4	28
F	8	8	8	6	6	10	34

Note: columns (4) and (5) are subheadings under *Resources*.

The question is now which option to choose.

The clear choice is Option *F*. It reflects a strong personal and community need, and both net benefits and apparent feasibility are as high as any other choice. Some real-life situations will resemble this one. One option stands out clearly from the rest, and there is no decision problem.

But what if there were no Option *F*, and we had to make one choice from among *A* to *E*?[18] The overall value of *E* is slightly higher, but can we trust the numbers? The combined need for *E* is highest of all, but its benefits are relatively low, and its apparent feasibility is the lowest. Is there a better choice? We can eliminate *A*. *B*, *C*, and *D* all rank higher in benefits and feasibility, but *C* doesn't particularly excite the community, *D* doesn't excite you, and *B* doesn't excite anyone. Should you stay with a high-need project like *E* despite a strong possibility it will fail? Should you make the safe choice of *B* even though no one really wants it? Or should you steer toward the middle, placing your needs above the community's (*C*), or sacrificing them (*D*)?

In these situations, and there are many of them, our decision system breaks down. It's easy to spot the glaring defects in the formula we've set up: (1) Assigning scale scores to each factor is a chancy and unreliable business; (2) We have no solid grounds for assigning weights to each of the four main factors (Why should all be equal here? But if otherwise, by what criteria is the inequality determined?); (3) There's no inherent reason to add up the scale scores rather than to multiply them, or to subject them to other mathematical operations which would change the overall results; (4) In a group decision situation, different assessors may reach different conclusions. Under these conditions, the numbers lose their power, and you tend to base your real choice on other factors.

Don't be misled into thinking that this is the state of the art in decision making. Modern decision theorists are a lot more sophisticated, prone to write in superscripts and subscripts, to rely on some fairly high-powered math, and to use terms I can't do justice to here.[19] But I'm not convinced that they satisfactorily address the defects mentioned above. No formula and no verbal exposition can camouflage the fact that you or your group, the prime movers in your back-home situation, will ultimately have to assign values to the information that's in front of you and come up with some way of combining that information that makes practical sense.

I can understand how someone could become annoyed at this example, especially given all its faults. Who in one's right mind would make decisions this way? The whole example is silly, a complete waste of time. Playing with numbers may be fun and games, but making decisions by formula is ridiculous. No one operates like this. And (the protest continues) it's for sure all this number magic has nothing to do with my own work. My job is to get these phone calls made today. Or our group has to send out this month's bulletin. Or someone asked for a presentation over at their place, and that's reason enough for me. I don't have to make many starting-out decisions, and if I do, I'll follow the leader, or I'll play it by ear. I'll get by okay. Somehow, things work out . . .

I sympathize with this point of view, yet I don't share it. It's true that very few people decide on community work (or anything else) this way, but that doesn't mean you shouldn't. It's true that very few people are this linear and methodical (mechanical? computerlike?), but that doesn't mean you shouldn't be. What are your real alternatives – choosing by whim, or expediency, or following someone else and abdicating decision-making power altogether? Are these your preferences?

There's value in formalization, in assigning numerical weights for each identified factor within each option as precisely as possible, and then combining them. Formalization raises consciousness. Using *any* formal decision-making model means that you are taking responsibility for making decisions, which is worthwhile in itself. There's added value in quantification, for this pushes your assumptions out into the open, where you and others can examine them by daylight, and revise them as necessary. There's practical value too, not just moral and intellectual consolation, for formalization also improves accuracy of choice, and accurate choice increases community impact. If you had to make a single choice among A to E, might you not be slightly better off choosing E (and using the outcome to adjust your model)? Would you really rather flip a coin?

I'm not arguing that you should use this particular decision-making approach, nor that all community decisions should be preceded by communion with your pocket calculator. I am saying that you should use *some* formal, written-out approach for fitting your activity choice to the situation, perhaps making a few concessions to daily pressures, but ideally not too many. I must also advise you that the approach I've laid out here is about as far as I can take you in this chapter, and I must leave it to you to adapt it to your situation and to make needed improvements.

SETTING A GOAL

We've traveled a long route, over the peaks of assessment and then through the valley of decision. One small but crucial step remains: to convert your decision into a goal statement. In other words, once you have figured out what to do, you are responsible for translating it into one or more specific objectives. For example, if you decide to work on a neighborhood newsletter, two specific (and in this case complementary) objectives for your group might be:

1. to distribute 1,000 copies of a four-page newsletter door-to-door in your neighborhood within three months, and monthly after that

2. to collect enough donations, subscription payments, and/or advertising revenue to cover costs for each issue prior to printing

Similar logic applies across the board. Forming specific objectives means asking and telling yourself exactly what you would like to see accomplished by the end of a given time period. It involves specifying the exact benefits of your chosen activity, another reason to think in terms of benefits if you haven't been doing so already. Putting it another way, it involves answering a pointed set of questions (cf. chapter 2):

What?
By whom?
To whom?
How many?
How often?
For how long?
By what method?
Where?
By when?

Answering isn't particularly hard. The task simply calls for you to be thoughtful and precise, not to *do* anything yet. And the answers you give, the objectives you set, can usually be modified later on if truly necessary. In community work, objectives are generally non-binding.

Why bother setting objectives, then, if you're not positive you can live up to them? Because fate will provide its own answers for you, will set its own "objectives," if you don't choose first; you might as well beat it to the punch. There are also three more practical reasons. Specific objectives motivate you, by giving you a clear target to shoot at. Specific objectives help you evaluate your work, by providing you with ready-made criteria (the *primary* criteria) for judging your performance (chapter 6). And finally, specific objectives assist you in planning the details of your work (chapter 4). They focus your energy and make you more efficient. Once you've got a clear outline in front of you, it's much easier to fill in the rest of the blanks.

We're ready now to move into the next chapter, on planning. Planning amounts to filling in those blanks, figuring out the specific steps to meet your specific objectives. Planning is like assessment, in being preparation work which depends on concentrated thinking. Planning also has its own techniques, which we will review. One thing more: planning hints at a deeper commitment, an implied obligation to carry out the finished plan. To make that commitment requires an act of will.

4
Planning

PLANNING MAKES SENSE, BUT...

After you have figured out what you are going to do, the next step is to figure out how you are going to do it. In other words, you need to plan.

This sounds right. But it also sounds as if it means more head work, like the kind we described in the last chapter. Is this really necessary? Isn't it time to stop thinking about what to do, to stop talking about it, and to take the plunge? Once you are wet all over, things will follow from there.

Let's see if we can clarify the issue. I'll set down some statements about planning your course of action; you decide whether or not you agree. These statements apply to planning in general, but especially to planning in community work, and they assume that the plan is actually followed in practice.

1. A good plan will utilize the resources you have with greater efficiency.
2. A good plan will be more likely to overcome the obstacles you face.
3. A good plan will be more likely to stimulate the support and participation of others.
4. A good plan will in the long run save you time.
5. A good plan will in the long run conserve your emotional energy.
6. A good plan will strengthen both your confidence in and motivation for doing community work in the future.
7. A good plan will increase your probability of success.

Think over your answers carefully, then add up your score. I will guess – and I would bet my next royalty check if we were collecting

75

real data—that you and most other readers will agree to five or more of these statements. Two reasons support my belief. First, most people think of planning—at least in the abstract—as a productive and socially desirable activity, something they ought to be doing themselves, like morning sit-ups. Second, the catch word is "good"; we are not talking about *any* plan, which might be a waste of everyone's time, but only about a "good" plan, the pick of the crop. (It's also possible that the tone of the material presented so far may have biased you in favor.)

Suppose you did respond to most statements affirmatively. Consider the meaning of your answers. You have essentially stated that a "good" plan would be helpful to you. By implication, I think you may also have agreed to put a reasonable portion of your time and energy into advance planning on how to reach your goal. Is that fair to say? Planning may not be your favorite activity, and you may have to live with your feelings of restlessness for a while; I share your feelings; but a good plan may be worth the effort. And of course a good plan is what we are after, too; that explains the inclusion of this chapter.

Now, if good planning is liable to pay off, then where is your own plan? I mean the plan for the activity you're engaged in now, or the one you're getting ready to start. Does it exist physically? Does someone else have it? Can you point to it, in the same sense that an architect can point to a blueprint, or a playwright to a script? Is it scribbled on the back of an envelope? Or is it stored inside your head, in rough-draft form, subject to recall if you can find the right button to push? Or is it just a hazy background intention? Or is there a plan at all?

I'll make another bet, double or nothing if you like, that if you gather together all the community programs and activities that take place during a given year, whether in your own community or in the entire world, the percentage of those with a prior documented plan will be a single-digit number. I'll ask you to check which category you fall into. I'll also suggest that of all the potential community interventions thought up in the same time period, lack of careful advance planning ranks as a primary reason why the great majority of them never get off the ground. We believe planning is both valuable and virtuous, but we don't plan. The difference between belief and practice is genuinely impressive.[1] A good plan is hard to find.

The mystery of planning failure is worth dramatizing a bit more. On the one hand, it's not as if we don't make plans in our everyday lives, or that we don't sometimes take great pains to do so. Before the wedding party, we are likely to make up a seating plan; before changing around the bathroom, a remodeling plan; before going on a diet, a weight-loss plan—each one complete with charts and numbers. We're certainly capable of drawing up these plans, often quite talented at them, sometimes even emotionally involved.

We can also move up or down the scale of planning complexity with relative ease. We may set aside some evenings to sketch out a college-education plan, or a career plan, or a retirement plan, plans almost as big as life itself. On a much smaller scale, shopping at the supermarket, studying for an exam, thinking about what to do this weekend require planning too, or at least could profit from it. Even walking to the post office or returning a book to the library contains plans in miniature, though we normally don't associate the term "planning" with events so routine. But each one involves specification of a future goal and preparation of a sequence of responses to achieve it—planning, by more glamorous definition.

And to cap the argument, when we observe or consult a professional, we expect to see evidence of a carefully drawn-up plan. Planning is a hallmark of the professional, a substantial part of what we value in any professional activity. No self-respecting football coach would meet any rival without a game plan; no financial advisor could keep a client without proposing an investment plan; no choreographer would allow dancers on stage without their knowing what sequence of movements to follow. The dance is planned, just as pass plays and sell orders. Pure improvisation, in life as in art, is rare. Plans are woven tightly into daily existence. Conscious plans determine the more significant things we do. Planning, in fact, is a distinguishing characteristic of human behavior.

On the other hand, when it comes to making plans for social interventions, for community activities of even the humblest kind, the lights flicker and grow dim. You may pick out whatever reasons you find most appealing: lack of goal clarity; too long a time period needed to reach the goal; too many variables beyond personal control; insufficient personal payoff for the activity in question; little or no experience in social planning; few or no rewards for past efforts; or treatment of community activity as a hobby or diversion, rather than as a serious enterprise. I am myself partial to all of these, though each reason leads essentially to the same result: failure to plan adequately.

When serious, intentional planning does occur, the plans frequently get shunted off to the side, away from the mainstream of activity. Social agencies, in particular, are prone to designating one staff member as their "planner," almost as if to absolve other staff of planning responsibility. The planner, who frequently inherits the position by process of elimination, and who rarely has real power, sits faithfully in an office and eventually hatches a "plan." The plan is admired by all, then placed in the trophy case, where visitors so inclined can admire it too. Meanwhile, agency work goes on as before, unmindful of the plan, apparently unaware that it even exists. While this may be a little extreme, it doesn't miss by much; similar situations abound in grass-roots organizations as well.

Merely to describe someone as a "planner" touches off the ambivalence we feel about the planning process. A planner is a bit of a shady character, a misfit, someone not entirely to be trusted, someone who may be taking advantage and not really doing the work of an adult. The plans produced are liable to be starry-eyed, unworkable, and costly to boot. What's more, isn't the planner risking interference with some basic human rights? A pretty reliable applause line: "We've got to stop listening to all those social planners and other do-gooders who think they can tell us how to run our lives . . . ." These and other barely submerged negative feelings complement the positive feelings connected with the social desirability and potential utility of planning. Both sets of feelings are real; yet since rigorous social planning with follow-through is rare, it's not uncommon to find in the same person a sense of obligation to plan, guilt at not meeting the obligation, and displaced resentment directed at the entire planning process.

We could go on discussing planning in general or digging deeper into our ambivalent feelings about it. But our more important concerns are these: if a good plan will be useful for you, if it will increase your chances for success, we first want to understand what a good plan is and how to make one. Then we want to translate this knowledge into practice. These are our main purposes. To accomplish them, we could follow the outline of the last chapter, here laying out criteria for plan analysis and rules for plan construction, then giving some illustrations. But this time let's get down to cases sooner rather than later. We'll try reversing the procedure, starting with some concrete examples, critiquing them, and seeing if the rules, criteria, and value judgments will follow from there.

SAMPLE PLANS AND CRITIQUES

There's no end to possible planning situations, but since similar general principles will apply in each case, we can feel comfortable focusing in on the first one that happens to come to mind.

Visualize your own community. It probably has a fair mixture of age groupings, with children, young adults, middle-aged people, and older persons sharing the same community space. Of the older persons, some are productively working; some are happily retired; some are cared for by their families; some are institutionalized; others fall into none of these categories, and these are often people who live out their lives in poor health, with little money, and alone. They are the isolated elderly; by definition, they are not visible in their communities. Sickness or poverty or fear keeps them shut in their rooms most of the day.

Suppose that you decide to do something about this situation. You can't give the isolated elderly money or medical care yourself, but you can give them companionship. You can drop in to say hello and to pass the time, with no greater expectations. Specifically, suppose after some deliberate thought (and assessment) you decide to set up a program where you and others who are interested agree to make periodic visits to those isolated elderly wanting to receive you (cf. the church needs assessment in chapter 3). This is your general goal.

The next step is to figure out how you are going to reach your goal – that is, to plan. You're not an experienced planner, but you're willing to believe that a plan may help you get what you want. So you find a quiet place, and after a short while you emerge with something like this:

Table 4

Plan 1

1. Find isolated elderly.
2. Find people to visit them.
3. Match one to the other.
4. Begin visits.

In beginning a program – or anything else for that matter – a useful skill to acquire is the ability to critique your own plan. Let's try then to move back a few paces and comment on this one. The plan is simple – it sets out very plainly what needs to be done – and this is a virtue, for in more complicated plans there's a danger of losing the forest for the trees. The plan is clear. It lists the desired actions in chronological order. And at first glance the actions proposed tie in well with the starting goal.

But even an untrained eye can spot some deficiencies too. There is no mention of program size – your approach will probably be different if you are talking about five visitors as compared to fifty.

There's no indication of how long the planning process will take, which is important if you are serious about committing your own time. And it's not at all apparent how either the elderly people or the visitors will be found, or how they will be matched with each other. You may notice other faults yourself, mostly errors of omission, and you will probably be right.

The plan is too vague to be workable in practice; yet it is far from worthless. The very act of getting something down in black and white can clarify your thoughts. Seeing your ideas in print can also make them seem more real for you, thus strengthening your own motivation. Finally, once you have something to go on, something to criticize, you can study the critical comments and account for them in the next draft. We'll do this here and try again.

Table 5
Plan 2

1. Recruit people to help you plan the program.
2. Decide on the scale and the content of the program.
3. Devise a method of locating isolated elderly.
4. Locate isolated elderly.
5. Devise a method of recruiting visitors.
6. Recruit visitors.
7. Devise a method of matching isolated persons and visitors.
8. Match accordingly.
9. Devise a method for starting visits.
10. Begin visits.

(Time from #1 to #10: 3 months)

A better plan than the first? Yes, in several respects. The first improvement lies in finding some other people to help you plan the program (step 1). This is not the best idea in every case, for it takes more time, and there may be occasions when despite your own motivation you cannot track down a group of like-minded co-conspirators. Still, you are not obliged to bear the whole burden yourself; distributing it is usually to the program's advantage in the short run, almost always in the long run. The early involvement of others is especially helpful when you are inexperienced; and veterans know that if others participate in planning, they will also be more likely to participate in execution.

A second improvement is in the prior specification of the scale and the content of the program (step 2), even though the plan itself does not detail these precisely. A third is in the specification of a time frame, here three months; even this much will help us organize and prioritize our time. A fourth improvement involves paying attention to devising methods for locating the elderly, recruiting the visitors, matching them up, and getting started (steps 3, 5, 7, and 9). Note that the basic elements in the plan remain— steps 4, 6, 8, and 10 in this plan are equivalent to the four steps in plan 1—but this revised plan makes matters one level more specific.

Some deficiencies:

1. Task responsibility is undefined. Since there is now a core planning group, you are not going to do everything yourself. In that case, who is going to do what?

2. The time frame is too vague. Specifying three months from today to the first visit is like having a term paper due at the end of the semester: in both cases, the due date will be more easily met, and time will be more efficiently spent, if guidelines are set up for various stages of its completion. In other words, who will do what by when?

3. The plan ends too soon. After the visits begin, we hope that the planners do not slip away from the scene. A program once out of the nest still needs a parent's love. More precisely, the program needs someone to make certain that the visits were made and to evaluate how well they went. The plan should identify these activities and specify how they will be carried out.

4. The methods are unclear. It's right to include a method for locating the elderly, locating the visitors, and so on, but at some point we want to know what that method *involves*. That point may as well be now. For example, just *how* are you going to locate the isolated elderly? What specific actions should take place? These actions probably ought to be pinned down, and then written into the plan. In more general terms, and to anticipate later discussion, we should aim for a level of planning specificity most appropriate to the task.

Do you agree that these are real flaws? If so, is it worth the energy to correct for them in advance? If you say yes to both questions, then planning passes from a casual affair into a serious relationship. But planning is not casual; it is serious. Entering into a relationship with planning means work; when you take it for granted, you get into trouble.

Plan 3 meets the objections raised to the last plan. Task responsibility is spread out among a core group of seven, headed by the initiator, Buddy. Time guidelines are established for each individual task. Some attention is paid to the review and correction procedure, as noted in step 6. The methods for selection and match-up, while not entirely spelled out, are outlined a little more clearly. In addition, tasks in this draft are grouped under subheadings, which

Table 6

Plan 3

Step #	What	Who	By when (# weeks from today)
1. Develop core group			
	A. List potential core group members	Buddy	1
	B. Contact potential core group members	Buddy	2

	C. Meet with consenting core group members: discuss and define
	  1. goal
	  2. scale
	  3. content
	  4. next planning steps [included here]
		Buddy, Eva, Tom, Tricia, Eric, Rachel, Pat ↓	4

2. Obtain list of isolated elderly	Buddy	
	A. Identify possible sources of names or locations of elderly	Eva Tom	5
	B. Investigate sources	Tricia	7
	C. Compile tentative lists of names and locations		9

	D. Refine list
	  1. check for accuracy
	  2. pare down to desired size
		↓	10

3. Obtain list of visitors (repeat steps A-D above for identifying isolated elderly, applying each one instead to "visitors")	Buddy Eric Rachel Pat	3A = 5 3B = 7 3C = 9 3D = 10
4. Match isolated persons and visitors	Buddy Eva	11
	A. Assign approximately equal number of elderly persons to each visitor, on random basis	↓	
5. Start visits			
	A. Contact elderly persons; arrange first visits	All visitors	11
	B. Visit elderly persons	All visitors	12
6. Review visits			

	A. Arrange meeting of core group and visitors
	  1. review outcome of visits
	  2. adjust program procedure accordingly
		Core group and visitors ↓	14

	B. Continue with program as adjusted	All visitors	15, and indefinitely

shows a conceptual advance. And the time guidelines make it apparent that several essential tasks (here, steps 2 and 3) can go on simultaneously, through division of labor. The plan as a whole is longer, more detailed, more specific in its component parts. I think we can safely claim it is superior to its predecessors.

But it is far from flawless, and it may not even be sufficient. Among the major areas not covered are testing out the visit procedure, screening both parties to the visit, training the visitors, and ongoing evaluation. Rather than go into detail now, we'll take a deep breath and draw up a fourth version, inserting some new material in parentheses, and commenting on it subsequently. In reviewing this next plan – prepare yourself for some detail – here are some key questions to keep in mind: (a) Is this plan an improvement over the one before it? Why or why not?; (b) Is planning at this level of complexity worth the effort? and (c) If you've liked each plan better than each one before it, how much further do you want to go? (See Table 7, Plan 4.)

This fourth plan is far from a casual affair; it's dead serious. And we need to take it seriously, for other programs you might construct are going to run up against much the same issues, though differently garbed. We're not primarily interested in the specifics of visitation programs here; we're interested in general planning procedures, which the visitation example allows us to illustrate.

An excellent way for us to learn about planning in general is to examine this plan piece by piece. So what follows is a running commentary, emphasizing the newly included material, in order of appearance. As we proceed, think of how the comments here might generalize to and apply in your own setting; think too of how your own reactions add to or vary from mine.

Need (step 1-C-1).

You should already have independent evidence supporting the need for the program (cf. chapter 3). That evidence should be collected and documented before you pick up the phone. But the evidence may be weak, or one-sided, or of doubtful validity. Even if you think it is strong, it still is sensible to reestablish the underlying need in the earliest core group discussions. The perspectives of others will help make sure the resulting program responds to a need that is objectively there; and clarifying the need will also help bond the group together.

Target group (step 1-C-5).

At about this point, not much later, the term "isolated elderly" – the target group – needs to be clearly defined. Obviously, more is

Table 7
Plan 4

Step #	What	Who	By when (# weeks from today)
1. Develop core group			
	A. List potential core group members	Lee	1
	B. Contact potential core group members; (invite to meeting)	Lee	2
	C. Meet with consenting core group members: discuss and define	Lee, Alan, Nanette, Steve, Amelia, Roger, Ellen	4
	1. (need)		
	2. goal		
	3. scale		
	4. content		
	5. (target group)		
	6. (visit procedure)		
	7. next planning steps [included here]	↓	
2. (Conduct test visits)			
	A. (Obtain small sample of representative isolated elderly, from nearest convenient source)	Full core group	5
	B. (Contact elderly persons)		6
	C. (Arrange visits)		6
	D. (Conduct visits)		7
	E. (Review visits in core group meeting)		8
	F. (Modify procedure as necessary)	↓	8
3. Obtain list of isolated elderly (as defined)			
	A. Identify possible sources of names or locations of elderly	Lee, Alan, Nanette, Steve	9
	B. Investigate sources		11
	1. (town hall [town census])	Lee	
	2. (senior citizen clubs)	Alan	
	3. (elderly housing projects)	Nanette	
	4. (visiting nurses association)	Steve	
	5. (key neighborhood/block contact people)	Lee, Alan, Nanette, Steve	
	C. Compile tentative list of names and locations		13
	D. Refine list		14
	1. check for accuracy		
	2. pare down to desired size (and priority order)	↓	
4. Obtain list of visitors			
	A. Identify possible sources of names or locations of visitors	Lee, Amelia, Roger, Ellen	9
	B. Investigate sources; (recruit visitors)		11

1. (family, friends, neighbors)	Lee, Amelia, Roger, Ellen	
2. (churches)	Lee	
3. (clubs)	Amelia	
4. (posters)	Roger	
5. (newspaper story)	Ellen	
C. Compile tentative list of visitors	Lee, Amelia	13
D. (Screen visitors, via individual interview)	Roger, Ellen	15
E. (Pare list to desired size, to match number of elderly, including "most qualified" visitors)		16

5. (Develop visitation group)
   - A. (Contact selected visitors; arrange meeting) — Full core group — 17
   - B. (At meeting or meetings): — and visitors — 18-19
     1. (build solidarity)
     2. (train visitors)
        - a. (visit goals)
        - b. (visit techniques)
        - c. (local resources)
     3. (discuss all procedures)
     4. (clarify commitment)
     5. (answer questons)

6. Match isolated persons and visitors
   - A. Assign approximately equal number of elderly persons to each visitor (on basis of visitor preference, or proximity) — Lee, Alan — 18-19 [can be done at meeting in 5-B above]

7. (Contact elderly persons on list)
   - A. (Explain program) — All visitors — 20
   - B. (Determine if person falls within target group)
   - C. (Determine if person wants visit: if yes, explain next steps and arrange first visits)
   - D. (If necessary, solicit other prospective elderly)
   - E. (Revise list accordingly)

8. Start visits — All visitors — 21

9. Review visits
   - A. Arrange meeting of core group and visitors — Full core group and visitors — 23
     1. review outcome of visits
     2. adjust program and procedure accordingly
   - B. Continue with program as adjusted — All visitors — 23, and
   - C. (Repeat cycle of 9A and 9B above, with possible separate additional meetings for core group) — Core group (as modified) and visitors — indefinitely (monthly meetings)

meant than an older person who lives alone. The specifics might best be left up to the core group members, but they ought to agree precisely on what kind of person they are talking about.

Visit procedure (step 1-C-6).

The actual visit procedure should be roughed out in advance, scene by scene if not line by line. This is especially true if some test visits will be made, as indicated in step 2.

Test visits (step 2).

Even experienced scientists conduct pilot tests before launching full-scale investigations. Unless you have done this particular kind of work before, there's every reason for you to do the same. The people you have chosen to help may want no part of you; you may want no part of them; or, if mutual sympathies remain, you may find the generation gap is larger than you think. The more inexperienced or unsure you are, and the more novel the plan, the more test visits you should make. The test visits will give you an idea of what percent of people will be receptive, before the visits actually begin, and they will also help you to work some bugs out of your procedure. It's better that you do this now, rather than involve a full group of visitors and visitees in a well-intentioned but not very perceptive operation. If a few extra weeks of trials will lower the discomfort index all around and help you fix the scope of your visitor recruitment efforts, this is more than a fair exchange.[2]

Obtain list of isolated elderly (step 3).

This step assumes that the test visits in step 2 show enough positive results to keep you going. If the visits are a complete bust, you certainly want to reexamine your basic premises. You can go back to the drawing board, very carefully this time, or you can abandon the project altogether. Program trials are neither a mere formality nor a delaying tactic; they should supply essential corrective feedback. Not all ideas are good ones, even if they are yours, and not all good ideas work. If after sufficient trial the program does not take hold, you can let go of it with no stigma attached.

Time frame (step 3).

Note that there is no time overlap between steps 2 and 3. In this plan, the decision to go ahead with the program depends upon completion of the trial visit analysis in step 2. Such a planning approach is conservative, but usually justifiable. It's possible to have steps 2 and 3 overlap, or even go on together. This accelerated early effort will tend to bias the program into continuing, even when it shouldn't. If it does continue, some time can be saved; if not, some additional time will be wasted.

Investigate sources (step 3-B).

Division of labor is made more specific here. A similar situation applies for step 4-B.

Priority order (step 3-D-2).

If a program cannot affect the entire target population, the intended targets should be prioritized according to their need and your capacity to provide service. Which persons are the best candidates for a visit? If you can specify them, overall program impact per unit of time spent will improve. (Cf. also step 4-E.)

Compile tentative list of visitors (step 4-C).

The number of visitors to be recruited should be tied to the planned size of the program, which in turn should be determined in advance by need, available resources, and pretesting. To recruit many more visitors than you can possibly use is a poor use of your time as well as discouraging to those who volunteer to help. Note also that if the number of visitors is to be equal to or less than the size of the core group, visitor recruitment and specialized visitor training become less necessary and time consuming. This plan assumes a somewhat bigger program, to meet more of the purported need sooner. However, a smaller program, which may more easily build upon its successes, may be perfectly justified and in some cases preferred.

Screen visitors (step 4-D).

Not all people who want to help will turn out to be good helpers. Potential visitors should be screened by one or more core group members via preset criteria, especially if you are fortunate enough to find more recruits than you can handle. Persons who are obviously not suited for this task can perhaps be given something else to do. Even if no one gets screened out, as may well happen, the act of screening still helps convince the visitor (and the screener) of the program's seriousness, while the fact of selection raises both self-esteem and connection to the program by a degree or two.

Time frame (step 4).

Recruiting visitors can legitimately take place at the same time the listing of isolated elderly is compiled. These are parallel tasks, neither depending upon the prior completion of the other. A planner may portion out as many parallel tasks for which there are human resources to execute.

Develop visitation group (step 5).

A prospective visitor should receive some prior training. The plan should include one or more previsit occasions for the visitors to meet together, to experience themselves as a group about to embark on a socially important mission, and, most importantly, to get some grounding in visit techniques and procedures from those who have made visits before. Proper training will enhance program impact by strengthening visitor skill and commitment.

Match isolated person and visitor (step 6).

Matching on the basis of visitor preference, or proximity, is probably preferable to matching on a random basis. If those about to be visited should express or imply a preference of their own, that of course should be honored too.

Contact persons on list (step 7).

You don't want to walk into a person's home cold turkey. There is an ethical issue here, one of consent, which suggests a prior contact. And there is a practical issue, one of how best to make the first contact so as to gain at least provisional acceptance. No matter how carefully planned and sensitive the prior contact, some people, for varied reasons of their own, will not want to be visited, certainly not by strangers. You as program planner first need to verify their number, and then – while fully respecting those who decline – to minimize it. Working out the contact details, making the prospect attractive, is in many ways the most delicate part of the whole program – though those details are not spelled out even in this plan.

Repeat cycle (step 9-C).

The review and correction process is not a one-time event, as suggested in plan 3, but a process which ought to continue for the life of the program. Very rare is the program which cannot improve, or which can run without adjustments for any period of time. Improvements and adjustments can best occur within regular group meetings. Even if the program were operating at peak efficiency, and maintenance-free, its membership would inevitably change; ongoing meetings are necessary both to reassess the value of the program and to reaffirm the value of its participants.

Time frame (step 9).

Compared to plan 3, this plan takes eight weeks longer from the time someone is first contacted to the completion of the first round of visits. (This is not the same as eight full weeks more work.)

Given the quality difference between the two plans, the extra time appears warranted. The plan could probably be executed somewhat sooner, without compromising quality, if the core group committed itself to moving faster.

What grade would you assign this plan? If I were pushed, I'd rate it about B-plus, possibly higher. I think it's a solidly constructed plan, one which has a fighting chance of working out in practice. I have reservations about it, though I have no doubt that it is the best of the four plans we've seen. I do feel confident in claiming that if all community workers began by drawing up plans akin to this, the infant mortality rate of programs would drop by at least half. Is such intensity of planning effort worth it? I definitely think so, even though a plan of this complexity may seem like far more than you bargained for when you began this chapter. But that is all right.

Still, there are reservations. To begin, this is surely not the *only* adequate plan that could be devised for this program; others, perhaps yourself included, might construct a plan with somewhat different language, content, or sequence that would be at least as good, as judged by criteria we shall identify later. The plan is also imperfect as it stands. Specifically, I would like to see more safeguards in the test visit procedure, so as to lessen the chances of bias affecting subsequent program decisions; I have doubts about recruiting and training the visitors (steps 4 and 5) before contacting the persons to be visited (step 7), even though reversing the process could keep the potential visitees on the hook too long; and, given its crucial nature, I would put more thinking into the contact procedure in step 7. You undoubtedly can add critical comments of your own.

And you will always be able to. You may have come to appreciate by now that plans are like most human endeavors – they are never perfect. High grade approximations, even brilliant ones, can be found, but a detail can always be changed, a refinement always added. Any plan can be picked apart. If you doubt it, consider plan 5 (actually a plan segment) designed to tighten up the step 7 contact procedure mentioned in the last paragraph.

We can admire the precision of this plan segment. It is more detailed than the previous version, and this detail may help us when it comes time to make the first call. But this plan, like its ancestors and its possible descendants, is vulnerable to criticism. Just how do you explain the need, or the history of the program? What exact language do you use to make the request? Even if all the dialogue were typed and handed out as a script, there would still be the vocal nuances, the pauses, the rhythm of speech, the tone of voice to account for. And even if the dialogue were rehearsed, as a scene in a play, the caller would still need planned responses for each possible answer one might receive. Compared to other possible plan segments, this one is among the easiest to script out. Yet even here planning eventually breaks down, and spontaneity takes over. Human beings are limited in their ability to chart the future.

But something is more disturbing about this plan segment than its lack of finality. The plan at this level seems too complicated, too rich, like a chocolate cake when we wanted a cookie. It is more than we need, at least before we have actually started. It chokes off the free expression of our personality. It weighs us down. The ideas in this plan may not even be good ideas, though that raises a different issue altogether. . . .

Table 8

Plan 5 (partial version)

Step #	What	Who	By when (# weeks from today)
		Elderly Persons' #	(Day: 108)
7.	Contact persons on list	#1-10:	1/11/21/31/41/51/61:
	A. Have list of phone numbers	Willie	Tues., July 29, 10 a.m.*
	B. Dial first number	#11-20:	2/12/22/32/42/52/62:
	C. Make opening remarks	Opal	Tues., July 29, 10:15
	1. hello		3/13/23/33/43/53/63:
	2. is this (person's name)?	#21-30:	Tues., July 29, 10:30
	3. your name	Ray	4/14/24/34/44/54/64:
	4. your affiliation	#31-40:	Wed., July 30, 10:00
	D. Explain why you are calling	Tanya	5/15/25/35/45/55/65:
	1. nature of need		Wed., July 30, 10:30
	2. history of program	#41-50:	6/16/26/36/46/56/66:
	3. what is involved	Hank	Wed., July 30, 10:15
	E. State request	#51-60:	7/17/27/37/47/57/67:
	1. would it be okay if I stopped by?	Irene	Thurs., July 31, 10:00
	2. (if yes) arrange date and time	#61-70: Tony	8/18/28/38/48/58/68: Thurs., July 31, 10:15 9/19/29/39/49/59/69:
	3. (if no) would it be okay if I sent something to you in the mail about this program?		Thurs., July 31, 10:30 10/20/30/40/50/60/70: Thurs., July 31, 10:45
			Friday, Aug. 1: missed calls, not-at-homes, busy signals, etc.
	. . .		
	. . .		
	. . .		

*Schedule indicates that Willie makes a call to person #1 on Tuesday, July 29, at 10:00 a.m. (Day 108 of program); Opal calls person #11 at the same time, etc.

Pages ago, we began looking at sample plans in the hope of understanding what makes for a good one. Our tour may have turned into a jungle expedition, but we have seen the eyes of the beast. By now, we should be ready to draw some conclusions that might be useful to you in your own work, whether you are leading a community activity, or simply participating as a group member.

WHAT MAKES A GOOD PLAN?

In judging a plan, we apply standards of form, scale, and content. Form: does this plan display proper structural characteristics? Does it meet the formal definition of a plan? Scale: is the level of complexity of the plan proportional to both the requirements of the program and the needs of the user? Content: will the ideas in the plan work out in practice? If these same standards are also used to judge artistic merit, this is no surprise, for a plan is a handcrafted, one-of-a-kind composition, with origins in the creative soul.

Form.

A plan has to start with certain materials, then arrange them following certain broadly interpreted rules of design. If you're going to build a wooden cabinet, you will need to get wood, and then shape it into shelves, walls, and doors. If you want to write a sonnet, you start with thoughts and images, and then shape them into fourteen lines of rhymed iambic pentameter. In a plan for a social program, and for many other human activities, the raw materials are actions, people, and time. The design rules involve shaping these materials so as to answer the formal questions:

(actions)	1. What?	(What will be done?)
(people)	2. Who?	(Who will do it?)
(time)	3. When?	(When will it happen?)

and then putting these materials in sequence, in chronological order. The putting-in-sequence is the crucial factor. We've encountered these three questions before, most recently at the end of the last chapter when we discussed goal setting. But goal setting is static (a snapshot); planning is dynamic (a movie). Planning involves answering these questions *repeatedly* through time, for each anticipated action. Any plan meeting these conditions passes the first and most important test for form.

To pass the second and last test, another set of by-now-familiar questions must be addressed. Specifically:

4. To whom?	(Who will be affected?)
5. To how many?	(How many will be affected?)
6. How often?	(How often will action occur?)

7. For how long?   (. . .will action occur?)
8. By what method?   (. . .will action occur?)
9. Where?   (Where will action take place?)

Quite often, answering the first set of questions above will by itself suggest specific answers to the second, again for each action step in sequence. At other times, the answers may be implicitly understood by all. If neither is the case, then the answers should be clearly specified in the plan. When they are, that is it, as far as form is concerned.

When planners put plans to paper, they may adopt one of several different layouts. Some like time bars:

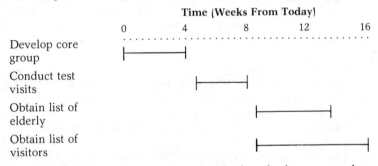

Others are partial to flow diagrams, critical path charts, or color-coded graphics. I like the layout originally presented here, but the differences among all of them are essentially minor.[3] Whatever manner of visual presentation suits your taste will probably do very nicely. The point to remember is that regardless of format your plan must respond to the basic questions of who, what, and when.

The design rules we have suggested for form apply to all social program plans, whether they are plans to start something brand new, as in our example, or to maintain a program that has been running for years. The last few draft plans for the visitation program in general do satisfy these standards. But the standards are not difficult at all, and I can assure you that you don't have to be a mental giant to meet them. What you do have to be is precise, but that is mostly an issue of personal self-mobilization. Your specific choices of actions and actors will undeniably make a difference, but that too is a different matter, a matter of content, one which we will take up after we have examined the criterion of scale.

Scale.

The plan should be on a scale that is well proportioned to the task. Another word for "scale" as used here is "complexity," and another way of stating the criterion is that the complexity level of the plan should match up well with the complexity of the program you hope to operate. Some illustrations may bring this out more clearly.

If you are planning a family picnic, your mind may check off: sandwiches, fruit, dessert, drink, napkins, thermos, basket, blanket; and you may dwell a little on what food you are going to make, or when you can get to the store. It probably won't please your family if you grab the first thing you find in the refrigerator, but it would seem quite odd to spend the whole morning drafting the picnic menu. On the other hand, if you are drawing up a master plan for park development in your town, a morning's work is nowhere near enough. The task here calls for a multi-page, possibly a multi-chapter document, which can easily fill up months. There is a certain scale to planning picnics, or parks, or anything else. Most of the time we can sense approximately what that scale is, even though we rarely have occasion to verbalize it, and don't always follow it.

A community-based social program usually falls in between these two examples. The program will surely involve more than one family, but probably fewer than all potential park users. The period between day one of planning and day one of implementation will generally be measured in weeks or months, instead of hours (picnics), or possibly years (parks). Accordingly, the scale of the program plan should fall somewhere in the middle, too. Of the visitation plans we studied, the first and second drafts seem on too small a scale for the task – they aren't complex enough. The fifth draft may be on too large a scale – it spells out more than we require at the start. The third and fourth drafts appear to be close to the scale we need. They are appropriate technology for the task at hand.

The vagueness of "seem," "may," and "appear" in the last three sentences may trouble you as it troubles me. Judging scale is harder than judging form, where we proposed a standard checklist. No checklist stands out from the rest this time; what we offer instead are some guidelines which may help in deciding how detailed your own plan should be. These guidelines suggest that a more complex, larger-scale plan will be of more value when:

- You and your associates have never been involved in a program resembling this one.
- The people in the target group (on the receiving end) have never been involved in a program resembling this one.
- The program is novel in your area, with few precedents to fall back on.

- Many people are involved on the giving end of the program.
- Many people are involved on the receiving end of the program.
- Many parallel tasks (tasks that can be performed at approximately the same time) can reasonably be assigned.
- A long period is anticipated between initial planning and program implementation.
- The program is expected to continue for a long time, or indefinitely.
- The program, for reasons unique to your particular situation, requires an above-average amount of groundwork before it can hope to start.

A personal factor enters in, too, for the plan must meet the needs of its creators as well as its target group. The scale of the plan should feel comfortable to you; if it overwhelms you, if you feel consumed by it, if you are losing sleep over it, you can try not worrying quite so hard over every detail. (If the plan seems too simple, you might consider worrying some more.) You are very likely the one who will have to implement the plan, and it won't profit you to be at odds with your own creation. If you resist it, you won't believe in it; and if you don't believe in it, why do it at all?

Choosing scale has few firm rules – the guidelines are rough, not absolute. And while we might prefer more exactness, there is still a place for "feel." The scale of plan 4 for the visitation program – given the program's general goal, its method, and a sense of the number of people involved – appears to match the guidelines and also feels right, at least for me. There is some room for error and for difference of opinion, in that a modest departure from proper scale (or from another person's opinion of it) will probably not bring down the entire program. But since ning is hard work, you as planner must guard against being too easy on yourself, against getting by with less planning than is really needed. With practice, your ability to construct and deal with larger-scale, more complex plans will gradually increase, and the extra precision gained will be to your eventual advantage.

Content.

If a plan is expressed in proper form and appropriate scale, it satisfies two criteria of "good." But neither criterion has much to do with how well the plan will stand up to reality. We are not just interested in easy-to-follow, well-proportioned designs, but also in designs that *work*. Will the content of the plan, the planning steps when carried out as specified, lead to the desired results? Will the plan perform under game conditions?

Judging plan content can be tricky. This is because judgment depends on how well the plan responds to variables unique to your specific situation. A strong extended-family tradition in your area, for example, or an especially high concentration of recent retirees, should each affect a visitation plan, each in a different way. If you are really planning a program in your own setting, I can't judge your plan properly unless I first know what those variables are, and then examine how well your plan takes them into account. Neither can you. This means that a plan that dazzles in one setting can fizzle in another, that more than one specific program plan can share the honors in a given program category, and that you as planner/craftsperson must avoid the temptation of mass production and be able to customize plan content for your own situation and your own clientele.

But judging content is not entirely relative, either. There are some common rules of thumb, features and procedures which make a plan more likely to succeed, and they transfer across most planning situations we encounter. We list them below, again as guidelines rather than absolute standards.

The first three guidelines review material covered in the previous chapter:

1. A clear goal. Specific, measurable objectives.
2. Identification of resources. This includes planning to maximize the impact of resources you have and to take advantage of any unexpected resources you might find along the way.
3. Identification of obstacles. This includes planning to minimize the impact of obstacles you anticipate and to protect against those which are unlikely. For each new cost, you need resources to cover; for each possible objection, a reply; for each potential blocking move, a countermove, that shakes you loose toward the goal.

Goals, resources, and obstacles are part of the planning process, but – as we saw at the end of chapter 3 – they should be established *before* the planning of the step-by-step sequence of actions takes place. In other words, planning steps should follow upon, and be directly keyed to, the goals, resources, and obstacles you have identified in advance. We have done this implicitly, but not explicitly, in the visitation plans we sketched out here. We could have, perhaps should have, prefaced each plan draft with a goal statement and resource/obstacle inventory. Such a preface would lock in plan content closer to objectives (the very act of writing directs one's aim), and would also make it easier for an outsider to judge how well the planning steps which followed were adapted to the situation.

The remaining guidelines relate to this chapter and apply to the step-by-step action sequence itself:

4. Development of participation in the planning process. Participation not only lightens your load, but also grooms future program leaders. Establishing a core planning group (or steering committee, or advisory board) at the very beginning often helps bring about the involvement you want.

5. Development of awareness of the ends and means of the program plan—if it's not already there—by your target group prior to implementation. Before people are willing either to give or to receive, they have to be aware of what you are trying to do. The less your target group knows about your plan, the greater the necessity of planning to build advance awareness.

6. Development of prior support for the program plan, if it's not already there. Support follows after awareness (cf. chapter 5). It too must be in place before target group members will participate and conceivably assume responsibility.

7. A fair test of the plan on a small sample, with further actions contingent upon test results.

8. Careful recruitment, screening, and training of those who will give service. Since the quality of the program will obviously hinge on the quality of the service providers, diligent planning ought to go into recruiting the very best people you can find, into screening of others, and into training of all.

9. Consent of those who will be receiving service. The plan ought to contain procedures for verifying at least tacit consent, and for securing explicit consent when the service goal may be misunderstood, controversial, or accompanied by risk. Naturally, the primary method for securing consent is through prior contact with the proposed recipients.

10. Review and evaluation of the plan throughout, together with review of timelines and monitoring of assigned responsibilities for task accomplishment. In this case, we mean review and evaluation checkpoints within the plan itself. These activities should of course also continue for the entire duration of the program and be carried out at least once after it ends. (See chapters 5 and 6.)

An effective planner of social programs will incorporate most or all of these guidelines into plan content. With exceptions noted, our later draft plans do so. If you can do so as well, tailoring the guidelines to fit your own plan or that of your group, you will be learning not only how to recognize a good plan but also how to do the actual planning itself. And there is another bonus. Once plan content has been firmed up, it needs to be acted on. These planning guidelines (paragraphs 4 through 10 above) are at the same time highly desirable action steps. If you can internalize them, start thinking about them now, you will have a leg up on the next chapter, where we discuss program action in some detail. But, more importantly, you will have a head start on making your plans really work.

THE VALUE OF PLANNING

We are now ready to return specifically to the question of value. We have seen that a good plan meets certain standards for form, scale, and content. Ideally, we have also learned something about how we might apply these standards in day-to-day practice – not that big a jump. The question of value is the question of whether all this planning activity is worth it. At the beginning of the chapter, I suggested to you (or was it you who agreed?) that a good plan would conserve your energy, enhance your success, yield all kinds of positive dividends. Can this be proven?

The most convincing proof might be for you to try serious planning in your own work and compare results with and without. Other solid evidence could be derived from research studies evaluating program benefits and costs as a function of prior planning time or planning quality. But I can't point with confidence to any such studies, and you may not yet be seasoned enough or mindful enough to supply evidence from your own experience. In that case, the author must resort to deductive argument.

A ballpark estimate of planning time for the visitation program we discussed is a morning's work, say 3 to 5 hours. This is the time necessary for an average person to draw up the initial plan, not to act on it. We'll assume that we're aiming for a plan similar in scale to plan 4, and we'll count only original sit-down planning time, not later ongoing planning, and not stray thoughts which occur while lying in bed or boarding the bus. Suppose in the first year you want to see an average of 10 visitors spend an average of 2 hours a week making visits for 40 weeks (although your actual intent is to have the program run indefinitely). This initial expectation comes to 10 x 2 x 40, or 800 service hours. Suppose that you also anticipate a combined total of 200 hours, including core planning meetings, recruitment, visitor training, etc., before the program gets off the ground. Four hours of drafting the original plan, then, represents 4/200, or 2 percent, of anticipated subsequent planning time, and 4/800, or 0.5 percent, of anticipated service time.

Some questions of interest: (a) Will the time spent in drawing up the original plan result in an equal or greater reduction in hours of subsequent program planning? (b) Will the time spent in drawing up the original plan result in an equal or greater gain in hours of eventual service generated? and (c) Will the time spent in drawing up the original plan result in an equal or greater gain in program quality?

I think the answer to all three questions is "yes." Note that for (a), the reduction need only exceed 2 percent (4 hours) of later planning time, and that for (**b**) the gain need only exceed 0.5 percent of first-year service time. These are surely very modest expectations; we would hope that the payback would be considerably greater. For (**c**), no firm percentages can be assigned, since time and quality are nonequivalent dimensions. So we rephrase the question: Would it be worth four hours of your time if you could improve your program's quality by even a few percentage points? I think it would be. And should such a time expenditure be expected to produce such a gain? I think with any kind of intelligent planning it should, though that is perhaps as much an article of faith as a scientifically proven fact.

The visitation program is only one example, and the numbers supplied are arbitrary. But the visitation program seems somewhere near the typical size of programs you yourself might undertake, and the sample numbers given are probably quite conservative. We would expect to draw similar conclusions for virtually all types and sizes of community programs. The larger the program, the greater the potential planning advantage. Good planning should genuinely give you more control over your environment, help you reach your goals more easily, strengthen your motivation for your work and your commitment to it, and actually live up to all the claims advertised for it at the beginning of this chapter.

Satisfaction, of course, is not guaranteed. Burns's couplet,

> The best laid schemes o' mice an' men
> . Gang aft a-gley

did not become famous without reason. An exquisitely crafted plan will not necessarily lead to a comparably exquisite program, and may in fact lead to no program at all. Delivery of actual services depends upon skills and qualities over and above planning activity, and often upon factors beyond your own control. Yet men are craftier than mice. While planning and outcome are not perfectly associated, they are strongly and positively correlated. From that fact morals flow.

The main moral is that planning is almost always worth the effort that goes into it. Yet this moral is based upon rational analysis, and such analysis has its limits as a persuasive tool. Otherwise the basements and kitchen tables of America would be awash in plans right now. Most people are not particularly rational when it comes to investing their time, any more than they are in investing their money. The barriers to planning are as much emotional as rational, and it is these emotional barriers we will have to trim down to size.

OVERCOMING BARRIERS

Now, overcoming emotional barriers is an impressive feat to pull off on paper. But what if I remind you that the information presented in this chapter is information many of you know already? The skills involved in planning, and in most community work, are fundamentally simple skills, combined and repeated many times over; they are also naturally occurring skills, part of our neurological equipment. If you were truly lost in the woods, the first thing you would do after calming down would be to devise a plan to get out. You wouldn't need this book. Planning is a survival skill, a biological adaptation, part of our evolutionary heritage.

And you don't have to be lost in the woods to be pressed into planning. It's not as if you've never put together a plan before, for you have, and the majority of you have constructed plans similar or superior to the program plans we've described. True, the plans illustrated here are gussied up, wearing their party clothes, trained in refinement and in attention to detail – all of which is appropriate, since planning is a formal event. But ask yourself: How much can someone else teach you about planning that you don't already know – "know" at least on one level? Gradually, you realize that the teacher does not just reveal what is new, but brings you closer to what is already within. That in itself is a powerful teaching. It may be a little unsettling to see authority figures you rely on get knocked down a few pegs. But ultimately the teaching is confidence-building and liberating.

Taking a different tack: planning is no more a matter of skill than one of mental determination, a kind of internal discipline. The "inner way" of planning – of involvement in any community activity – is to develop and strengthen the discipline that will help you do the work. This teaching is as powerful as the first. Unfortunately, it does not seem too comforting if to stimulate planning is our goal. We know that getting ourselves to do something is often tougher than actually doing it. Imposing discipline on oneself is a rugged job, something we are very good at postponing or avoiding altogether.

There are particular difficulties in disciplining oneself to plan, and they must be faced squarely. Planning is hard mental labor, harder than we are used to; even though advanced brainpower may not be required, deep concentration is. Planning is time spent thinking when you could be doing, reaching for glory out there in the world. Planning can be solitary and lonely. Planning by itself is infrequently rewarded. Planning at best means long-term delay of gratification, for the fruits of one's efforts may not ripen for some time. Planning usually receives very little social sanction and less social support. Planning must often get smuggled in, in between pressures to do something right now.

It's no wonder planning is rarely chosen as a leisure-time pursuit. Yet these difficulties should not be overstated. If planning rests upon discipline, it rests upon a personal quality which is within personal control. And just as you can receive instruction in how to get yourself to diet ("Don't bring sweet foods into the house . . ."), or to meditate ("Pay attention to your breath . . ."), or to discipline yourself to do anything else, you can learn – or recall – some techniques to facilitate planning activities and to make the act of planning more natural and more rewarding.

We have shaded into a discussion of the how-to of planning. The argument I'm advancing here is that good planning (good community work) depends upon two already introduced factors, technical skill and personal will. You already had some planning skills before you approached this chapter, though the material here may have added to them and sharpened your thinking. "Will" is the present topic of our analysis, and what follows is a collection of ideas to enhance its operation. They are not intended as revelations or miniature sermons or character builders, but rather as some well-tested thoughts to pick and choose from that may make it easier for you to plan.

1. Reserve some planning time. Book it as you would a dinner reservation or business meeting. Planning is much like a business meeting, the person you are meeting being yourself. Mark the time down in your calendar or appointment book, and don't cancel.

2. Make sure you reserve enough planning time, so you don't rush. While an honest morning's work should get you most of the way through the startup stages of most social program plans you will ever construct, if you need more time, take it. If you work better in bite-size snatches, break up the time accordingly.

3. Take care that the time you reserve is quiet, free from distraction. Working in the quietest room you can find, at a desk, with the door closed, should improve your efficiency. If you are an outdoor planner, head for a park bench or a shady tree where kids don't play.

4. Use your planning space only for planning and closely related activities if you possibly can. In that manner, when you enter your chosen environment, the stimuli there will by association help put you in the proper frame of mind.

5. Reward yourself for completing a planning session, or a significant part of it. A cup of coffee, a chance to read the newspaper, or a walk around the block should do the trick, unless you are inclined

to treat yourself more lavishly. Reminder: reward strengthens the behavior that precedes it.

6. Write your plan down. There are at least three good reasons why: (**a**) A written plan does not forget; (**b**) A written plan can more easily be critiqued by others; and, most importantly, (**c**) A written plan helps to clarify your thoughts. Writing *anything* down helps to clarify your thoughts. What's fuzzy in your head is likely to become clear on paper (though sometimes vice versa, in which case you need to check your starting premises).

7. Keep a planning notebook close at hand to jot down thoughts and reminders along the way, as do the more meticulous (compulsive?) planners among us. When they don't have a notebook, they use napkins or candy wrappers. And they always have a list. But the list makers of the world should be around at the finish, even though they may seem to act superior to the rest of us.

8. Start with the broad outline, then fill in the blanks. The earlier choices are the most consequential, hence require the most thought. If you outline an elephant, you will soon have to include tusks and a trunk, not flippers or wings. So make rough sketches, to be sure that a metaphorical elephant is what you want. If it is not, don't be afraid to use the wastebasket. If it is, then block out the major elements, take care that they fit well together, and move steadily from the general to the specific.

9. Visualize the plan as it would unfold in practice. Walk yourself slowly and feelingly through each step, imagining yourself as a participant in the action. ("What would really happen if . . . ?") Take on different participant roles; note your own reactions, then modify the plan appropriately. When something does not make sense to you in your own fantasy, it may also not make sense in someone else's reality.

10. If you are planning with others, maintain a climate of openness so that criticism can be freely given and accepted. It's often helpful to generate a lot of uncriticized, rapid-fire ideas first, as is done in brainstorming, before honing in on those ideas which fit your situation best.

11. If you are planning by yourself, you can still ask others to review your plan, and you should. It's not beyond reason that you missed a point here or there; and even if you didn't, someone else may still have some better ideas or know some short cuts. Look for reviewers who are experienced in planning and who know the community, who are familiar with your program type and who could be in a position to assist in program operation. Take the time to track them down. Their criticisms will not only improve your plan, but may also tie them more closely to what you are planning.

12.   Whether you are planning with others or by yourself, you should review your own plans. Do this when you are rested, and when the ink has had a chance to dry. The visualization technique mentioned in paragraph 9 above can be employed again here.

13.   Develop support for spending time on planning, and for the planning process as a whole. If you can profit from a steady, measured approach to planning, so can others working with you, especially if their first inclination is to rush into the breach. Mutual support will act as a stabilizer. If you are working in an agency setting, support is especially necessary; you can mandate planning activity among people you may supervise, and promote it at all other organizational levels.

14.   Be certain that the plan is closely linked with what you will actually *do*. The plan must never be allowed to become a showpiece, far removed from what is really going on. Actions should stem from what has been planned out beforehand. The linkage will be firmer if this has been agreed on at the outset, and if the planners and the doers are the same people, or at least next of kin.

This list covers most of the field. If you have assimilated it, together with the previous material, then by this time you have increased your awareness of (**a**) the value of planning, (**b**) what a good plan is, (**c**) how to create one, and (**d**) how to get yourself to create one. These are commendable achievements; they constitute the graduation requirements from this chapter. But there are a few loose ends left over, and before you get your diploma, it's important that we tie them up. We can do so in question-and-answer form.

QUESTIONS AND ANSWERS

You've spent most of the time talking about planning in the beginning stages of a project, before any service actually starts. But isn't it also true that planning should continue for as long as the project lasts?

Absolutely. Though we have stressed the formative stages, planning should be no less an ongoing activity. You'll see that planning is embedded in the material of the next two chapters, just as it was in the one before. Specifically, planning is needed throughout the action stages of a project, to develop awareness and support, to make sure the program runs and keeps running smoothly, and to build new leadership if others will be taking over. Planning is needed to design and conduct a proper evaluation as well. The question is very well taken. Planning and doing should stream from the same power source, cycling like alternating current.

Ongoing planning is the primary concern in helping agencies, in institutions, and in the corporate world. Established organizations pay more attention to maintaining what is already in place rather than to beginning something new, for organizational survival (with due respect for innovation) most often depends on doing well what one has done well before. Most organizations also deliver a variety of services, or manufacture a variety of products; each may have its own plan. An extra layer of ongoing, centralized planning is then needed to adjust goals, and to coordinate and monitor the mixture of organizational functions. Annual plans, long-range plans and five-year plans are a common tangible result.

Compared with startup planning, ongoing planning more often involves subplans, multiple and detailed extensions and variations of the founding idea. An original plan taken root can be expected to send off branches. Many different plans can be off and running at the same time. But ongoing planning involves the same basic principles we have discussed before. The standards of form, scale, and content, the value of planning, the how-to's all apply, regardless of starting point or organizational size. Wherever you are in your own work, your starting point can be considered as today, and your planning skills and discipline exercised from there.

Isn't it possible to plan too much as well as too little?

Yes. This is less common, but it does happen. In designing any program, zero hour eventually arrives. Fussing too much over the plan yields progressively diminishing returns. Planning should occupy a significant but not all-absorbing percentage of time in the overall program operation. The thought-to-action ratio should not be allowed to climb out of sight.

There's no sense in going overboard on planning scale, in blocking out tomorrow's events by the minute, or in planning for tiny details six months ahead. We are, after all, not commanding combat troops in a military operation; and our ability to predict the future is just not that great. Much of the filigree work can be saved for later. The planner can be satisfied with that level of precision needed now.

Sometimes planning is also used as an excuse for inaction. Planners and planning groups can become overcautious or overly self-doubting. They can decide to study, test, or revise some more, thereby missing the best time to act, and dampening everyone's enthusiasm in the process. By choosing to wait, they avoid failure, but also success. Some risk is inherent in developing a new program, in putting anything new on the market—there's no getting around it. Yet if your plan reflects your best effort under the circumstances, you might as well test it in the real world.

Is it all right to deviate from a plan once you have set it up?

Within limits, yes. A plan is based upon agreement; it does not normally have the force of law. Even if it is "the law" where you are, it should always be open to amendment. Although your job as planner is to anticipate the future, unless you are a prophet, or very lucky, some unanticipated events will happen. If an unplanned obstacle turns up, you will have to detour around it. If an unexpected resource comes along, you will probably be eager to use it. Either way, your plan must be modified accordingly. This again highlights the need for ongoing planning.

Changing an established plan should not be taken lightly. A thoughtful plan will minimize the prospect of deviation in the first place. A thoughtful planner will also want to visualize and plan for all futures which might occur, even if their probability is slim. The more backup plans – contingency plans – you have lined up and primed for implementation, the better the job you are doing. But if you take a sudden turn toward the rocks, flexibility, spontaneity, and the ability to improvise on the spot are also virtues. Your contract does not oblige you to stay on a collision course.

The knottier problem is when you start out wanting **X**, but as you proceed, you realize you prefer **X¹**, or even **Y**, instead. Or you may still want **X**, but **Y** looks more feasible given the conditions. Or **Y** presents itself as a golden but fleeting opportunity. Do you change plans then?

A helpful strategy here is to think about combining the alternatives. **Y** may be incorporated as part of **X**, or vice versa, thus broadening the scope of your activity. Others working with you may be able to tackle **Y** right now, as a separate project. Alternatively, **X** or **Y** may be postponable, the next item on the agenda. The choice may not be either-or.

But if it is, the answer lies in the measuring of costs and gains. Do the advantages of **Y** clearly outweigh those of **X**? Can you give up your own investment in **X**, and any commitments to others you may have made, without penalty? What about the long-range consequences of your choice? Will you feel more personal satisfaction for having accomplished **X** or **Y**? These are some of the questions to ask yourself. There's value in being an opportunist – that is, someone who takes advantage of an opportunity. There's less value in abandoning something that's working well, or in violating the letter or spirit of your commitment, for an uncertain promise. Making final judgments in these cases can be painful, yet it's part of what you bought into. My own feeling is to switch if and only if the scale points unmistakably in that direction, to stay with what you have otherwise, and don't look back.

Aren't you rambling on oblivious to social reality? You are telling people to plan, but to do anything about those plans takes money and power. Everyday people, the people you claim you are writing for, have little of either. To tell them to plan when they haven't the resources to put plans into action is just another con; it's naive at best, and it probably does damage. To get the community you say you want will require a full-scale restructuring of the economic and political system.

This is a fundamental issue. I'm glad you didn't mince words.

Money and power help; who will doubt it? Money means you can buy staff time and the physical materials you need. Power – formal power – means you can legitimately tell some people what to do, and influence a bunch of others as well. Few of us don't appreciate these benefits. Agencies, institutions, most organizations hold on dearly to money and power, relying upon them to provide basic services; yet even they say they never have enough. Meanwhile, you as an ordinary person may not have the money for stamps; you can hardly think then about putting out a mailing. Money and power give you some stuff to plan with; in different words, planning is a luxury item reserved for the wealthy and powerful buyer.

I'll agree to all of this up to the last semicolon; yet I must add some more. Barring a revolution, money and power are not going to be equally distributed among us in the near future. However desirable, however necessary, it may be to strive toward economic and political redistribution, both inside and outside the system, such redistribution is not the only way to create social change. What can more easily be equally distributed are planning skills, plus other program skills, together with the motivation to use them. Planning can be a weapon of the disenfranchised, of the underclass. Planning can serve as one of the few equalizers they have. Planning combined with related program skills can be used to meet local community needs, many of which stand apart from the money and power centers of our social system – needs neither favored nor opposed, but simply ignored.

Meaningful social change can come about with very little money and no formal power. The visitation program we spoke of is one of literally thousands of activities which can succeed without dollars and without prior "position" in the community. The Lowell Cooperative Learning Center was another example. What these programs demand are not money and power, but (again) skill and will. The plan, tapping those very qualities, *makes* you powerful. It can also win you powerful supporters. If money is a concern, planning can bring that your way as well.

That's helpful to know, since "very little" money is not the same as no money at all. The homeliest of community activities is liable to cost you something, even if it's only for coffee, magic markers, or the aforementioned stamps. If you need a telephone, grown-up office supplies, and a place to keep them, you will have to pay for the efficiency and legitimacy they confer. Should you or your associates not be able to supply that money out of pocket, you will have to hustle it, or barter for it, one way or another. Raising money on that scale is not extraordinarily difficult, and many good books can teach you how to do it. (See bibliography.)

However, if you are starting a community program, you ought to take a hard look at whether you need more than a few thousand dollars a year at the maximum. It's not that voluntary poverty makes you morally pure, or that having money to spend chews away at your soul. It's simply that most of the time you don't need that much money to do the job. Maybe you do, if paid staff are absolutely essential, or if some facility must be built from scratch. In those cases, you can try to get an existing agency to subsidize the program, or lure local money and power sources your way, or chase after outside funding by writing a grant.

But think three times before setting your sights that high. Money and power can bog you down in petty detail and uninvited obligations. They can muffle your creativity and your social conscience, for now you have something to lose. The record of those with money and power to burn has not exactly lit up the sky.

Of course, if you already have money and power, you are going to use them more wisely. If they can be easily courted, you will turn on the charm. And if they fall into your lap, you will not shoo them away. But if you are neither rich nor powerful, you don't have to be. A program may or may not be better with big money and formal power, but that's not the issue here. The point is that the lack of either one does not bar you from effective social planning, nor from effective social action.

All this material about planning is neatly presented, and I applaud it. But is this really what I need to know, and does it apply to me? And I'm not sure it's practical. Do you honestly think that people like me are going to sit down in quiet places and draw up step-by-step plans?

You don't have a moment in the day to call your own. Or the only time you can plan is in the shower or driving to work. Or you go with the flow. Or you can put together a masterful plan in sixty seconds flat. Or you've already tried the ideas presented here, and they have disappointed you.

Readers will enter into this chapter material from different backgrounds and with different needs. The writer has only one bag of arrows to shoot. Some of his arrows may miss your mark. In that case, there are other valid approaches to planning, other marksmen to seek out. Perhaps your own need is to study time management or public policy formation, to pursue a business degree, or to start with some deep reflection on your personal goals. All of this is to be expected, and encouraged.

The general theme here has been that planning is important, that it's neglected, that it's possible to improve it, and that it pays off to do so. Any increase in serious time devoted to planning should help. There's more than one way to plan. I value the ideas expressed here as much as any, and think they will help you; but if you find others will serve you better, then choose them. Ideas are tools in a hardware store. You can listen to the salesperson's recommendations, but ultimately it's up to you to pick out those best suited to you and your own job.

5
Action

GETTING YOUR WAY

Eventually, the time comes to act. Neither the most diligent needs assessment nor the most exquisite plan by itself provides services to people or creates change. Both assessments and plans are necessary preliminaries, and both may properly have taken a good deal of time; but neither is a substitute for social action.

Let's be clear from the start about what action involves. At bottom, it means trying to get your own way. You've established a socially valuable goal (with input from others), and have thought hard about how to reach it. Now you have to go out and do the reaching, then the grasping, then the holding on. All of this in an environment which could be supportive, which might be hostile, but which is most likely to be indifferent.

In other words, if what you seek has social value, especially if it will create something where nothing existed before, the chances are you will need to exert all the influence you possibly can. You will need to control the environment, and specifically to get other people to do what you want. You can compromise, or even reverse your field. But if you really want change, you are going to have to change people; and since most people approach change slowly, cautiously, with their brakes on, you can't pussyfoot around.

This sounds manipulative, and it is. And it sounds almost unethical, but it shouldn't be. You can't act without manipulation. Failure to act is what may be "unethical." Influence – manipulation politely put – is ethical when it aims at fulfilling a community need, when it empowers others to fulfill that need, when the targets of your influence are aware of it, when they are not coerced by it, and when they are encouraged to respond with influence attempts of their own. These handed-down criteria barely scratch the surface of social ethics (to probe further, see bibliography); for now, we can simply acknowledge that social action in virtually any form brings us face-to-face with attempts to control and with their ethical consequences.

The purpose of this chapter is to help you get what you want, consistent with your own ethical standards. We'll begin by trying to understand the action stages in a social program or activity, introducing a framework for that purpose. We'll consider how these stages relate to different types of activities you might be involved in. Then we'll spend the most time discussing each of the stages in turn, itemizing some specific principles, techniques, traps, edges, and general reminders along the way. The material here should apply if you are leading a social program or activity, but also if you are just following along as a group member – for there too you will have tasks to carry out.

Before pushing off, a note on how this chapter links up with those surrounding it. Most planning (last chapter) may occur prior to action, and most evaluation (next chapter) may come later, but planning and evaluation should both go on during the action period itself. Planning, action, and evaluation overlap in time; all three are part of the same overall change-making process. They are conceptually and often chronologically distinct, but not tightly compartmentalized.

A FRAMEWORK FOR ACTION

Stages for the community worker.

From the viewpoint of the community worker, action can be separated into three consecutive stages. In the first stage, you enter into your chosen setting, lay down the necessary groundwork. In the second, you carry out the planned activity. And in the third, you leave the setting, ending your personal involvement and perhaps the activity itself. This action sequence corresponds to getting in, staying in, and getting out – entry, execution, and exit. It's as simple as that.

In other words, a social program has a life cycle, like individuals, organizations, all living systems. It is born, it prospers, and eventually it dies. A program is not forever, though some will outlive you. If your program weakens and fails, your involvement needn't continue. Your role as program initiator is like that of a parent; you nurture your offspring at each stage till maturity, then let them go free.

Stages for the respondent.

Another way of looking at social action is from the viewpoint of the respondent, the person in your target group who will get involved in your program or activity. As a community worker, stop and think for a moment: What do you want the respondent to do?

If you have a program that's working out well, most times you'd like to see the program continue, with other people helping to run it. That is, you would like others to take some responsibility for it, both because your goal as change agent is to empower others, and because you may not be able to continue your own leadership indefinitely. But of course responsibility sharing does not happen automatically. Before people are willing to take responsibility, they are usually participants. Before they are participants, they are usually supporters. And before they can be supporters, they must become aware that the program exists in the first place; of all the stimuli competing for entry into consciousness, those belonging to your program must be among the favored few.

So the sequence you desire for the respondent goes from ignorance to awareness to support to participation to responsibility sharing. As a community worker, your goal is to move as many people through these stages as you can. But it's hard to move people so far; the path from ignorance to responsibility is washed out and buried under. You must therefore build a bridge to get people across. The bridge can be shaky at first, like a rope bridge, possibly spanning only one stream at a time. But it will have well-placed footholds, and guiderails to lean on. Gradually, your bridge should become longer and stronger, part of a main-traveled road. Bridging is one of the most important concepts in community work. The gap between awareness and action, even intention and action, is immense. To close it, you have to pave it over firmly, allow many chances to take small steps, then lead people across, at their own speed, from wherever they happen to be.

Integrating the two sequences.

The action stages for the community worker and the respondent roughly parallel each other, and can be sketched as shown in Figure 4. The entry stage is most closely associated with developing awareness and support. Actual program execution occurs just as people have begun to participate, to receive program services and benefits. When there is sufficient responsibility sharing, the community worker may decide to leave.

In practice, events will probably not be quite so clean-cut. Time relationships between rows will not be as rigid; the stages within each row will overlap; and the stages themselves may not apply in

Figure 4
Action Stages in Social Programs and Activities

TIME ⟶

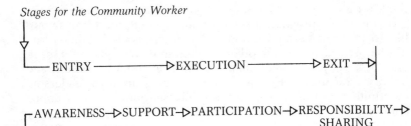

Stages for the Community Worker

ENTRY ⟶EXECUTION ⟶EXIT

AWARENESS⟶SUPPORT⟶PARTICIPATION⟶RESPONSIBILITY⟶
SHARING

Stages for the Respondent in the Target Group

every case. The figure above is a framework for understanding social action stages in broadly general terms. It's only one conceptual hook to hang your thoughts on. But let's see how it applies to programs or activities you might be part of.

Types of programs.

Not all programs or change activities require the same amount of attention to each stage. The amount of effort you put into each will depend upon whether your program:

• is reacting to specific negative events, or acting to create something new. Many community actions are responses to immediate adversity. A school closing is proposed; a rent increase is scheduled; a zoning variance is requested. Often these events are perceived as threats, often accurately, and when people feel personally threatened, they can react quickly. There is no trouble gaining support, participation, even leadership. A reactive program is one case where you can skip the preliminaries and sail right into execution. This type of program, however, is ordinarily defensive, aimed toward restoring the status quo, while the cutting edge of social change lies in program *initiation*, in creating something fresh and new. Yet when something new is proposed, people rarely rush forward with the same commitment as when something that already exists is being taken away. They have experienced no benefits from the proposed activity; they may not be able to see what those benefits are. As an initiator, you will have to start much nearer the beginning, to do some fairly detailed bridgework, to make those benefits clear.

• is meant to involve a small or large number of people. In small-scale settings – a local club or association, a block, a compact neighborhood – entry problems are less troublesome. Since most of your target group knows you, you can assume that they have a basic respect for you and a trust in your good intentions. Many are likely to back you from the start; some others will help out of personal obligation. If you are working within a group or organization, established traditions and informal group pressures may get you the awareness and support you need right away.[1] But the larger the target group you want to serve, the smaller the percentage of group members you will know personally, and the smaller the percentage who will know you. Accordingly, the greatest effort at the beginning will need to go into building awareness and support. The more novel your ideas, or the more you are asking, the more this is so.

• takes place in a familiar or unfamiliar setting. Much of the time, even when working in a large setting, the setting is "yours" – your neighborhood, your town, your chapter of a bigger organization. You are yourself a member of it, and you know most of the rules of the road. To this extent, less constituency building is necessary. However, on occasion you may find yourself operating in unfamiliar territory, where you are an outsider, where people do not know who you are or what you stand for. Like any visible outsider, your presence will arouse curiosity (at a minimum), and sometimes varying degrees of resentment, most of which will not be directly expressed in front of you. These reactions are natural, a product of a long evolutionary process. They should be anticipated. In such circumstances, building initial awareness and support – brick by brick if necessary – will clearly take first priority.[2]

In sum, an intervention which is reactive, small-scale, and home based generally involves less preparation time than a first-time, large-scale intervention on foreign soil.[3] But while program types differ, and program stages are not always uniform, virtually all real-life programs require a good measure of awareness and support building. If this is not your main need right now, it certainly will be at some other time. And entry stages are often the hardest, just as it takes more energy to pull out of the station than to roll down the track. So we'll switch on to Entry here, staying with it until we are rolling, and picking up actual program Execution and Exit in proper time. But first, a story.

ENTRY: BUILDING AWARENESS

The outreach program I directed several years ago provided consultation, education, and program development services to a broad range of community groups and individuals. We had a staff – we told ourselves – overflowing with talent and motivation. When we first started out, most of us kept busy enough, but our phone wasn't ringing off the hook. We could do more – we wanted to do more, if more people would ask. Why didn't they? We reasoned that we were a brand-new program, not very visible, and that our services were not in keeping with the traditional image of a mental health center. We worked pretty hard at developing community contacts, but it was frustrating at times to realize that our skills and ideas were not universally recognized.   .

Some time after the program began, I went to a conference in Vermont to meet and hear my counterparts throughout the New England region. One groggy morning (late night party), I wandered into a talk on publicizing services. I remember waking up fast. Where we sent out routine press releases and occasional bulk mailings, the speaker talked of computerized mailing lists and envelope addressing services. Where we had a sturdy card file of community contacts, he advocated market segmentation studies. Where we considered ourselves lucky to collect token fees, he had designed skills-training programs around vacation packages complete with hotels and sightseeing trips. He had made his program financially self-sufficient in two years. Listening to him was mindexpanding. Human service workers were not supposed to be so sophisticated.

The underlying message, though, could not have been simpler. No matter how outstanding your program ideas may be, they are useless if people do not know about them. In other words, your program, like any other service or product, must be publicized and sold.

For several reasons other than plain ignorance, many professional and nonprofessional community workers alike tend to keep a safe distance from awareness-building techniques. Awareness building smacks of promotion. Promotion is a corporate business practice, and such practices are to be avoided. Promotion carries the aroma of false advertising, of promising more than you can deliver. Promotion can be seen as blowing your own horn, and as such is inconsistent with your personal or professional dignity. And, pragmatically, promotion may bring you more business than you can handle, devouring you in the process. If what you have to

offer is any good, people will eventually find out about it themselves.

There's a contrasting view, which holds that if you are committed
to a particular social goal, and believe that your program or action
will help reach that goal, then you have a practical obligation to
communicate your ideas to others. The cold fact is that most people
could not care less; or, less harshly, that people will stay uninformed unless someone informs them. Your obligation may be
moral as well, tracing back at least to Jesus's instruction not to hide
your light under a bushel basket. To publicize your ideas does not
require high-priced gadgetry, and you don't have to trick others, or
beg them, or beat them over the head; but you ought to give them a
full and fair chance to hear what you're about. If excessive demand
is a real possibility, then the amount of awareness building can be
scaled to current program capability (as long as no needy group is
systematically excluded). Awareness building, publicizing, promotion, "marketing" if you will, can be carried out in a way which is
neither shoddy nor demeaning, but rather socially responsible and
productive. This is the view taken here.[4]

The next question then is how you go about developing awareness in practice. A list of major awareness-building options is given
in Table 9.

Some notes on the information in this list: (**a**) All face-to-face
contact can be either one-on-one, or in groups; (**b**) Much self-
published print contact can occur via several reproduction methods
(handwritten, ditto, mimeograph, photocopy, electrostencil, offset,
silkscreen, etc.), and can be either hand-delivered or mailed; (**c**) For
all entries in categories 1 to 3a, contact can be made with any or all of
the target group members, community leaders (as you define
them), and other selected persons or groups you want to influence;
and (**d**) For each case in **c**, contact can be made to all or some of the
persons or groups, and if to some, via selected or random sample.
These alternatives should keep the budding publicist happy for a
while.

And some more general comments. First, this list is not the only
way of classifying awareness building or publicity options. Second,
no listing of this size can account for all the possible improvisations
from basic technique – making an announcement over the school
public address system, taping up hand-written flyers at the local
supermarket, convincing local ministers to deliver your message
from their pulpits, and so on. Third, the list itself does not include
specific instructions on how to utilize any of its items; that is, there
are specific skills in writing a press release, designing a brochure,

Table 9
Major Awareness-building (Publicity) Options

1. *Face-to-Face Contact*
   a. You to other
      1. prearranged
      2. incidental (on the spot)

   b. Other to other
      1. prearranged
      2. incidental/spontaneous (word of mouth)

2. *Telephone Contact*
   (same categories as face-to-face)

3. *Print Contact* (See also #5)
   a. You publish
      1. letters/postcards
         – first class or bulk
         – personal or mass-printed
      2. flyers/leaflets/handbills
      3. brochures
      4. catalogs
      5. posters
      6. newsletters/bulletins

   b. Others publish (print media)
      1. daily newspapers
      2. specialty newspapers or newsletters (e.g., suburban, college, ethnic, union, corporate, other house organ, church bulletins, shoppers', etc.)
      3. magazines (e.g., of cities)

   Forms of Print Media Coverage
      1. news articles (releases)
      2. features (from interviews)
      3. columns (you write), guest or regular
      4. letters to editor
      5. editorials (you stimulate)
      6. press campaigns (ditto)
      7. photographs
      8. community calendar
      9. volunteer opportunities
      10. press conferences
      11. paid ads

4. *Radio/TV Contact* (most options as for print media, and in addition):
   a. Talk shows
      1. you call in
      2. as guest
      3. your own show (especially on cable)
   b. Radio feeds via beeper
   c. Public service announcements
   d. Citizen editorials
   e. Station campaigns

5. *Specialty Options* (partial list)
   a. Ad books
   b. Balloons
   c. Banners
   d. Billboards
   e. Bumper stickers
   f. Buttons
   g. Car caravans
   h. Contests
   i. Conventions
   j. Costumed people
   k. Demonstrations
   l. Embossed items
   m. Entertainments
   n. Exhibits (sponsor or participant)
   o. Fairs
   p. Films and videotapes
   q. Floodlights
   r. Fund-raisers
   s. Graffiti
   t. Handbill passer-outers
   u. Milk cartons
   v. Mobile vans
   w. Open-air debates
   x. Parades
   y. Pickets
   z. Rallies
   a' Skywriting
   b' Slide shows
   c' Sound trucks
   d' Special events
   e' Street art or theater
   f' Tent cards (coffee shops)
   g' Transit ads
   h' T-shirts

even conducting a telephone conversation (see bibliography). Finally, the list does not address questions of whom the publicity should be aimed toward, how much, and when.

Where do we go from here? We have an impressive array of options and techniques at our disposal, but many or most of them may not suit our particular circumstances. Our time is valuable, so we don't want to put in any more effort than we have to. We might get by very well with a few well-placed phone calls and a reminder postcard in the mail; but it's also possible that we need something one or two cuts more extensive and/or more eye-catching. Which techniques should we use?

I wish I could provide you with a handy formula, but I'm afraid there is none. Asking which techniques to use is like asking what you should have for dinner tonight. The actual choice of awareness-building techniques will depend (once again) upon analysis of a number of variables in your own situation. We can identify those variables, show how certain situations go more easily with certain methods of publicizing, and give an example or two. Beyond that, you as a community change agent must design an awareness-building plan calibrated to your own particular goals. The planning here is an extension of the planning process described in the last chapter. There, you drew up broad-gauge plans on paper. Here, you refine your plans, leave your desk, test them out, and modify as necessary. Effective community work takes planning, up and down the line.

Among the variables which should determine your own publicity plan are:

1. The response you desire from the people you wish to influence

In other words, what is the goal of your awareness-building efforts? Do you want others for now simply to know that you exist, or to do something more?

2. The number of people you wish to influence

That is, your "audience." This should correspond roughly with the size of your target group.

3. The kind of people you wish to influence

That is, what demographics? Your message form and content may need to vary with different subgroups.

4. The general level of familiarity with programs like yours

How much does your audience know about your type of ideas?

5. The general level of acceptance of programs like yours

Are you speaking to a generally sympathetic, antagonistic, or neutral audience, and how sharply polarized is its opinion?

6. Your personal relationship with the people you wish to influence

Are you friend, colleague, authority figure, outsider, none of the above?

7. The amount of time you have available

Both total calendar days and the amount of time within each day.

8. The number of other people who can help you, and their available time

For posting material, making phone calls, stuffing envelopes, etc.

9. The amount of money you have available

You can do a lot for free, and usually a lot more with money.

Can you determine where you stand on these variables on an issue that concerns you? Different answers sug~ different awareness-building techniques. That is, we can now combine information on these variables, together with the options we know are available, to propose some general guidelines for building positive awareness. These guidelines should hold up for most, though not necessarily all, situations you may encounter. They are not novel, not 100 percent complete, but they are tested by time, and together they should serve you well in forming your own plans.

Awareness-building Guidelines

Overall Effort

Overall effort put into awareness building should be greater:
1. the greater the magnitude of response desired.
2. the more people you wish to influence.
3. the longer the time you wish the influence to last.
4. the less familiar your target group is with programs like yours.
5. the less accepting your target group is of programs like yours.
6. the less personal a relationship you have with your target group.
7. the more resources – time, money, people – you have at your disposal (though you should not spend more resources than necessary to create the degree of awareness you want).

Contact Type

Personal contact.

8. The more personal a given contact, the more effective it is. Specifically, a given face-to-face contact is more effective than a letter; a given letter is more effective than a handbill, etc.
9. The more personal a given contact, the more time-consuming it is. As a rule of thumb, you can contact three to four people by

form-letter mail in the time it takes you to contact one person by phone. The ratio is higher for mail as versus in-person contact, and higher still when flyers or posters replace mailed announcements.

Personal contact is especially helpful when:
10. target group size is small.
11. you have a good supply of personal contacts to begin with; they should be used.
12. your target group is less familiar with or accepting of your ideas.
13. a greater magnitude of response is desired.
14. less money is available, since personal contact is free. (Media coverage is your other best bet in this case.)

"Impersonal" contact (i.e., by printed material or other media).

15. Generally, the more people you wish to influence, the more impersonal the typical contact must be, unless time and other resources are unlimited.

Impersonal contact may be more cost-effective:
16. the larger the size of the target group.
17. the fewer the personal contacts you have to rely on.
18. the greater the target group familiarity with or acceptance of your ideas.
19. the smaller the magnitude of response desired.
20. the less time available for you to work with (especially with a large target group).

Printed information. Whatever its form, print copy should:
21. specifically be mailed to, distributed to, or posted near the people in your target group you want most to reach.
22. have a physical appearance which if possible slightly exceeds, or at least matches, the average expectation of the audience.
23. have content slanted to match the reading level of the audience – neither over its head, nor talking down.
24. stress specific information (for example, time, date, place, response desired) and include a contact source for further details.

Mass media.
25. Mass media coverage is almost always valuable, for in addition to being free, it usually reaches a larger audience than any other home-distributed publicity source. For specific details on working with the media to maximize your coverage, see bibliography.

General Contact Efficiency

Prioritization.

When contact with all persons in your target group is not practical, those contacts which can be made should be directed to:

26. those persons or groups who need most to become aware of what you have to offer.

27. those persons or groups who you feel are most likely to support you.

28. those who can best leverage your impact (cf. #31 below).

Leveraging.

The effect of a given contact is greater if it can be leveraged. Specifically:

29. Each contact recipient should in most cases be indirectly or directly encouraged to share the information with others.

30. Others in your current task group, or willing new recruits, may be enlisted to help you publicize.

31. Special effort should be made to contact those who are in the best position to spread your message to others, especially to those who need to know. These persons can rebroadcast your concerns and requests through their own networks, thus multiplying your effectiveness.

Diversification.

32. More than one method can and usually should be employed to reach a given audience, especially a larger one. For example, personal techniques can be used for some subgroups, less personal techniques for others – or both can be combined for the same group.

Skill utilization.

33. Publicity efforts should take advantage of any special skills you or others in your task group may have in writing, speaking, artwork, etc. The same applies to connections you may have in the media, in print shops, or elsewhere.

To compress these guidelines into a nutshell, in building awareness you should start by defining the goal of your awareness campaign, then figure out who it is you need to reach, and what resources you have (time, people, money) to reach them. After that, it's a matter of planning and specifying a series of awareness-building steps which make a pleasing match between your needs and your resources. These generalities sound a little lofty, though. Is there a way of bringing them down to cases?

- If your parent-teacher association wants to present a talk on learning disabilities, a good way of building awareness would be to print up a notice of the event and have it sent home with all children in the designated school or schools. Alternatively, or in addition, a notice could be included in the regular PTA newsletter. You might also contact personally those whom you knew had a specific interest in learning disabilities, as well as heads of any local organizations concerned with the issue. If you wanted to make the talk open to the general public, a short press release to the local newspaper would be both desirable and adequate. A bunch of inexpensive posters distributed around town could help. Unless the speaker were of particular eminence, or unless you had special reason for putting extra energy into drawing the largest possible crowd, that should pretty much do it. Your expected audience is relatively small, well-defined, and easy to reach; your publicity can be relatively simple, inexpensive, and painless.

- If you want to work out tool-sharing arrangements with other people on your street – I'll keep my extension ladder in a common place for common use, if you'll do the same with your garden tools, and so on – you must speak personally to each household potentially involved. That's all, in terms of awareness building itself. But here, you have an unfamiliar and untraditional program which calls for a fairly high-magnitude response. Exactly how, when, and where you broach the subject will need to be very well thought out. You will also need to build long-lasting support for and participation in your project, and we will soon discuss some possible ways of doing so.

- If you are organizing a community drop-in center for mothers and preschool children, you have a different situation again. Your target group is relatively large (unlike tool-sharing), and the program aims to be long-lasting (unlike the PTA talk). Here are some possible opening strategies: You can start simply with people you know and move outwards from there; you can design a standard publicity mix of flyers, posters, and news releases; you can recruit through social service agencies; you can pinpoint your efforts by searching through the town census, or even through birth announcements; or you can adopt some combination of all of these. So many of your exact choices depend on your starting goal and current resources. But once the center opens, you will probably want to rely heavily on word-of-mouth publicity from its users, because a steady supply of new members will be needed as older ones graduate. A program like this has a special need for ongoing awareness building – a continuous keeping in touch.

How would you have publicized each of the three programs above? What elaborations or corrections would you have made to the suggestions given? It usually helps to think in terms of case examples, and I wish there were space for more detailed examples to give. But as homework, you might want to think of what specific awareness-building actions you would take if you wanted to: (a) sponsor a pancake breakfast; (b) establish bicycle lanes on main streets; (c) find private homes for foster children; (d) start a softball league in the poorer part of town; (e) run for sheriff; or (f) stop the closing of a branch fire station. How would you fit these actions into a plan? And what general conclusions would you draw?

It's humdrum but true that different situations lend themselves to different solutions. Each case is so unique that it's not possible to prescribe a single all-purpose awareness-building package. Publicity then needs first of all to be tailored to the individual event. But more: just as several different suits in the store are likely to fit you well, so several different awareness-building solutions are likely to be appropriate for the same occasion. A helpful philosophy here is to avoid shopping too hard for the elusive "one best," and instead to seek out something comfortable yet becoming (cf. community needs assessment). With practice, you will become skilled at fashioning your approach to the situation at hand. You will also become more confident in your own judgment. Both these qualities will make it easier for you to move on to other stages, as we do now.

ENTRY: BUILDING SUPPORT

Awareness building ought to continue throughout the length of any social service or community change program. New people will move into your target group; some target group members who were oblivious to your efforts may now be able to respond; and current participants need to be kept abreast of what you are doing. Even in well-established programs, publicity must go on. But after a while, the relative percentage of effort devoted to building awareness alone should decline. Attention needs to shift to creating positive support.[5]

In creating support for your ideas and activities, you are after people's emotion, not just their attention. Awareness is a necessary precondition, but it's not sufficient. If you want people to care about your proposals, to care inside themselves, then you must aim consciously at getting them to agree with you and to back you, even if not yet overtly. You must move them another step across the bridge. As in the case of awareness building, the amount of support you need to generate will depend upon the nature of your program, and more particularly upon the discrepancy between the support you want and the support you now have. Most of the time the two are not the same.

Support and awareness overlap. Sometimes both can be increased through the same communication. A TV commercial, for example, has the dual intent of raising your awareness about a product and encouraging you to buy it. Or when neighborhood kids come by your door with raffle tickets, they want your awareness, your support, and your participation all at the same time. If you can pull off this triple achievement with one stroke in your own work, congratulations. It's possible; but when you want to get involvement in a social program, it's less likely. You seek an internal and a longer-lasting commitment, and you can't be bought off with a dollar or two. Generating support for a new program idea usually takes more time. But unless you are able to point to an existing support base or to put in the necessary time to secure one, your intervention will have little chance of succeeding.

Techniques for creating support can be readily derived from the social psychology and community organization literature. We list several here, again as guidelines, keeping with an itemized format for efficiency of presentation. They can sometimes be combined with each other, and with awareness-building techniques. Think of them as added tools that you can call upon when the job warrants.[6]

1. Respond to need.

Your program ought to be responsive to a community need, certainly to a need of your target group. We've stressed this in the past two chapters. But this value-based principle has a practical side as well. People will not support you with more than a few grams of conviction unless they see your plans as meeting their needs. If they haven't already expressed an overt need for what you want to do, that's a yellow flag. If you run through it, then you must convince them, in part through applying the next principle below.

2. Maximize user benefits.

You should spell out as clearly as possible what the target person has to gain by following your suggested course of action. The axioms here are that individuals will seek to maximize their own self-interest, and so will groups. Why should the student dropout join a high school equivalency program, and why should the Chamber of Commerce sponsor band concerts? What benefits will follow for them? More crudely, what's in it for them? Crude as it is, this last question cuts near the core of human nature. It's always asked, and it always has to be answered.

To answer it, consider what kinds of benefits people want. In psychological terms, what reinforces human social behavior? A short but comprehensive list:

- Food, sleep, pain avoidance, etc.
  (basic physiological needs)
- Safety/Security
- Approval of others
- Prestige/Status
- Money (earned or saved)
- Time (saved)
- Achievement/Accomplishment
- Approval of self (self-esteem)

Consequently, you must show your potential supporters how your program or your proposal will give them one or more benefits similar or related to those above. Getting an equivalency degree should in the long run lead to a higher-paying job, with all the connected advantages that brings. Sponsoring the concerts should add some prestige to the Chamber, as well as gain it approval from concert-goers and band alike. If you have difficulty citing benefits, you must make a hard and possibly painful reappraisal of your own program design. But assuming you can identify real rewards, the more vividly you can point them out the better, as long as you avoid promising more than you can deliver.

3. Minimize user costs.

Unfortunately, benefits have a way of mingling with costs. Usually if a potential supporter is to receive some benefit, some price will have to be paid, be it in dollars, hours, sweat of the brow, or risk of failure. Once in a while, especially when an outside angel is footing the bills, you can put together a program which is virtually cost-free. This ideal cannot always be met. Your more common task is to design a program in which the benefits to potential supporters outweigh the costs (honestly pointed out) by the widest possible margin. Not only potential supporters must be convinced the margin is wide, but *you* must be convinced too, for otherwise you are only deceiving yourself as well as others.

Designing programs with high benefits and low costs requires planning and imagination, especially since the benefit frequently arrives only after some cost is expended. Supporters may well have to make some real efforts before reaping any rewards. Ideally, the time period between cost (effort) and benefit should be as short as possible. It helps if you can provide some benefits along the way, or even before cost begins, as an inducement, a free sample. But for many, it's still easier to stay home. And so you must look around for other support-generating techniques.

4. Work within the experience of your target group.

The benefits you are offering must be real, but also communicated so that they can be understood and appreciated by the people they are intended for.[7] The stress is on shared values, and shared experiences, since people show more belief in and support for others whom they see as similar to themselves. When you are in home territory, working within your group's experience will be less of a problem. But if you are slow to identify the values and experiences you share, then you need to stop, look, and listen before you leap. So if you want to draw unemployed people into a job counseling group, you should display (or first acquire) sensitivity to the life space of your potential group members. Or if you want to persuade your local hospital to rotate health promotion clinics through different neighborhoods, you should know who your hospital administrators are and what they stand for, then be able to present your proposal as if it fit perfectly into their own plans.

You needn't try to erase every possible difference between yourself and others, nor to pretend that real differences may not exist. Poses of similarity can backfire, while some honestly stated differences can win respect without threatening support. You should speak the language of the people you wish to serve, but you don't have to mimic their words. Your social and ethnic backgrounds may vary, your stances on some issues may be diametrically opposed, but others should realize that you appreciate their experience, that you are working for the same ultimate goals, and that on *this* occasion you can work very well together.

5. Have a clear issue.

Sometimes, your issue is already sharply drawn, as in the case of reactive programs. But sometimes, the general topic is clear, yet the specific issue is fuzzy. You may want to do something about nutrition, but that worthy sentiment alone will prompt only nods of approval. Nothing else can happen. But if you decide on a food co-op, then you have an issue, something that people can reject, passively support, or actively participate in. Similarly, if you want to work in "alcoholism" or "energy conservation" or in another generic category, your specific issue or project first needs to be defined, the goal and the steps to it made clear. You are then in a far better position to acquire specific support, and you can go on to the next point.

6. Start with small requests.

At the beginning, most requests you make of potential supporters should be small ones. Sometimes very small, and sometimes you should allow incubation time before making any requests at all. When you are building support, especially for a new idea, most of your target group will want to take a nibble (or a sniff) before a full bite. They should have plenty of time to ease into the situation gradually. For example, someone may not be ready or willing to make a contribution right away, or to come to a planning meeting; so you can ask if he or she would be willing to be placed on the mailing list, or to receive another contact after a while. If properly phrased, it's hard to turn down those kind of requests; and there is good evidence that agreeing to a small and manageable request increases the probability of agreeing to a larger one later on.[8]

A minority of people will be ready to take larger steps from the start. Such people need to be recognized, recruited when possible, and brought along at their own pace – all these tasks take percep- tiveness and skill. Those ready to pitch right in can become part of a working core group and gently speed up the program (see princi- ple 8 below). Make this happen when you can. But be aware that pushing people too hard too soon can easily stimulate anxiety, resistance, and withdrawal. Especially for longer-lasting activities, it's usually preferable to divide into subgoals, start out small, and work up gradually.

7. Make your requests specific.

Many good ideas lose steam or fizzle out entirely because a target group is presented with nothing specific to do. The proposed action (the request) may be small, but it has to be as clear-cut as you can possibly make it. That way, the gap between intention and partici- pation can be most effectively bridged. Faced with a barrage of information, worthy causes, demands without end, most of us never get around to doing all the things we want to do. We file generalized requests for support under the heading "things I might consider doing if I had more time." Requests so filed disintegrate like clouds rolling by. To transform a vague intention into a useful social activity means providing specific action opportunities, and attempting to gain specific commitments, at every occasion.

So, a person you contact might be asked to speak to the next-door neighbor (and to confirm this out loud). A person reading a news- paper article might be encouraged to call such-and-such a number for further information. A person picking up a flyer might be persuaded to send in a coupon. A person attending a committee meeting might agree to hang up some notices at work. Get a verbal commitment whenever you can, as this raises the possibility of action. Sometimes your requests will not take hold – not everyone is going to mail in a coupon – but it has cost you very little to make them, some people will respond, and those who don't may do so the next time around.

Community work is open-ended; there is plenty for everybody to do. Those not ready for one task can be offered another – the more open invitations, the better. When potential supporters do something specific, however small, their action not only advances your (their) cause, but also ties them closer to the program – since when people act, they invest ego in seeing that their action turns out well. Your base of support is thus doubly strengthened.

8. Develop a core group.

You should consider recruiting a core group of interested people in the community who will work together with you. Their defining characteristic is that they already support you, and are now willing to help generate support and participation from others. A core group can enhance your own effectiveness and make your life easier; in addition, it can provide a training ground for others to take over your program should you decide to leave it. Remember that we talked at some length about the merits of a core group in the previous chapter.

9. Solicit the support of influential people.

Influential people – they may or may not be "community leaders," and they may or may not be in your core group – can open up doors for you. They may even *want* to. You needn't feel that you will inevitably be compromised, or your ideas watered down, by speaking with someone who has Power. Your goal is to get the most mileage out of your support-building activities. So it makes sense first to identify those persons who have the most influence on your target group, regardless of whether they are *in* it. Depending on the situation, they could include the parish priest, the Brownie troop leader, the Rotary Club president, or the family across the street. Then seek them out, explain your ideas, listen well, and if possible ask for their help in a small but specific way.

If they are willing to help, they can use their contacts, their credibility, and their position to generate much more support for you than you could ever hope to accomplish in the same time. This is leverage, which operates as surely for social programs as it does for machines. (See also principle 8 above, and awareness guidelines 29 through 31.) As suggested before, their own positive action will bind them more closely to your interests. If they are not willing to help actively, perhaps they can help behind the scenes, or at least give you silent assent. Even if you can't get approval, your courtesy call may forestall passive or active opposition. But with a carefully planned approach to influential people, you should find your impact extended more often than not.

10. Repeat your message.

If you honestly feel yourself getting nowhere after putting in a reasonable amount of time and effort, then you may question sincerely whether your plans are appropriate to this moment and place. But on the other hand, most people are not going to swear undying loyalty the first time they are asked for support. Your message may need to be repeated a number of times before it catches hold. Anticipate this, spread your messages out if necessary, and think about how you might vary your approach. Well-established research evidence suggests that repetition of a communication frequently increases attraction to it.[9] So repeat if it's called for, being careful not to overkill.

11. Use good timing.

Single nerve cells vary in their receptivity to stimulation over time; so do individuals, groups, and organizations. Good timing means delivering your message when target-group receptivity is at its peak. This has at least five aspects. One is avoidance of natural low periods: you don't want to schedule key planning meetings during Christmas week, or to launch a new fund-raising drive right after people are tapped out from the last one. A second involves foresight—keeping aware of social concerns about to reach local attention, and having specific ideas for dealing with them when they do. (This applies both to national concerns filtering down, and to local concerns welling up.) A third involves capitalizing on unexpected community events, not only expected ones; being quick, for example, to propose a regular newspaper feature to follow up on an angry editorial, or being first to suggest community uses for a recently-abandoned building. A fourth is piggybacking: hitching your star to a popular cause or event, and showing—if you can fairly do so—how your ideas promote the one or enhance the other. A fifth is developing a sense of when the best moment is to step forward. Some would call this intuition; to others, it's simply keeping your eyes and ears open and having the confidence to act on what they tell you.

12. Thank people for any support received.

No matter what kind or how small. This point is so obvious, yet so often overlooked in our running around. Local change work operates on an economy of trust and good will; you probably can't pay people in cash, but appreciation is almost as good as gold. Appreciation is durable, divisible, transferable, and scarce; better yet, it's also infinitely renewable and free. Not only do people love to be appreciated, and like those who appreciate them, but they deserve it. Someone who makes a personal contact for you, or who is the trunk of the telephone tree, or who brings the packages to the post office is supporting you out of free will, and merits your gratitude. Even someone willing to listen to you state your case should be honestly thanked for time given. And if there's a chance for you to reciprocate support received, or to do a favor, even if unasked, so much the better.

Which specific principles to use, and how to combine them within your overall effort, will again depend upon your particular situation. Just as in building awareness, you need to custom design your own plan for generating support, based upon your goal, your target group, and your resources. Embed your support-generating techniques within your awareness-building strategy when you can. Then check to see if your overall plan meshes well with your nature and your particular circumstances. Don't expect these principles alone, even when expertly applied, to move mountains. But if you have a good plan, you should be able to alter the community landscape.

All this detail may seem to put too much emphasis on the entry stage – too much rehearsal, not enough show. Is it really necessary to pay so much attention to creating awareness and support? Unless both are firmly established before you start, I think so. For any noteworthy act – building a house, playing a sonata, even robbing a bank – the stages of preparation are always the least visible and always take the largest amount of time. The house-building analogy is particularly apt here. To lay the foundation requires heavy-duty equipment. When built, the foundation is invisible. The casual observer sees only the house. Yet without a solid foundation, the house will not stand.

Support does not have to be 100 percent in place before services and benefits can begin. When enough people have crossed over from support to active participation, or at least when enough are right on the edge, you can start to concentrate more on program execution itself. Like awareness building, support generating is an ongoing process. You may need to keep attracting new supporters, and to maintain the support you have with booster shots. But when you have a sufficient support base, it's best to get going, for the merits of your program will draw additional people in, while too long a gestation period may scatter them away.

EXECUTION

Once people start coming through the doors, a new stage has begun. You have nurtured your program from the initial gleam in the eye; now it is ready for full-fledged competition in the marketplace of ideas and services. You have given your program an opportunity, for which you deserve credit; now the chances are that your work will be judged on its worth, by the benefits it delivers.

When your program begins, one of three general consequences is likely to follow. In the first case, you fail conspicuously, despite your best rationalizations. Nobody shows up. Those who do show up don't come back. Those who have supported you become discouraged, and quietly phase themselves out. When this happens – and it can happen to the best of us – you must trouble-shoot for the cause of failure. You may have begun too quickly, without sufficient public awareness and support. You may be operating at the wrong location or hours. You may have a gremlin in your program, an easily correctable flaw that has gummed up the works. Sometimes you can tinker around, make some minor adjustments, and win big on the second try.

Some other times, no amount of tinkering will make the program go. Your idea may just be fundamentally unsound – no one is a genius all the time. You may find it more comfortable to believe that your idea is a good one, but that conditions are not right, that your seed cannot germinate in this kind of soil. You may be quite correct, but what matters now is that your program has not worked in this time and this place, and that you need to think seriously about cutting your losses and moving on to different ground (see "Exit").

In a second case, your program takes right off. All kinds of people get excited, even people you never dreamed would care. Everybody wants to participate, to help, to grab some piece of the action. You have more demand than you can cope with. The press wants to make you a star. Sometimes your dreams really do come true – it can happen. Planning well, promoting an idea that gives significant low-cost benefits, and building a sturdy foundation will increase your dream-come-true percentage.

When you are a smash success and have achieved your goal, you can get off right at the top. But if you still have more to do, you may need to contain the enthusiasm of your supporters, to channel their energies so that your work can continue on an even keel after the initial commotion dies down. You will want to maintain your efforts, but probably not at so intense a pace. You are in an excellent position now to build up new leadership, while casting around for another gleam.

The third case is most common, just as there are more shades of gray than of black and white. You make some progress, move some distance toward your ultimate goal. You may not yet have achieved all the participation you've wanted, but it's enough to keep you going, at least for a while. Give yourself some praise for having made something out of nothing. Now, if you're not done, you need to continue building awareness and support, to draw more people into your network. You need to groom some others to eventually take your place. You need to check that the services you are providing are of the highest possible quality (see next chapter). But most immediately, you need to keep on top of day-to-day program operations, to weave around daily obstacles, to make sure your work stays responsive and alive. This is Execution.

In some respects, it's easier to keep a program going than to begin one; in other respects, more difficult. Look at things first this way:

Once a program has begun, it develops its own momentum, takes on a life of its own. Once you see it breathing, then you yourself can breathe more gently. You still have effort to put in, depending in part upon how successful your program has been in terms of its goals. But there's less effort in stoking a fire than in starting one. You are now a regulator, a maintenance person, a fire stoker, whose task it is to know how much energy should be consumed, where, and when. This task is by no means trivial, but neither should it be over your head.

To a large extent, program execution is repetitive, a case of doing the same things over and over. You have to call another meeting, send out another mailing, put together another revised budget. These are the nuts and bolts; the nuts and bolts never stop coming at you; but if you've handled things once, you can handle them again. Program execution does require a daily discipline – you have to be there, you have to keep caring, you can't let matters slide – but that discipline is not so much a skill as a quality that comes from inside. If you can keep your own inner fire burning steadily, you are likely to do well.

There's an alternative point of view: when you start to execute, your troubles have just begun. You have many more things to do;

it's like being given a third ball to juggle after you've just managed juggling two. And it's not only the volume of tasks that faces you, but the varied skills required to dispatch them. There are too many skills to teach thoroughly in a single book. But if you take community work seriously, here are some that you should have on call:

- attitude-change skills
- behavior-shaping skills
- bookkeeping skills
- fund-raising skills
- grant-writing skills
- graphics and printing skills
- interpersonal sensitivity skills
- leadership and facilitating skills
- negotiation skills
- political skills
- publicity and public relations skills
- secretarial skills
- supervisory skills

Not to mention assessment skills (chapter 3), planning skills (chapter 4), and evaluation skills (chapter 6).

Though this list looks impressive, it shouldn't scare you away:

- You may not need a number of these skills in your particular program.
- You may already possess some of them. Any experience dealing with people teaches you basic techniques of persuasion, basic facts about groups, and so on. These common-sense principles transfer across settings more often than not. Community change work is working with people; there's no secret "X" factor; you don't have to learn an entire new psychology.
- Some desirable skills are really more like parts of one's personality, an issue we'll examine at greater length in chapter 7.
- What you need and don't have you may be able to draw from others. Someone who works with you may be superb at hustling donations; someone else may be a graphic artist, a press secretary, or a contract lawyer, or may know somebody who is.
- What you need, don't have, and can't find, you can learn. Each of the skill areas listed above has its own literature. The references in the bibliography can help you get started. Or you can take courses, apprentice yourself to someone you respect, or simply consult with someone who knows more than you do. Most such people are surprisingly gracious with their time.

The truth is probably that the execution stage is both easier and harder than entry. The "repetitive maintenance" and the "additional skill" arguments are both true, and offset each other. Execution does involve repetition, but it's a big mistake to put your program on automatic pilot and take a nap. On the other hand, if you've gotten this far, chances are you'll be able to cope with any new challenges heading your way. Each of the skills we've listed is worth learning – worth mastering, if you are dedicated – but any current gaps in your knowledge should not prevent you from getting by with what you have now.[10]

No amount of list making or reassuring prose can fully prepare you for having even a little executive responsibility in a real-life community intervention. You soon learn, if you haven't already, that the day does not drift sweetly by. Events come in flurries, sometimes in one king-sized wallop after another. Outside forces, beyond your anticipation and control, buffet you around – even though the more you can anticipate, and hence control, the better off you are. And things go wrong, maybe not even all that often, but enough of the time to keep Murphy's Law on the books. (Laws like Murphy's or Parkinson's or the Peter Principle are usually phrased in semi-humorous form, because the truths they reveal, if taken straight up, would be too painful to confront.)

On any given day in your program, your alarm may not go off; your car may not start; you may not be able to reach anyone on the phone; the phone may not stop ringing; your co-workers may take the day off; your long-awaited appointment may cancel; your kid may get sick at school; the copy machine may break down; your brochures may be lost at the printers; the bank may claim your program account is overdrawn. You may not receive any of these blessings today, but if you keep at it, you will get your share.

When you do, you are not being singled out for divine retribution; these events are part of the piquancy of life, not just of community change work. You should plan out your route as best you can, then steer with the bends in the road. To expect that everything will go perfectly all of the time may be morally admirable, but it does wear at you.

Traps.

There are, however, some traps to watch out for, some road hazards that you can avoid by foresight and by careful navigation. In my own experience, I've run across two particularly devious traps which I'd like to mention to you.

One of them is a time trap, a failure to allot sufficient time for whatever you are doing. Time traps come in two different varieties.

The first is a failure to budget enough time for the project on a day-to-day or week-to-week basis. Matters are invariably more complex from the inside than from the outside looking in. To execute just about any job well almost always takes more out of you than expected. But if you don't allow enough time, you can easily become overextended, overwhelmed, frustrated, resentful. Quality may suffer. And without enough attention, the odds of your work yielding a decent return are about the same as an undercapitalized business venture turning a profit. Few truths in community work are as compelling, or as ignored, even by those with combat ribbons. A wise change agent will calculate beforehand as closely as possible just how much time is needed from all concerned, then leave an ample margin for error so that calm will still prevail if the budget is exceeded.[11]

A second and related time trap is a failure to allow enough chronological time over the long haul. Change activities need their own time to take root and grow. A community program is a living organism that needs to be nurtured; its growth can often be hastened, but it can also be killed off with too much artificial stimulation. The more complex the program, the more exotic the plant, the longer nurturing is required, and the longer growth may need to take. So here are two hard but necessary lessons for the community worker: one must learn that moderation, even deliberate inaction, does not necessarily imply lack of concern (though of course it can). And one must be patient enough to wait for the blossoms. These are lessons for the less experienced, but for the supercharged as well.

The other major trap is one of delegation, the division of work responsibility between yourself and others. Delegation traps are also of two basic kinds, though this time opposite from each other. One mistake is not delegating enough, which may happen for several different reasons. You may be possessive, wanting to keep control of the action all to yourself; or you may find it hard to trust others to follow your suggestions or meet your standards; or instead you may be fearful of asking other people for assistance, or unwilling to impose upon their time. As power-tripper or patsy, you wind up licking the stamps or mopping the floors, when others might be more than willing to help out. Unless you are deliberately working alone, there's almost always someone else who potentially could take part of the job.

The opposite error is delegating too much. In this trap, you spend half your waking hours in meetings, trying to reach a group decision.[12] When you stagger out around midnight, you may all agree it was a "good meeting," and it may have been good, but whether all the participant-hours consumed were consumed most efficiently is another question. Some meeting hours might better have gone toward actual service to people.

The moral here is not only to use meeting time constructively, but also to think through how much individual as versus group decision making there ought to be in your own case. Social psychologists have accumulated considerable evidence on decision-making efficiency, which you might want to acquaint yourself with.[13] Value judgments aside for the moment, many times having one person take responsibility for a particular task or a particular set of decisions is just out-and-out easier. I can remember so many meetings when I devoutly wished we would stop and *do* something, instead of talking, talking, talking, talking.

But there are tradeoffs. First, part of your goal in doing community work with others may be to build up their confidence and skill, to give them more power and responsibility. This comes about largely through participation in group discussions. You could make the decisions (or assign them), maybe do so more quickly and better, but ultimately you would be defeating your own purpose. The rest of the group has to sit at the switch. They may hesitate, they may fumble around; but, especially if you are teaching others, you may need to encourage group decision making, at least initially, and to accept potential short-term inefficiency as an acceptable cost of potential long-term empowerment.

Second, group meetings and group decision making usually strengthen commitment to the group's cause, to the group itself, and to individual members within it. As a result of meeting and deciding together, group members may come to support each other outside the group, in ways having nothing to do with the original group purpose. These side effects may do more to build community closeness than the original group meetings themselves.

Third, some groups favor group decision making for ideological as well as (or instead of) practical reasons. More activist groups in particular are partial to making decisions by consensus, where often the entire group must agree before action is taken. Reaching consensus can be an epic struggle, but more often than not it's simpler than expected. Most informal groups rarely take formal votes anyway. Consensus decision making may take more time; but if reduction of hierarchy, more equal distribution of power, and strengthening of in-group solidarity are central to the purpose of your work, then you may choose to live with the extra expense.

A middle path can probably be plotted between the traps of under- and overdelegation. By following that path, you will be able to exert maximum feasible leverage, promote individual responsibility among your supporters, and keep group ties tight, yet avoid the swamplands of endless discussion. The path's exact location may vary according to your own destination, and in any case it may not be very wide. But by thinking ahead, by trial and error, and by proceeding with caution, you will be able to find it and to stay on course.

Both time and delegation traps are essentially failures of planning. If time and delegation issues are not thought through and squared away in advance, program priorities are harder to maintain. You tend to focus more on the crisis of the day. Your work setting becomes a fire station, alarm bells constantly ringing. It is exciting and fun to be a fire chief, to send off crews to quench the blazes. But if you are only stamping out unwanted fires, responding to one crisis after another, you are in trouble. You should work harder at fire prevention. More accurately, as a social change agent, you really want to start stoking fires of your own, where you control the time, the place, the heat, and the light. You are a responsible arsonist, a professional firebug. In keeping with your professional standing, you need to plan.

Edges.

An ardent collector could set out a truckful of other traps, but program execution involves more than defending against every threat that might arise. The community worker also takes the offense, looks for the extra edge. Even if you have advanced training in management, even if you have mastered the execution skills mentioned previously, you may still need something to make your program stand out from the rest, in a manner consistent with its dignity. Fundamentals will sometimes take you only so far. In a paper blizzard, you must be the golden snowflake.

"Edges" are specific techniques, angles, approaches, or bits of knowledge that can increase the probability of program success. They are no substitute for well-conceived and well-managed programs, and certainly not for goodwill and friendliness toward others, but are rather small points that collectively can add up to a large advantage. The edges that follow, a partial list, dovetail with previously noted principles for building awareness and support. They apply particularly to medium-sized programs and larger (when you can't fit all program members into the living room). Many of them are common sense; several of them you may be using now; some of them may not now apply. But since we often misplace or ignore our common sense, and since one or more edges may be essential to you, a summing up may be helpful.

Access to materials	Applies to printing and duplicating equipment, data analysis equipment, office supplies, etc. Rule: if you desire it, don't own it, and cannot buy it, then hire it, loan it, or come in and try it.
Addressing envelopes	Handwritten/typed addresses, hand-applied photocopied adhesive mailing labels, machine-applied labels, or mailing service. Are you using the right technique for your situation?
Advisory board	For your program, or a steering committee, board of directors, etc. A formally-constituted board can not only help publicize and generate support, but can give you more perceived community power and heighten in-group sense of program importance and worth.
After the event	Sign-up sheets, for volunteers, future participants, or mailing list additions; literature to distribute or sell.
Agendas	Distributed in advance, with, if possible, the approximate time to be devoted to each item stipulated.
Barter	With other agencies, groups, or individuals: (a) goods for goods; (b) goods for service; (c) service for goods; (d) service for service; (e) goods instead of money; (f) service instead of money.
Bulk mail	For mailings of 200 or more pieces. Rate is approximately 25 percent of first class rate for qualified nonprofit organizations. Rules are fairly complex. Your postmaster can provide you with details.[14]
Bulletin board(s)	In your office. Plenty of space, divided into sections. Cleaned regularly.
Clip file	Regular reading, clipping, dating, and filing of items from your local paper about your activities and the activities of related others. Ditto for reports. (See also chapter 3.)
Coffee and tea (regular and herbal)	For participants, visitors, staff.
Contact list (1)	Complete and up to date. For all people in your target group (if it's small), or all potentially interested people (if it's large). Choose file cards over printed lists, but both are better than one alone.
Contact list (2)	Include procedures for: (a) *reaching* all people on your list (via mail or phone); (b) *adding* new names (including program attendees, visitors,

	people you help, people who help you); (c) *removing* outdated names (say once a year).
Contact list (3)	If you have a good one, you can share it with other groups.
Contribution box	When appropriate.
Coupons	Those receiving mailings for public events can be asked to return a coupon to reserve a place, thus potentially adding to the event's perceived legitimacy and importance.
Critiques	At the end of a meeting can make the next one better.
Donations	To groups or causes similar to yours will pay eventual dividends. Need not be in cash (see Barter).
Electrostencil machine	A potentially superior alternative to photocopy for reproducing multiple copies of good quality.
Fearless scrounger	An invaluable asset to any group. Feed sparingly and keep hungry.
Good working relationships	With all people on your contact and resource lists. (Needs saying once.)
Growth	Both personal and professional, for you and your co-workers. Courses, workshops, inservice training, use of consultants, professional reading, subscription to relevant journals, retreats, far-off vacations, some time to play.
Guest book	For your records, and for additions to mailing list.
Junk mail	A free education in mailing techniques and brochure design. Keep selected examples for reference.
Literature rack	In your office (possibly elsewhere, too), containing your publications (free and/or for sale) plus other materials relating to your cause, in case a visitor has to wait or wants to browse.
Logging	Of phone calls and letters by source and type can be a useful evaluative tool.
Logo	For your organization's printed matter; and/or motto (written equivalent).
Mailing lists (other organizations)	Place yourself on the lists of those organizations which mail out materials relevant to your concerns.
Meetings	That end slightly ahead of schedule will often reinforce feelings of group accomplishment.
Message system (1)	Someone to answer the phone (best). Answering

	service (if necessary). Answering machine (if absolutely necessary).
Message system (2)	Cubbyholes or other divided message spaces for offices of more than a few. Also: bulletin board space nearby noting whereabouts and estimated arrival time for each absent group member.
Newsletter	For moderate-sized organizations on up; in-house and/or for outsiders. Particularly good for neighborhood groups.
Newsprint (large pads)	Or chalkboards, or other visual aids. For writing down ideas, agendas, things to be done in group meetings. The more options or tasks, the more desirable for group members to *see* them written out.
Nonprofit status	Converting your group into a nonprofit corporation can bring with it such advantages as expanded fundraising capacity, low-cost bulk mailing privileges, grant eligibility, increased visibility and status in your community, and greater self-esteem. Laws vary from state to state, but generally nonprofit incorporation is not that hard to accomplish.
Orientation sheet (or handbook)	For new members or staff.
Passion	"We may affirm absolutely that nothing great in the world has been accomplished without passion" – Hegel.
Personal relationships	Never hurt.
Personal touches	For example, a handwritten note; remembering a special day; a personal visit when a card would do; dropping a clipping in the mail; an unexpected grace.
Postal system	Understand different classes of mail and their price structures. (Get a free descriptive circular on this from your post office.) A postal clerk you know can make judgment calls in your favor.
Posters	Variations: **(a)** attached pockets, kangaroo-style, with small cards to remove and keep: **(b)** printed on thinner paper, in writing-pad form; reader rips off and keeps one sheet of pad.
Printers	Find a friendly and reliable local printer who is willing to answer your questions and strike up a relationship.
Proofreading	Regularly and carefully. (Respect for the English language.)

Quality *(of printed* *materials)*	When communicating with outsiders, and if you can afford it, pitch quality a notch or two above what would normally be expected for a group of your type. Not overly fancy, though.
Recognition	Of everyone connected with your work. Both informal/ongoing, and also formal/structured—for example, potlucks, outings, banquets, certificates, group pictures, recognition nights, thank-you notes.
Resource directory	Own one for your community. If your community doesn't already have one, make one and distribute it yourself, as a combination in-house and community project.
Resource lists	Of other agencies and groups; of media people; of others who have specific skills you can tap if necessary. May be covered in part by Contact List and Resource Directory.
Review	Of drafts of brochures, mass-printed materials, important letters, etc., for style and content by at least one other person prior to printing or typing.
Rooms	For public grass-roots organizing events, book one slightly smaller than expected capacity so as to give the appearance of a crowd.
Signs	Identifying your workplace. Prominent, attractive, beckoning.
"Speakers' bureau"	You or someone in your group should be readily available for community talks and should publicize this fact to local groups and the general public.
Speedy replies	To all requests and correspondence. Same day if possible.
Stamps	Commemorative stamps on first class mail are no more expensive. If you find a stamp whose message ties into your program concerns, buy in quantity.
Stationery	Letterhead, with logo; high-quality paper for important correspondence; standard paper for standard correspondence; colored paper for flyers.
Students	To work with you, from high school students on up. Don't forget continuing education students. Can help themselves and you via internships, field placements, research studies, class assignments, full class projects.

Suggestions	A suggestion box, or often better, an open suggestion logbook where people write comments and you reply publicly to them.
Support	Someone who will listen and give back kind words. Co-workers, friends – and in institutional settings a good boss will help. In any setting, an organized support group may be feasible.
Tasks	A list of useful but nonpriority tasks for slow moments or when a volunteer walks through the door.
Tax-exempt status	One step beyond nonprofit status (a prerequisite). Harder to get, and more time-consuming, but exempts you from corporate, sales, and property taxes and makes you eligible for tax-free donations. For details, see Internal Revenue Service Publication #557, free on request.
Telephone company	Will give you free literature and free consultation on phone systems suitable for your needs and budget, and on how to use the phone for maximum efficiency and responsiveness.
Telephone trees	Each member calls several others according to a pre-established branching plan. A quick and cheap contact method if branches don't snap. For any close-knit, medium-sized group or larger.
Telephone voice	Pleasant and courteous, however clichéd this is. First-time callers who don't know you well must necessarily judge you by your phone personality. (Try tape recording and listening to some of your own phone conversations.)
Testing	Actual testing of ideas and techniques, especially new ones. On a small scale, but scientifically.
Typeface	Pica (10 characters to the inch) is generally more readable than elite (12 characters).
Typewriters	Those with interchangeable type balls (for example, Selectrics) are worth owning or loaning.
Volunteers	To help, expecially in agency efforts. Can be recruited via media contacts and trained in-house. Will also arrive through establishing good working relationships with others. (See also Recognition.)

As you keep adding to and sharpening the edges in your collection, success will inevitably begin to trickle your way. Enough success, perhaps, for you to start thinking seriously about getting out.

EXIT

The life expectancy of community programs varies, but all are mortal. All programs are destined to end at one time or another in their present form. Some are intended simply to be reactive or one-time events; others are completed when a specific longer-term goal is reached; others still are designed to last indefinitely, though none will. Even public helping agencies, many of them younger than you, change their functions or close their doors. As for grass-roots activities—neighborhood organizations, ad hoc coalitions—a few years is a long time. This is not to justify the situation, but rather to point out what seems to be a fact of organizational life.

Even if the program carries on, you may not want to carry on along with it. You may have private reasons for leaving, or you may just want to give others an opportunity to lead or serve. Whatever your reasons, endings and exits should be a concern for you soon after your program begins, if not before. You should be able to anticipate both the termination of your program and your own departure from it. Just as we have raised our consciousness about personal death and dying, so should we become more sensitive to programmatic death and withdrawal. Sensitivity can blend with compassion. Your general goal should be to set up conditions so that the best aspects of your program will continue, if it will continue, or to have everything packed up, if it will not. You should aim to leave without loose strings or frayed connections, rather with feelings of completion, satisfaction, and ease.

Both actual program length and the management of your own leave-taking should depend on the type of program you are involved in and how successful it is. Quite often the answers to both questions are clear-cut:

1. If the program is a one-shot occurrence—a speech, a workshop, a benefit performance—there is usually no problem. When the show is over, the program ends, and so does your involvement. Exceptions are cases where you want to use the program event to generate another, longer-lasting community activity. For instance, you can set up a conference with an eye toward spurring a particular interest group, which could continue to meet and pitch into other projects long after the conference ends. Followups like this (good examples of leverage) are often excellent ideas; if you are successful here, and are also part of the new action, then the situation changes to that in paragraph 4 below.

2. If the program has a concrete longer-term goal, a foreseeable end point that most can agree on, then again there is no need to con-

tinue after the goal has been reached. When the school crossing guards are on the job, or when the housing violations have been corrected, or when disability benefits have been restored, then you can all stop. Other examples here include construction projects, resource acquisitions, and events with deadlines such as fund-raising drives and political campaigns. Many reactive programs also fall into this category or category 1 above. It's true that next year's fund-raising drive is just around the corner, that you may have to mount another campaign, or that your present success may be only one way station in a longer-term mission, but at least you can rest before you blast off again.

3. If the program is *meant* to carry on, but falls flat for lack of takers, then you may have no choice but to stop. Or you may elect to trim your losses and get out before things grind to an absolute halt. A third option is to keep plugging, despite what reality is telling you so far. If you take the third, you should believe that your decision is strategically wise, as well as virtuous; it could be neither, but it needs to be both.

4. If the program is meant to continue, and it succeeds well enough, that is where exit problems may come in. Not inevitably, for you may decide that you want to stay in your current role for the duration. Others may move on, for turnover is axiomatic, and you may have to seek replacements for them. But for you personally, once you have become precinct captain or car pool coordinator, volunteer chairperson or executive director, you may have found your niche. You like your job, others like you in it, you do it as well as anyone, and there's every reason to keep a good thing going.

Yet there is also advantage in leaving. First, because a more attractive niche may beckon. Your work may lose its challenge after a while, may become routine, even boring. You might get more satisfaction from starting something new and/or different, and your now-considerable talents might be a worthy match for those new ventures. If you were capable enough to handle X, you might be resourceful enough to take on X^2. That's where you may be needed, and that's where fulfillment may lie.

Second, because in any useful role you have the opportunity to guide others to take your place. We repeat: A basic purpose of community work is to strengthen others, to help them gain more control over their own lives. You build strength and control by giving away power and responsibility, and by establishing a supportive climate where those capacities can be exercised. It doesn't matter whether you are a professional change agent or not; nor is it crucial whether you are a leader or an ordinary group member. Either way, you have the chance to transfer your skills and talents to those now ready. Your heirs may be better than you, full of crackling ideas and bubbling energy. Hope that they are: Community workers of all kinds should eventually be looking for ways to make themselves less necessary. In this respect, community service work is fundamentally different from the production of goods.

If you decide to go, how do you make the transition and leave a successful program in the best possible place? In general, it's best to move gradually and methodically, with plenty of lead time. Ideally, it's also best – it's more empowering – for other participants to determine how your leadership will be assumed. A superior leader develops commitment in others so that they will be ready to make choices like these and motivated to take on more responsibility themselves. Here you are moving members the last step across the bridge. Even if you are less of a leader than an active participant, a similar responsibility-building replacement process may be called for.

Sometimes, though, others may not realistically be far enough along to take over responsibility or to select a replacement by themselves; or the dynamics of your situation may not easily allow such a choice. The next block parent may traditionally be self-nominated, or the next club treasurer may merely be the one who agrees to do the work. If you are the leader (or present block parent, or club treasurer) and you gauge this to be true, then you proceed somewhat differently. From the beginning, you should be keeping an eye out for those participants who have the interest, the skill, and the spirit you want; if you can't find them, you can recruit them from the outside. When the time is right, you can sound people out, in order of your preference, as to their willingness to accept more responsibility. (You also want to make sure beforehand that whomever you support can be approved by others.) Having found one or more candidates, you may then formalize your plans to leave, giving yourself and others enough advance notice to make the necessary adjustments.

In either case, it's essential to allow enough time to pass on your skills to others. You may be able to do this over coffee, or you may need to plan multiple training sessions that are fairly formal. The length and the formality of training will depend on how much new material has to be communicated and how technical it is. You will know. In executing the transition, you should be complete and explicit. And you should make sure that your successors get some hands-on experience, a chance to practice using their new responsibilities under your supervision, with your feedback. Some actual overlap between the time they assume their new role and your actual departure will be a plus; similarly, once they've started, you should make yourself available to meet with them as needed, at least at the beginning. Planning – once again – and gradualism are the keys.

Sometimes, exit dilemmas arise. If you want to stay and others want you to stay, that is fine. If you are ready to go and others are primed to take over, that is ideal. But if you want to go and others want you to stay, you have a problem, especially if you feel they are ready to carry on. Ideally, you can agree on transition steps together. In doing so, you will have to balance your commitment and affection for the established program against your probability estimate of its success in your absence, both factors against your attraction to new community involvements, and all three against your responsibility to yourself. No formulas apply; you alone will have to judge which way the scale tips. By instilling responsibility in others from the beginning, by making the intensity and duration of your commitments clear early on, you can reduce the chances of this situation occurring. Yet sometimes it will, and sometimes you may choose to untie the cords that bind you. This can leave raw skin.

Less commonly, it can happen that you want to stay and others want you to go. The more effort you put into anything, the more ego-involved you are going to be, and the harder it may become to wean yourself away. But especially if you came in as an outsider, or with some special skill that has since been transmitted, those you have taught may now be eager to try their wings, even if they are too polite to flap them in your presence.

If others are prepared to continue, you can probably swallow your personal preferences, view their willingness as healthy and desirable, and step aside. If others are not yet ready – if, for example, they want you to leave because they don't like you or your approach – your internal conflict is greater. You want to keep the program alive, but you can hardly give to people who don't want to be given to. You can look for some useful contribution you can make on their terms. Ultimately, though, you will not be helping anyone if you have outlived your welcome. Clear expectations and skill sharing from the beginning again would have helped. If you do leave reluctantly, it's a lesson for next time. Even at that, things may continue on very well, possibly better than before. You may already have made your best contribution, or overrated your importance, or both.

In practice, others' feelings about your staying or going are rarely so sharply polarized. If you stick around, that's okay, and if you leave, we'll manage. Here is one of the most frequent exit situations, if not an outright dilemma. Suppose you are helping to run a program which most people agree has some value. But there's less passion than indifference; the majority would surely opt for continuation, but if the program vanished tomorrow, no outcry would follow. You too may feel passion fading, and think that maybe you should pick up and move on. Where lies your greatest utility? Once again, no hard rules.

It may be better to stay; but suppose this time you make the decision to leave. You set up the program to continue as best you can, following the principles we discussed above. You say a little prayer for it, then gently loosen your grip and walk away. You hope that it survives. Maybe it will.

But if it dies, you may have done all you could. Program death is a part of program life. Program life and death are both parts of a higher-level natural selection process, operating with imperfect though better-than-chance accuracy to ensure that those change programs most responsive to people's needs stay alive. You, as social change agent, will try to propagate your species and to prolong life at its best. Your place is where the pulse is quickest. If life signs weaken, you can try to restore them. Should you fail, you can learn from your failure, at the same time accepting that program death makes room for new program life to be born and to flourish.

6
Evaluation

A SIMPLE(?) EXAMPLE

A community organization decides to conduct a training program for present or potential leaders of self-help groups. The program purposes are to have participants learn basic leadership and helping skills useful in support-group work, and to encourage them to start similar groups of their own. Trainers are to be organization staff. The sponsors recruit members mainly by press releases and mailed brochures.

About thirty people sign up, most paying twenty dollars for six morning or evening sessions. The training program goes off as scheduled. At the end of the sixth session, program staff pass out and collect a one-page evaluation form. Results indicate that twenty-three of twenty-five participants returning forms found the training program "useful" or "very useful," while all twenty-five said they were "sometimes" or "often" able to apply material they had learned to their real lives. All twenty-five also wanted the program offered again.

Questions:
1. Was the training program a good one?
2. What do you think of the evaluation method used?
3. How (if at all) might the evaluation have been improved?
Defend your positions.

We'll come back to these questions in a while. First, we have to set the stage.

147

THEORY VS. REAL LIFE

Suppose you have figured out what needs to be done in your own community setting. You've carefully drawn up a sequential plan of action to meet that need. You've put your plan into motion; you've built up sufficient awareness and support; you've actually begun what you set out to do. And suppose things seem to be humming right along. What's more, others are ready to assume responsibility so that your work can continue. You feel satisfied, and proud.

Congratulations, for you have come a long way. But there is one more step to take before you can come up and claim your prize. You have to evaluate your work, the program or activity you started. You have to answer the basic question: "How do I know it is any good?" Or, more specifically: "How do I know this activity is helping anybody, or changing anything for the better?"

It's hard to deny that the question is legitimate. And the answer to it is not self-evident. Not all birdhouses attract birds. The fact that something exists, hand-tooled or not, does not necessarily mean it is good, or valuable, or useful. If it were, life would be that much less of a puzzle.

So, if we write down some diverse examples of potentially useful community activities (from the vast repository available):

- starting a support group for single parents
- setting up a nutrition information center at your local supermarket
- producing a regular Spanish-language radio program
- beginning a parent visitation program at your neighborhood school
- finding private families to house former mental patients
- conducting a training program for nursing home aides
- establishing a 24-hour emergency line at city hall
- persuading the town recreation department to offer co-ed volleyball . . .

Does it make sense to evaluate these activities, to check on their basic worth?
Of course.

Should we take questions of evaluation seriously, so that overt evaluation efforts are on a scale with the amount of effort spent in implementing the original program?
Yes, that makes sense.

Should we actually budget time for evaluation, and plan evaluation steps, just as we planned the original program and its execution?

I guess we probably should. I can see where you have high expectations.

Perhaps, though high expectations are cheap. Now, in everyday practice, how well do you think programs like these are evaluated? *I don't know for sure. Maybe not very well.*

You are right. The fact is that most community activities or social change programs are hardly evaluated at all.[1] Many times evaluation is missing altogether. Most other times evaluation is cursory, glossed over, invested with all the spirit of going to the dentist. Serious evaluation by any professional standard is rarely attempted, even more rarely accomplished. With very few social science concepts (except maybe assessment, and planning) is there such a gap between theory and practice. In theory, evaluation is a program essential, a powerful tool, an unblemished virtue. In practice, it is none of these. Somehow, the translation has not been made.

But why not?

That's the question we need to tackle first. Clearly, people working in community settings, from agency directors right on down to the lowliest unpaid foot soldier, have problems in carrying out program evaluations. Their problems may center around external obstacles or internal resistances or both. If we can understand what these problems are, and why they exist, we may come a little closer to carrying out evaluations in practice. The techniques are available; they are admittedly imperfect, but they are not especially complex, and we will argue that they really can help you do a better job.

But before we discuss techniques – we'll do so later on, and apply them to cases – it might be best to focus on the problems, to demystify the evaluation process. The purpose of this next section is to loosen up some of the defenses and blockages regarding evaluation, so that new learning can later take place. If you have no such defenses, then come and help us review.

SOME REASONS WHY EVALUATIONS AREN'T DONE

Rephrasing the question: What gets in the way of doing evaluations of community programs and activities? (Not doing them *well* for now, but doing them *at all*.)

1. The term "evaluation" itself is poorly understood. "Evaluation" is a jargon term, like "needs assessment" or "cost effectiveness." It

sound technical, feels a little intimidating, looks as though it might be beyond the range of the average person. But it really isn't.

Evaluation has two aspects. The first aspect simply involves receiving and adjusting to feedback from the environment, a type of feedback we experience continuously throughout our waking lives. If "feedback" is unfamiliar to you, then think of evaluation as "checking"; you check the results of anything you do, consciously or not, and you adjust performance accordingly. Through checking, you learn. When you bang a nail, you guide the movement of the hammer so that you don't squash your thumb. When you fry an egg, you make sure it's neither too loose nor too rubbery. These activities, and hosts of others like them, are so natural, so matter-of-fact, that we barely expend conscious energy on them. Yet they all involve feedback, from eyes, muscles, or ears; we are checking, monitoring, evaluating them all the same.

The second aspect of evaluation is valuing (c.f. "*evalu*ation"). We assign a quality rating to the performance in question. True, we normally don't apply many different values to tasks as simple as banging a nail — it's either hammered home or not. But we are likely to utilize a value range for tasks which are one level more complex. For example, when we put in a shelf, or make a soufflé, we grade the results. Our judgments (evaluations) again are made easily and naturally, without any special difficulty or prior planning. And, as before, we adjust our actions depending upon how well we rate ourselves. We use evaluations as tools to improve performance. If the shelf collapses, next time we'll make sure to find the stud; if the soufflé falls, we'll remember not to open the oven door while it's cooking.

So checking that something was done and valuing how well it was done are part and parcel of daily life. These processes, taken together, are evaluation. Without them, we could hardly live, much less get better at living.

The same checking and valuing processes extend to social programs. Can you see how? All but the very simplest life events can be diagrammed like this:

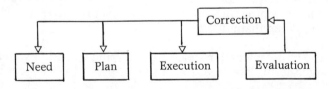

A preexisting need generates a plan; the plan is executed and evaluated; and the evaluation has a corrective impact upon subsequent execution as well as upon assessment of the need and formation of the plan. Evaluation is actually very much like assessment (chapter 3), only after the fact. This is all abstract, and perhaps too neatly packaged, but it's also quite real.

In analyzing social problems, the same feedback loop, the same progressive, correcting mechanism, are both present. The same basic concepts apply. The flow of this book (chapters 3 through 6) has been created precisely to mirror this sequential process. The key differences between evaluating social programs and personal life events are that social programs usually affect more people and are considerably more complex. Because they are more complex, goals are sometimes harder to define, criteria for evaluation are sometimes more difficult to establish, and, once established, the criteria are sometimes more difficult to measure. But because such programs are also more important for public welfare, it is all the more essential that evaluation effort be made.

2. Evaluation takes time. There's not much question about it. A comprehensive evaluation of an extensive social program – the operations of a medium-sized agency or a school system for example – can take weeks or even months of full-time work. What's more, if you really believe in evaluation, you will have to wait for the results to come in before instituting any major changes.

Your own community activities may not require that great an evaluation commitment. But someone is still going to have to plan any evaluation, design any evaluation instruments, collect any data, tabulate, analyze, communicate the findings, and ensure that those findings are really used to improve service delivery – all of this, ideally, on a regular, periodic basis. These hours will add up, and, as always, will probably add up to a larger figure than you first envisioned. You may not have that kind of time, and even if you do, you may not feel it is worth investing in program evaluation. Every hour spent designing questionnaires could be spent in counseling, training, educating, organizing, giving service to people. Evaluation makes sense, but. . . .

The rejoinder is simply that you are not being pushed into an either-or choice. You're not being told to spend your life toting up numbers, but rather to ask yourself this question: Assuming you believe that a well-conducted evaluation can strengthen your program, what percentage of total program time should formal (versus impressionistic) evaluation receive? Perhaps not 50 percent, or 25

percent, or even 10 percent; but do you really want to say 0 percent? Doesn't it seem proper that in your overall mix of activities a
finite if small percentage of time be blocked out and reserved for
evaluation? If you settle on 5 percent – one clock hour in each 20
program hours – shouldn't that amount of evaluation time be
expected to carry its weight? Shouldn't the results when in yield at
least commensurate program dividends?[2] I think they should.

3. The results of evaluation may be disappointing. If you are
involved in a program you like, one where things seem to be going
well and everyone appears more or less content, evaluation may
look to you as just extra frosting on the cake. You would foresee
little to gain except the confirmation of what you knew already. On
the other hand, you would surely have something to lose if for
some reason the evaluation turned out poorly. Your ego would take
a tumble. Your program would lose credibility if others found out.
Continued support, both personal and financial, could be jeopard-
ized. Your own position could be threatened. Any one of these consequences would be good reason to leave well enough alone.
Alternatively, if you know deep down that your program is only
limping along, then a thorough evaluation may be about the last
thing you want.

So you may drag your feet about evaluation. Priorities will go
elsewhere. You may not actively oppose evaluation, but neither
will you encourage it. You will try to fend off any planned assessment which seems threatening. If you can't fend it off – for
example, if you are required to produce evaluation data for outsiders, or if outsiders are required to come in and evaluate you –
you will showcase the most flattering results, put the best possible
face on the rest of the data, and explain away any negatives you
can't hide. You can try to discredit the credentials or motives of
those making external criticisms. If necessary, and if you can get
away with it, you may claim that your program can't be evaluated
by normal methods, because it deals with "intangibles."

There are exceptions, for not everyone is quite so self-protective.
Some program administrators or community workers welcome
honest feedback, may even take steps to seek it out. They really
want a dispassionate view of how they are doing; they admit their
accountability; they are ready to take the sting if they need to be
stung; they know that evaluation is almost guaranteed to point to
some program defects, yet they are genuinely primed to use those
same evaluation results to make their program better. They know
that if their program improves, their personal futures will take care

of themselves. Of course, we would like to include ourselves in their ranks.

To do so calls for not just a belief that evaluation will actually improve your program, but also a sense of security and openness for all involved – you and others working with you have to be solid enough to accept and learn from criticism without feeling put down or turned off. When infighting and one-upmanship are norms within the task group, evaluation will be used as a political rather than a corrective tool. When the climate is supportive and trusting, evaluation works best.

4. Evaluation is thought to require specialized techniques and methods. If you believe that it does, and that you don't have the needed knowledge, then you have prima facie grounds for not evaluating.

The response here is yes and no. Yes, in the sense that discourses about evaluation methodology will fill a wall-sized bookcase and none of them is bedtime reading. It is often feasible and usually desirable to evaluate social programs, especially new or complex ones, by sophisticated experimental designs. Evaluation special-ists – university professors, or think-tank consultants – do not venture forth without advanced knowledge of research design and statistics. The more you know about evaluation research tech-niques, about experimental design and analysis, the better off you are.

No, in the sense that most of the time you can perform a useful evaluation without particularly specialized knowledge. By a useful evaluation, I mean one which meets your current evaluation needs, or comes close. You can conduct such an evaluation by applying disciplined common sense, stretching your mind a little, asking for advice when you need it, and making do with what you have. If you don't have an electron microscope, you use a magnifying glass. With practice, your powers of observation will increase. You may not come out with a "perfect" evaluation, or a "professional" one (by professional standards), but you should be able to generate relevant data which are relatively free from bias and valuable to you. Later in the chapter we will give examples.

What evaluation does require, over and above technique, is a certain finesse – an ability to get cooperation in starting the evalua-tion, in carrying it out, and in putting at least some evaluative recommendations into practice. This finesse is more of a personal quality than a technical skill. We'll come back to this point later on as well.

SOME REASONS FOR EVALUATING

Ideally by now any of your resistances to evaluation have been at least momentarily weakened. You know that evaluation goes on constantly in daily living, that its corrective action improves performance, and that useful evaluation can take place without highly specialized training. But you are also aware that evaluation absorbs time and that the results may turn out poorly. You may now have fewer good reasons for not evaluating, but not enough good reasons for going ahead. And you may ask what relevance any of this has for your own work: How does this really apply to me? You may have a vague sense that evaluation is good for you, something you ought to do. But why should you get personally involved in evaluation, other than to fulfill some abstract standard of a "good" program, or to meet someone else's demands for accountability?

I'll try to explain, as clearly as I can. Virtually any human service agency effort, social program, or community activity is geared toward producing some kind of change. On examining your current work or your future intentions, you will find that you are almost always wanting to make something happen, to make something better.[3] Change means a difference in conditions, a difference in the level of some variable, compared to what existed before. Detecting change, then, implies some measurement of conditions, first at time A, later at time B.

Evaluation provides that measurement, by assessing change from one point in time to another. *Without evaluation of some kind, you cannot tell if change occurred.* Therefore, without evaluation you cannot say whether your program or activity did any good. That process – the only process – which can tell you how well you did is evaluation.

An illustration may help. Suppose you are running for local office, your second time out. The first time, you were an unknown. You didn't expect to win, and you got beaten badly. But in this contest, you've had a lot more exposure, you've campaigned twice as hard, and you think you have a real shot at victory.

How do you evaluate your campaign? Mainly by your percentage of the vote in this election, and in comparison to the last one. Vote counts are very precise evaluative measures; everyone accepts them as determining electoral success or failure. Try to picture a situation where everyone went home after the polls closed and no one bothered to tally up the ballots. That's hard to imagine; it would be ludicrous, bizarre. Yet it is hardly more rational to wage a hard-fought campaign for some nonelectoral cause you care deeply about and then walk away without trying to figure out how well you have done.

In both campaigns, you need evaluation of results to judge your effectiveness and to provide a stimulus for subsequent improvement. The difference between the two situations is that community activities are usually harder to evaluate than elections. Not only are evaluative criteria harder to sort out and to measure than votes, but no election officials will be on hand to do the evaluation for you. In these circumstances, we tend to get lazy; we rely on our subjective impressions, which more often than not will be molded to justify what we are already doing. But the proper action is clear: if you want to get past your own biases and make your program better, you have to take evaluation seriously and dig for harder information.

STEPS IN THE EVALUATION PROCESS

By now, you may be persuaded that you need to evaluate your own work. You may still have some well-founded reservations – I have a few myself, to be specified later. But I'd like to suggest that we lay our reservations aside for the moment and move on to the next question: If you want to evaluate your community activity or program, how do you do it?

We can identify eight steps in the process. Our plan will be to pick our way through them fairly carefully – step four especially – then to return to our opening example, plus some others. After that, we will describe some hitches and snags in many real-life evaluation settings, and examine ways of dealing with them. We'll key our discussion to the ordinary community worker, the small-time operator. Eventually, we hope to find an approach to evaluation which will be useful for us in most ordinary circumstances.

Step One is both the easist and the hardest. It is mental. You have to want to evaluate your own work – to open yourself to criticism and change, to collect evidence, to draw conclusions, to transfer your conclusions into practice, and to be utterly honest with yourself while doing so. Actually, "wanting to" is not enough, since our own inertia and our own constraints let too many wants slide by. There ought to be an intentional, written commitment to evaluate, to block out the specific time and resources to do the work, and to guard them from infringement. Commitment is the mainspring for any social action. No matter how convincing I may be, that commitment has to come from you.

Step Two is to specify the purpose of the evaluation. Why do you want to do it? Because you somehow think you should? Because you want to prove that things are going well? Because you have to produce results for an outside group, or for your own associates? Because you need to know how you are doing? Because you want to use the results to improve program operations? Determine what your position is and what its implications are. Then follow up by asking: "What will I do with the evaluation data when they have been analyzed?" Your answer will help clarify your motives and the way you proceed with the next steps.

Step Three is to identify the goals of the program. This ought to be an easy step, in that you should have identified these goals previously, in chapter 3. (You should also then have made sure that your goals are *worthwhile*, something evaluation in itself cannot do for you.) If you've already identified your goals, just retrieve them and lay them on the table. If you haven't, your failure to have done so comes back to haunt you now. It's important to understand why, and why step three is necessary.

Evaluation must be keyed to your starting overall goals. If your goal was to do **X**, evaluation must take place in terms of **X**. Without clear goals, it's not just that evaluation procedure becomes much more confusing; it also becomes much harder to know whether your goals were achieved. You can hardly tell whether your program succeeded, because it's not certain what is meant by success. We're not sure what evidence to look for, and so just about *any* evidence could be credited in your favor.

Note well the stress on *starting* goals. It's ethically and pragmatically dubious to do your work and then scout around for goals that match up well with the results you obtained. Evaluation serves the community best when it gives the most honest information possible. If it makes you look good in the process, so much the better, but that should not be the main purpose.

When goals are not clear-cut, it's your responsibility to clarify them as best you can. Demanding as this may be, it's always possible, for you are the one who is doing the choosing and clarifying. As you proceed, you will realize that a major side benefit of serious evaluation is to force you into making clear goal statements. This can be illuminating, though sometimes also humbling if you learn the hard way that goal clarification should have occurred well before you started.

Step Four is to select the specific criteria on which the goals will be assessed. This is a natural extension of step three. The point here is that evaluating in terms of overall program goals is only part of the battle. Evaluation must also be based upon specific preselected criteria. Again, a word of explanation is in order.

The more specific the goal, the less the problem in selecting a criterion measure. If your goal is to get the potholes in your street fixed, your sole criterion is whether they are filled in or not. If you aim to establish a community residence for the retarded, your criterion is a full house. Or if you want to see the school gym opened up on weekends, you can come by on Saturday and try the door. Especially when the goal is a physical goal, when the hoped-for change is a physical change, you may have narrow and clearly defined criterion measures which follow naturally from the goal itself. Evaluation can be a snap.

But the community worker is usually after more than a one-time physical change, and that is why most human service programs are not so tidy. More often than not, they have multiple goals. And they traffic heavily in feelings and attitudes, internal states which show up in sometimes peculiar ways and sometimes not at all. In other words, our aim usually goes beyond the simple outcome of getting a gym opened, or a residence built. We may want to see kids and families using the gym facilities, learning new skills, starting informal leagues; or we may aim for some particular level of client movement into and out of the residence, some definable educational improvement, some concrete gains in understanding by the residents and the neighborhood about each other. Getting the gym or the residence to open, the initial change event to happen, is like getting a balky engine to kick over; necessary, praiseworthy, but not sufficient. The engine then has to do some work, and you as evaluator have to find some criteria for assigning value to the work done.

How do you evaluate work output, or any performance? The evaluation will certainly include assessments on criteria related to specific performance goals. If our main concern is with specific behaviors, we'll try our best to measure them. Beyond that, evaluation will usually occur in more than one way, since we are usually interested in more than one performance dimension. Social scientists and community workers over time have compiled an extensive and broadly applicable list of criterion variables which can be used for small-scale program evaluation. There is a Chinese restaurant full of possibilities. Here is the menu. Suppose we first read through it and come back to make our choices when we've finished.

Table 10
Selected Evaluation Criteria

Outcome variables.

1. **Survival** (and survival time). If the program is intended to last over time, and it does, that in itself can be valued. Survival value and survival time should not be taken lightly. Without basic survival, you can't do anything else.[4]

2. **Awareness.** Awareness is almost as fundamental as survival itself. If the people you want to reach don't know about your work, they can't take advantage of it. Awareness breaks down into:
   a. the number of people who know about your program.
   b. the percent of the total target population which knows.

3. **Support.** Expressed attitudes about the program by:
   a. nonmembers/nonusers (external support)
      Considered by source, external support can come from:
      • outside agencies or institutions
      • community leaders
      • media
      • the general public
      Considered by form, support from most of the above groups can take the form of:
      • attitude surveys
      • interviews
      • letters
      • phone calls
      • published accounts, or other testimonials
      • statements at public hearings
      • votes
      • public awards or commendations
      • accreditations (that is, meeting the formal standards of some outside regulating agency)
   b. members/users (internal support)
      This can take the form of unsolicited testimonials. More frequently, and more desirably, such support occurs through expressed satisfaction via solicited attitude survey or feedback form; it can also be measured by interviews, letters, etc.[5]

4. **Attendance.** Attendance is an easily countable and especially revealing behavioral measure. When the dust has cleared, either people show up or they do not. Some subcategories:
   a. the number of people who come to an event
   b. the number of people who come as a percentage of those who signed up, or who said they would come
   c. the number of people who return for subsequent meetings which are part of the same program. (This can also be expressed as attrition rate.)

d. the number of people who sign up for and/or attend related future events. (This can also be measured by percent of capacity or by waiting lists.)

5. **Participation.** Another behavioral measure, for participation means membership, and members are often asked to become involved in some specific way, taking a more active role than mere passive support or attendance. Your own local definition of participation will suffice here. Participation can be measured by:
   a. the number of members
   b. the number of new members (for example, over a defined time period, and/or as a percentage of new membership – acquisition rate)
   c. the number of members who have dropped out (or, dropout rate)
   d. the percentage of members this year who were also members last year (that is, turnover rate; other time periods can substitute for "year")
   e. the average length of membership
   f. the number of responses to mailings or solicitations for a particular event (for example, coupon returns, phone calls, letters, walk-ins).

   Note: the term "users" can replace "members," especially if there is no membership in the program as such; occasionally, both categories may apply.

6. **Responsibility sharing,** or active help. This means people assuming some specific responsibility for, or making some tangible contribution to the program, over and above simple membership or participation. The precise definition will again have to be local. However, some specific indicators are:
   a. the number of active volunteers (also, the number of hours of volunteer service; acquisition, dropout, and turnover rates for volunteer helpers; average length of volunteer status)
   b. committee membership (for example, size; percent of memberships filled; attendance at meetings; amount of competition for available openings, etc.)
   c. board membership (cf. subcategories for committees).

   The amount and kind of responsibility sharing or active help can be further broken down into "spontaneous" and "solicited" categories (see footnote 5).

Note so far: The evaluation categories of awareness, support, attendance, participation, and responsibility sharing (#2 through #6 above) duplicate the stages of program implementation discussed in chapter 5. (The intermediate category of "attendance" has been added.) This is deliberate. *Each implementation stage can and should be separately evaluated.* The emphasis in your own evaluation will depend in part upon the stage you are in within your own program.

7. **Requests for new service** – the number of times people ask you for something that you are not now actually doing. This variable is significant, since in this case others are asking you to do something for them, instead of the other way around. By doing it, you build your reputation, and consequently increase the short-term probability of future requests coming in.

   While your ultimate goal may be to reduce dependence on you, and hence to lower the frequency of requests, at the beginning you usually seek high request volume; getting it is a sign that your program has taken hold. Specific request indicators will vary with the situation, but some requests frequently made include those for additions to your current program, consultation, speaking or training engagements, information and referral, membership in other groups or on ad hoc task forces, and assistance in starting a similar program in a different locale.

8. **Spin-offs.** Admirably, an effective social program can bear off-spring – true genetic variants – with no apparent prior fertilization. Colloquially, these offspring are often referred to as "spin-offs." Once the original program has reached a certain operating speed, there's a tendency for pockets of program energy to coalesce, spin themselves off from the parent body, and strike out in a nearby but diverging direction. The parent body itself can spin off, as when a work group has achieved its original goal, maintains its internal cohesion, and looks around for something else to do.

   In either case, a community garden project may blossom into neighborhood tree planting; a teen-age recreation program could evolve into a summer camp; a toys for tots campaign might phase into a second-hand toy store. Spin-offs are valuable by-products, to be stimulated, nurtured, and encouraged whenever possible. They count as bonus points.

9. **Incidental effects.** Quite often your program will yield effects you could never have anticipated. Who could have seen that a clean-up project would arise out of the Cub Scout picnic? Or that the town health fair would lead to changes in the school lunch program? Maybe no one. But a wise change agent knows that when people are brought together, they will talk to each other. They will have their own agendas; they will be looking to mate with other minds, and if conditions are right they may strike a match – with consequences far more significant than the original event which brought them together. The change agent, as match-maker, works to set up the optimal conditions for informal conversation as well as formal action. The incidental effects produced may be hard to spot, far removed from the original program intent; but they were partially caused by the program, and they count, too.

10. **Income.** Which could mean:

a. the number of people who pay for your services
b. the amount of money paid
c. the number of member or supporter financial contributions
d. the amount of those contributions
e. the amount of organizational, institutional, or grant-related contributions
f. the total program operating budget
g. the amount of program profit or loss.

Income is an "outcome" if it means survival; but program views on money vary, and evaluation criteria used will vary accordingly. Some programs need money to stay afloat, or at least define themselves that way. The total operating budget may then become a measure of success. Willingness to pay for services may also be seen as an indicator of how much that service is valued, and a program may make it a priority to collect what the traffic will bear. And external income, especially grants, may be life blood.

Other programs take the opposite tack, and want as little to do with money as they can. The service they provide is intended to be free; fees mean failure. External contributions, especially grants, are shunned, for they limit independence and drain energy. The program has little need for much money, expects to carry on as cheaply as possible, and will rely on out-of-pocket expenses, in-kind services, and loans, plus occasional donations from friends when absolutely necessary. Still other programs fall somewhere in between, and will (or should) have their own set of financial evaluation criteria.

Process variables.

All ten major criteria listed above deal with outcomes, or "products" of your work. Another mode of program evaluation, requiring quite a different mental set, focuses on process. The activities involved in producing the outcome—the meeting, the planning, the agonizing, the elation—are valued for themselves; the journey has its own worth, over and above the destination. Process variables are generally harder to pin down, and they generally apply only to the people who have constructed the social change activity—not to the "target population," as we have used that term.[6] Some commonly employed process variables (far from all) are:

11. **Accomplishment.** (that is, personal feelings of accomplishment)

12. **Learning.**

13. **Satisfaction.** (alternatively, "fun")

All of these derive from working on the program, as opposed to using it. These process variables, though subjective, can be measured by questionnaire or interview.

Input variables.

Yet another approach to evaluation considers the amount of effort (or input) that goes into the program. Input variables include:

14. **Time.**
    a. the total number of hours spent (for example, service hours)
    b. the total duration of effort (for example, calendar days).

15. **People.**
    a. the number of people working on the program
    b. the position, or rank of the people working on the program, and time spent by each. (In an agency setting, for example, is the work being handled by top administration or by lower-level line staff?)

16. **Contacts.** Frequency counts of:
    a. personal contacts made
    b. phone calls completed
    c. letters/brochures mailed
    d. pieces of literature distributed.

17. **Money.** The total amount of money spent (possibly broken down by budget category).

Cost-effectiveness variables.

If input data are collected, they can also serve to assess the amount of input required to produce a particular kind of output. The term commonly used here is "cost effectiveness" – that is, how much cost for a given effect? Since any cost may be matched up against any effect, there is no one single measure of cost effectiveness; there are really as many different measures as the number of cost variables and effect variables multiplied together. But some cost-effectiveness indicators most often used in practice are:

18. **Dollar cost per hour of service** – or, service hours per dollar. A similar exchange of comparison base is also possible for the other measures below.

19. **Time cost per hour of service.** (Time = total operating time, including nonservice hours)

20. **Average client fee per hour of service.**

21. **Dollar cost per contact.**

22. **Time cost per contact.** (In this case, and in #21 above, contact is treated as an "output" rather than an "input.")

23. **Number of contacts per respondent.** (That is, how may contacts are necessary to get one attendee, participant, return of a mailing, etc.?)

24. **Dollar cost per respondent.** (combines #21 and #23 above)

25. **Time cost per respondent.** (combines #22 and #23 above)

Additional choices.

There is more. For many or all of the indicators mentioned:

1. Diversity, or width of demographic representation, can be an additional criterion (for example, diversity of supporters, attendees, participants, responsibility sharers, contributors, etc.) Alternatively, you may desire only certain *kinds* of representation, and you can measure that too.

2. Where not already indicated, data collected may usually be expressed either in raw numbers or in percentages of an ideal, especially percentages of the total target group you intend to serve, or whom you have contacted.

3. Data may be stated in the form of either numerical or percentage change from the previous evaluation period or periods. For example, a dues-paying membership of fifty may be interpreted positively or negatively, depending upon how many dues payers there were the last time you checked. This is the central point. Evaluation data should be compared with previously collected data whenever possible.[7]

This list is only typology. You may know of a better one. And despite its length, the list does not encompass all possible evaluation measures. You can add others, or figure out more collected data whenever possible.

That is quite a menu. The variety of choices seems mindboggling. In fact, maybe we had better go someplace else . . . .

Don't go yet. You don't have to order everything you see. Some of these criteria overlap. Not all of them may be applicable to you. And those which do apply need not all be chosen right now. But which ones should you choose?

Once again, we have guidelines rather than hard-and-fast rules. One guideline, recalling step three, says that you should choose evaluation criteria consistent with your starting program goals. Translated into examples, this means that:

If your general goal involves:	*You should emphasize evaluation in terms of: (though not to the exclusion of other factors)*
publicizing the availability of a new service	awareness: service use
building a new community organization	members: supporters
grooming potential leaders within an organization	responsibility sharing
sponsoring a discussion series	attendees
counseling ex-offenders	recidivism rate: employment status

skills training	skills learning
fund raising	net income
increasing worker satisfaction	expressed satisfaction: other process variables
justifying your existence to outside funding sources	cost effectiveness

Evaluation criteria should also be governed by your evaluation resources and by ease of measurement. Specifically, if you have more people to help you, you can collect more data on more variables; and if two evaluative criteria are otherwise equal in value for you, you should pick the one which is easier to measure. (Your evaluation itself should be cost effective.) These guidelines are obviously general: more specific answers must be tailored to your particular situation. We will propose a few more specifics toward chapter's end. Right now, we ought to continue with our eight-step analysis. We've gotten past the most technical part, and can cover the remaining steps more rapidly.

Step Five is to set expected levels for each criterion selected. We're not just concerned with "membership," "requests," or "income," but with getting (say) 100 members, 10 new requests, and $1,000 for operating expenses. Numerical values are almost always specifiable. When criterion levels are given numerically, we have specific program objectives, like those cited at the end of chapter 3. We have targets, which may not affect the evaluation results themselves (though indirectly they can), but which will certainly affect the interpretation we place on them. At the very beginning, you may not know what levels to set – your first estimates may be way too high or too low, and you shouldn't live or die by them. But as things settle down, take target practice more seriously. Your reward will be a clearer shot at success.

Evaluation steps one through five – intention, purpose, goal, criterion, level – have three features in common. They all go on inside your head: you needn't yet have made a move in the outside world. Properly, they should all go on before the program starts. And properly, they should all fit together in a preexisting plan. With concentration and clear thinking, this plan can be completed, a first draft anyway, in several hours or less. Successful completion will be time well spent. The next step leads us outside in space and forward in time.

Step Six is to take measurements on each criterion variable after the program has been operating. The tip here is to do this while creating the minimum amount of extra work for yourself. Much measuring can be done by simple counting; all you need is someone adding up the people as they walk in, or tallying the yeas and nays, or reading the bank balance, or logging requests. These countings are of naturally occurring events, without any special intervention on your part. On occasion, you may have to devise a measuring tool of your own, such as a feedback form. Such forms must be precise and unambiguous, but need not be overly elaborate nor meet scientific journal standards. And someone you know or know about may have devised a similar instrument that you can borrow from. Feel free to borrow; community work isn't copyrighted.

Think in advance about when to take measurements and whom to include. Measure before (as well as after) your program starts when at all possible. Measure similar persons not involved in the program at the same measurement times, when such persons can be located. And measure more than once after the program has been operating, to get at any long-term effects. In scientific research, these are requirements, or near-requirements, which help verify the causes of any change. In homespun evaluation, they are ideals, definitely worth approximating so long as efforts are in proportion to the program and do not throw the program itself out of joint.

Keep records of any and all measurements you collect, including any measurements of unplanned events. Label them clearly and file them carefully. Records will cost you little to keep. They can be helpful in future program planning, and, more important for our present purposes, they will provide a comparative baseline for any subsequent evaluations you or others undertake. Old program records have a way of coming in handy. At worst, they will gather nostalgia value.

Step Seven is to analyze the results, draw out conclusions, and form recommendations. These three actions combine naturally into one. The results you get will typically be numerical, having the same approximate status as retail prices or miles per gallon. To interpret them, they need to be placed in context, matched up against some standard – relative or absolute, or, ideally, both. If you were to go for a physical checkup and had a series of tests, the results would come back as a series of numbers, which the physician (evaluator) would have to interpret, place in the form of a diagnosis (conclusion), and possibly translate into a prescribed course of treatment (recommendation). It's much the same idea with social program checkups. Your test results might come back in a chart looking something like this:[8]

Table 11
Evaluation Test Report

Program name:	*Your*	**Program birthdate:**
Contact person:	*program's*	**Prior test report?**
Address:	*vital*	Yes____ No____
Phone:	*statistics*	**If yes, date of latest:**
	should	**Period covered:**
Target population size:	*fit*	**Date of evaluation:**
Target population location:	*in*	**Date of report:**
Other target characteristics:	*here*	**Evaluator:**

(Previous year's ratings in brackets: blank = no measurement)

I. *Outcome Variables*
1. Survival time:
2. Awareness:
    Number aware:
    % of target pop.:
3. Support:
    External (nonmember/user):
    agency/institution:
    community leaders:
    media:
    general public:
    Internal (member/user):
    unsolicited:
    survey results:
4. Attendance:
    Number attending:
    # as % of signers:
    # returnees/attrition rate:
    Future signups/attendees:
5. Participation:
    Number of members/users:
    Acquisition rate:
    Dropout rate:
    Turnover rate:
    Average length member/user:
    Response to solicitations:
6. Active help:
    Volunteers: # =   hours =
    Committees: # =
    Boards: # =   (members)
7. Requests for new service:
8. Spin-offs:
9. Incidental effects:

10. Income:
    Number paying for service:
    Amount paid:
    Number of member contributions:
    Amount of member contributions:
    Amount of external contributions:
    Profitability:
    Operating budget:

II. *Process Variables*
11. Accomplishment:
12. Learning:
13. Satisfaction:

III. *Input Variables*
14. Time:
    Hours: total =   service =
    Length:
15. People:
    Number:
    Position:
16. Contacts:
    Personal:
    Phone:
    Mailings:
    Literature distribution:
17. Money:

IV. *Cost-Effectiveness Variables*
18. Dollar cost per hour:
19. Time cost per hour:
20. Average client fee per hour:
21. Dollar cost per contact:
22. Time cost per contact:
23. # contacts per respondent:
24. Dollar cost per respondent:
25. Time cost per respondent:

Other evaluation variables
(including specific goals):

You as program doctor will have to look at the data (not shown here), judge them in terms of the program's history and preset targets, and figure out what to do next.

Program maladies are not hard to spot; diagnostic skills here can be largely self-taught. With just a little experience, you will become adept at sensing problems and prescribing useful treatments for them. Physical and program health are different, though, in two key respects. First, with social programs, there are fewer standards for "normality"; the standards instead are typically ones which you set in advance, based on your own goals. Second, program health means more than being "normal," or even being "well"; programs almost always have room for improvement.

Step Eight is to use the recommendations in practice. This usage step corresponds to the backward-pointing arrows in the chapter diagram earlier on. These arrows must connect firmly, so that subsequent plans and actions may be corrected and improved. If there is medicine to be taken, you must take it. Unless recommendations are put into practice, the whole evaluation exercise is pointless.

Unfortunately, many well-carried-out evaluations never get beyond step seven. Small wonder: many of the same obstacles to beginning evaluation in the first place also apply here. Provided that your past program actions were at least minimally acceptable, the path of least resistance is always to do the same things over again. A critical evaluation – and most are in varying degrees critical – will confront you with the desirability of, or the imperative for, change. Change will require commitment of new energy, to form revised plans, and to put plans into motion once again. Meanwhile, egos may be deflated, feelings may be hurt, and heads may roll. Some changes may come easily, but others may demand hard cognitive and emotional work. The best procedure is to build evaluation into your program operation so that it becomes second nature (hints later on). The major alternative is to praise everyone for an evaluation well done, file, forget, and carry on as if you had never heard of evaluation at all.

By this time, you may know more than you wanted to know about how to conduct an evaluation. On the other hand, the eight-step procedure does appear logical, generally feasible, perhaps useful for you, maybe just a slight formalization of what you may already be doing. The steps outlined may even seem too simple, too by-the-numbers. Well, they are. Book knowledge should be valued for supplying core concepts and ideal standards; but real life situations are often too ornery to be tamed entirely by fixed rules.

Some case examples will add dimension to our discussion. We're now ready for them.

FURTHER EXAMPLES

Case One. Remember our opening example – the support group leader training program – and the questions about its evaluation we asked then. What answers would we give to them now?[9]

Look at some of the positives. In the first place, people signed up, filling both a morning and an evening group. They also were willing to pay; the twenty-dollar charge for six sessions was bargain-basement for institutional training programs, yet probably a think-twice fee for many people around Lowell, not a wealthy area. And the people who came – about half general public and half representatives from other community agencies – tended to keep coming. Dropout rates were remembered as low, though data here were not permanently kept.

The course evaluations received at the end of the sixth session were favorable. (The evaluation form used is shown on an adjacent page.) Twenty-five of thirty people attending the last class returned forms. Of these, eleven found the course "very useful," twelve "useful," and two "sometimes useful" (question 2); thirteen were "often" able to apply things they had learned in their real lives, and twelve "sometimes" (question 3); all respondents wanted the program to be offered again, nineteen as it was, the rest with changes (question 9). The qualitative comments were widely scattered, but on balance were decidedly on the plus side.[10]

The training program brought in about $500 to the agency sponsors. Several hundred staff hours went into program planning, execution, and evaluation. Cost effectiveness, as measured by dollars per hour, was low. But at the time, the sponsors were externally funded and were not obliged to earn large sums of money. Actually, the income received buoyed the staff trainers, who now knew first hand that there were specks of gold at the end of some rainbows.[11]

So far, so good. But now consider the starting goals of the program: to teach people basic helping skills and to encourage them to become involved in support groups of their own. Was there any direct evidence that helping skills were learned? There was not. Was there any evidence *from the evaluation conducted* that helping ability, leadership ability, or any other type of ability improved? There was none. Helping skills were presumably *taught*; helping skills *may* have been learned; some students *claimed* they learned. But direct evidence? No.

Figure 5
Course Evaluation

1. General Comments _____

_____

_____

_____

(Use back if you need more space.)

2. I found this course ____ very useful ____ useful ____ not useful
____ sometimes useful

3. I was able to apply things I had learned in my real life ____ often
____ sometimes ____ never

4. The things I found most helpful about the course were: _____

_____

_____

_____

5. The things I found least helpful about this course were: _____

_____

_____

_____

6. If this course is offered again, I suggest the following change(s):

_____

_____

_____

7. What was the most important thing that happened to you as a result of
taking this course? _____

_____

_____

8. Are there other kinds of training programs which you can think of that
would be helpful to you in your work or in your own personal life?

9. Should this course be offered again? ____ Yes ____ No ____ With
Changes

Next: did students become more involved in support groups, either as leaders or members, as a result of the training? We don't know. One student evaluation volunteered (in question 7) that a previous group which had ended badly had decided to start again. That was all. Was there a follow-up to determine what group involvements might have started? There was not. Was there any evidence that students subsequently joined or started any support groups? None. In sum, how well did the training program do with respect to its starting goals? Unknown.

This is harsh, biting, but true criticism, and we search for some soothing words to ease the sting.

To evaluate learning – to evaluate any change convincingly – the trainers would have had to measure performance both before and after the training program. This means that they would have had to devise some kind of helping-skill test. A fair test would have needed to include some overt demonstration of helping skills, at two different points in time; multiple-choice knowledge alone would not have been sufficient. The test itself would have had to have been reliable, in that qualified trainers would have to arrive at approximately the same test ratings after observing helping behaviors in practice; and valid, in that independent evidence (such as predictive capacity) would be required to back the claim that helping was in fact being measured.

Technically, at least one control group should also have been employed, approximately equal to the training group before the program started with respect to demographic characteristics, motivation, experience, and other factors which might influence learning.[12] The control group should have received no training, but should nevertheless have been tested both before and after the training sessions to guard against the possibility that any gain of the training group was due to some extraneous factors other than the training program itself. The entire testing procedure would have had to have been presented to participants in an open, nonthreatening way, without endangering the supportive group atmosphere the trainers were trying to create.

To evaluate later involvement, the trainers could have contacted the participants six months, a year, two years after the program or more. The follow-ups, possibly more than one, and including any control group originally tested, should then have been conducted by phone rather than by mail, to maximize response percentage. Results from a somewhat related prior program did suggest that few students would go right out and start a support group, or even join one. Training might not have increased direct involvement, or the impact of training might have been long-term and subtle – both of which, in terms of *evaluation of effect*, amount to pretty much the same thing.

Would both program goal evaluations have been feasible here? Probably yes, though with considerable mental stretch and some technical difficulty. They could probably have been performed as suggested, without damaging program trust and rapport. Would they have been desirable? Yes, other things being equal, except that the evaluations would have consumed an additional 20(?), 50(?), 100(?) staff hours, necessarily expropriated from some other service activity. The amount of time devoted to evaluation might have been out of proportion to the time devoted to the entire program. Was the actual evaluation as conducted adequate in terms of program goals? No, as we have seen. Was the evaluation as conducted *justifiable* under the circumstances? A key question. To say "yes" is to say that inadequate evaluation may nevertheless be justified. To say "no" is to demand uncompromising evaluation of much greater breadth and depth than is found in virtually every existing grass-roots social program. Hold your own fire until you have read about cases two and three.

Case Two. The program under review here is a Women's Film Series. This came together because some members of my work group felt the enormous untapped creative potential of women in our service area. One general goal of the film series was to tap it. The program brochure described:

> A Series of Programs to bring together women and friends to discuss common concerns, to share new understandings of what it's like to be a woman today and to look at what women have done and can do . . .

The program coordinators borrowed five films on women's careers, women's health, and women's social roles, divided them into three program dates, and publicized accordingly. Cost was two dollars per program date, or five dollars for the series, enough to cover expenses plus a little extra. Each film program was followed by refreshments and group discussion. Total attendance at all showings was eighty-nine.

The main evaluation tool was again a post-event questionnaire, distributed and collected after each film. Once more, results were positive:[13]

	Yes	Somewhat	No
Were the films interesting?	70	0	4
Were the films helpful?	62	0	10

Women's Film & Discussion

LNS/cpf

A Series of Programs to bring together women and friends to discuss common concerns, to share new understandings of what it's like to be a women today and to look at what women have done and can do. Each program will include film(s) focusing on specific aspects of women's experience and discussion will focus on the specific experiences of participants.

On JULY 18   MOTHER/WORKER

What happens when a woman is balancing her role as a mother with her need for productive and rewarding work outside the home, or with her need to provide family income? Two films will be shown: one highlighting single motherhood and one about being a wife, mother, and worker.

On AUGUST 1   TAKING OUR BODIES BACK

Women are America's most frequent consumers of health services. Often women have felt out of control in the hands of the medical world. Film will show what women have done to regain control of their own health care, focusing on self-examination, the breast cancer controversy, unnecessary surgery, prescription abuses and other topics.

On AUGUST 15   WOMEN BECOMING

One film will examine what it's like to grow up female. Another will take a look at the effects passage of the Equals Rights Amendment would have on the lives of women and men. Discussion will focus on women's consciousness raising and political action.

Refreshments Will Be Served

Join Us ---- Bring a Friend

To Be Held on July 18, August 1 & August 15

10 AM - Noon at Solomon Mental Health Center
391 Varnum Avenue (Next to Lowell General Hospital)

7:30 - 9:30 PM at Lowell YWCA
Rogers Street - (In the Gym)

A donation of $2 per program or $5 for the entire series is requested to help cover expenses.

For more information, contact Kathy Desilets at 459-6454 or 454-8851 (Ext. 26)

This Program is co-sponsored by the Consultation and Education Service at Solomon Mental Health Center (a federally funded program in partnership with the Mental Health Association of Greater Lowell) and the Lowell YWCA.

REGISTRATION - Return to: Consultation and Education Service, Solomon Mental Health Center, 391 Varnum Avenue, Lowell, MA 01854

I plan to attend: MOTHER/WORKER (July 18)	___ AM	___ PM
TAKING OUR BODIES BACK (August 1)	___ AM	___ PM
WOMEN BECOMING (August 15)	___ AM	___ PM
ENTIRE SERIES (Three Programs)	___ AM	___ PM

Enclosed is a check for my donation of $ _____

Name _____ Phone _____

Address _____

Was the discussion interesting?	68	2	2
Was the discussion helpful?	58	2	7
Would you attend a similar series in the future?	59	0	2

Qualitative comments (generally favorable) and suggestions for future programs were also collected. In addition, the film series provided the stimulus for a broader-based planning group to crystallize and to plan a large-scale, two-day women's conference with name speakers, which was held nine months later with two hundred attendees.

Except for the conference spin-off, the strengths of this evaluation parallel the strengths of case one. The weaknesses are different. The training program in case one had semi-specific goals which could be assessed. The Women's Film Series had no specific outcome goals at all. To "tap potential," "to share new understandings," "to look at what women have done and can do" are not objective goal statements. They cannot be measured, and to this extent the program cannot be evaluated. The support group training program could have been evaluated in terms of its goals, but wasn't; the film series wasn't, because it couldn't have been.

Rebuttal: what would you have done differently? Would the film series have been "better" or "more effective" if precise goals had been formulated in advance? Would there have been more long-run community impact? Should the films not have been shown? Isn't it legitimate to hold an event because it feels like a good idea, with no specific goal other than the holding of the event itself? And if, for example, "sharing new understandings" cannot be reliably measured, does this mean that such understandings were not in fact shared, or that participants did not benefit in some real way? More generally, if something cannot be evaluated, does that by itself mean it is less valuable?

Case Three. Lowell's human service delivery system was all tentacles and no head. Many such systems are. Communication among agencies ranged from mediocre to zero. Communication between agencies and public was worse. Centralized planning was nonexistent. The time was ripe, then, for *Seasons*. Truthfully, the time had been ripe for the past dozen years, only no one had come forth to pluck the fruit.

Seasons was a quarterly newsletter, designed to breach the communications gap mentioned above. Its editors began simply by soliciting news and notes through the mail, then arranging the tidbits received into appetizing form. Two to three thousand copies of each issue were offset-printed. Perhaps one-third were posted to agencies and to other people on an existing mailing list, while the rest were hand-delivered in small stacks to wherever it was thought they would be picked up. Copies were free. Page one of the first issue (photo-reduced) is reproduced here.

Seasons lasted through its first year largely because its editors had fun putting it together. Stray community comments which filtered back were also reinforcing. Money was not a big problem then, for even though four quarterly issues cost about $1,200 and 200 staff hours, the office where the editors worked put up the (federal) dollars and permitted the time. But after a year, dollars got cut back sharply. If *Seasons* were to continue, it would have to justify its existence and/or find a new funding source.

The editors shopped around for someone else to foot the bill. To add credibility to their search, they also sent out one-page evaluation forms as part of the first birthday issue. More than 2,000 were mailed or delivered; about 30 came back. Those returning forms said in part that *Seasons* was helpful to them (25 yes, 1 no), that they had referred others to it (20 yes, 2 no), that it was not duplicating a service provided elsewhere (1 yes, 25 no), and that they would pay at least $5 a year to subscribe (17 yes, 7 no). Seven said they would come to a meeting to broaden *Seasons's* organizational base of support; when the meeting was called, one or two actually did.

The program gods did bless *Seasons* with a new agency sponsor. The new sponsor most likely did not go by the reviews, but was rather looking to get involved in interagency planning for reasons of its own. *Seasons* was cast out, and the bait was taken. The newsletter came to look a little different, with somewhat more interagency and less agency-community focus, but regular issues continued to appear. It was one issue at a time; the long-run future of community projects is never assured.

But what about the evaluation? Survival counts, and the comments on the feedback form were nice. Yet as in case one, evaluation via program goals was not conducted; no attempt was made, for example, to find out how successfully *Seasons* "provided a way for people to share information and ideas" (though at best this would have been technically difficult to do). And as in case two, program-goal evaluation was not always possible; for instance, "communication between agencies and public" is a concept so broad as to all but defy objective measurement. However, in this case, these two problems take a back seat to a third.

Obviously, those returning evaluation forms comprised only a tiny percentage of the full group. Almost as obviously, they were

SEASONS

A NEWSLETTER TO LET YOU KNOW WHAT'S HAPPENING IN
GREATER LOWELL COMMUNITY AGENCIES
AND PROGRAMS

....things to help you grow, change, enjoy life more....

************ SUMMER FUN FOR KIDS ************

Area Libraries offer fun things for your kids to do. Below are activities offered in two towns. Call your local library to see what they are offering.

WESTFORD - Fletcher Library - From July 11:
*SPECIAL ACTIVITIES - Puppetry, Dinosaur Lecture etc., Tues., AMs, 10:30
*MOVIES - 7PM. Weds., 50¢ for children
*CHILDREN'S LITERATURE FILM FESTIVAL - Thurs., 11AM
*READING PROGRAM - July 10 to August 18

All programs except movies are free. For more information call the library at 692-6263.

TEWKSBURY - Patten Library - From July:
*SUMMER READING CLUB - 1st to 6th graders, Weds., from July 5 to August 9
*TUESDAY'S CRAFTS - Ages 7 to 12, 2PM July 11 to August 15
*FILM PROGRAM for ages 7 and up, Weds., 10:15 AM

For more information, call Kathleen McLeod at 851-6071.

****

LOWELL MUSEUM
560 Suffolk St.
Lowell

OPEN: Tues. - Sat., 10AM - 5PM, Sun. 1 - 5PM
ADMISSION: $1. Adults, 50¢ children & elders
SPECIAL FOR SUMMER - July 10 to August 28, an exhibit on J. C. Ayer and Patent Medicine.
****

BILINGUAL SUMMER CAMP

Camp UNITAS is for any child between the ages of 7 and 13. The day program will meet from 9AM to 3PM during the month of July. It costs $20 per child or $25 per family. For information or an application, call Fr. Crahen at UNITAS, 458-8793 or stop by the office at 48 Lawrence St. in Lowell.

WOULD YOU LIKE TO MEET WITH OTHER WOMEN FOR DISCUSSION AND WORKSHOPS? CARO, Inc., 21 Central Square in Chelmsford, will be running a free weekly series that will let you do just that. The series will meet at 8PM. If you want to know more, or sign up, call Judith Harrison at 256-0369.

WELCOME TO THE READERSHIP OF SEASONS . . . .

As the seasons change, so do the programs that are offered in our community. Often we hear, particularly from agencies, how hard it is to keep up with these changes. This newsletter, which will be published each season, is intended to help by providing a way for people to share information and ideas.

The things listed here were responses to a letter we sent inviting area agencies to participate. We would like SEASONS to become your newsletter, so please don't hesitate to use the tear-off on the back of this page to let us know how you like it, and to share your ideas.

SEASONS will next appear in September. If you would like to contribute, call Gayle Letourneau or Kathy Desilets at 459-6454.

C * H * A * N * G * E * S

IS THIS SUMMER A TIME WHEN YOU WANT TO MAKE SOME CHANGES IN YOUR LIFE? Are you ready to be healthier? Happier? If the answer is YES, here are some programs you may be interested in:

****

STEPS to Good Health (Smoking Termination and Education Program)

This program, offered as a public service by the Dracut Board of Health. is designed to increase public awareness of the health hazards of cigarette smoking and help people in kicking the habit.

Services include: Information & Referrals, Self-help Kits, Quit Smoking Workshops, presentations and workshops for schools, and businesses. All FREE. For more information call 453-4450.

****

HABITS NOT DIETS (Weight Control Program)

Lose weight for good by changing the way you eat. Introductory session on June 22 at 4:30 PM. Classes begin on June 29. Registration fee: $25.00. Weekly fee: $7.50 (includes book).

****

DRINKING PROBLEMS?

If you or someone you care about is troubled by drinking, you can get some help from Lowell General Hospital Outpatient Alcoholism Services. They run free weekly films and alcohol education programs, and offer counseling and referral service.

not a representative sample. (The responses on the actual returns may themselves have been biased, but that is another matter.) What about the remaining readers? We don't know who most of them were. From the moment the hand-delivered copies of *Seasons* touched down, their fate was unknown. We don't know who, if anyone, picked them up, whether the picked-up copies were read, or whether the information read was used. The truth is that we can never know. The situation is like tying messages onto balloons, gauging wind speed and direction, releasing them into the air, and hoping someone finds a message and advises you about it.

In cases one and two, target groups were sitting right in front of us. For all the evaluation deficiencies, we could still see and hear them, pick up on our nonverbal channels various inklings of whether or not things were going well. In this case, the audience was largely unknown. Short of a door-to-door or telephone survey of a random sample of the total potential population, it will stay unknown. Unlike the owners of mass media, we probably can neither afford nor justify such a survey. Television has its Nielsen ratings; we have faith. Yet because we have little more than faith, should *Seasons* be scrapped?

EVALUATION ON TRIAL

The evaluation in each one of these three cases was defective. Let's say highly defective. But what should we expect? It's one thing if you have a fat evaluation budget, or if the evaluation becomes more important than the program itself. It's quite another if you are a low-budget service organization with untrained staff, or if you are a lone citizen just wanting to help in some small way. At least in the above cases, unlike many others, evaluation was attempted. Considering grass-roots community activities as a whole, I believe only a small minority, maybe a tiny minority, is truthfully evaluated more thoroughly.

There's another point, a vital one: Evaluation of real-life social programs and activities brings us face-to-face with problems so challenging that they threaten the worth of the entire evaluation enterprise. Some of them are problems of ignorance, laziness, and protective bias, *but others are largely inherent in evaluation methodology.* We have observed some of these problems directly in discussing cases, while others have been backstage. All of them are important enough to bring out for a curtain call.

1. Serious program evaluation can take a great deal of work, so much work as to be out-of-scale with program planning and execution, and as to take away from other valuable service delivery time.

2. The more complex the program, the more far-reaching and visionary, the harder it usually is to evaluate. For one thing, original goal statements tend to be more vague. For another, there are more evaluation criteria to employ. For a third, effects sought are more likely to be long-term (cf. #9 below). Social vision in this case is negatively rewarded.

3. Because of the difficulty in assessing complex programs, evaluators may settle for easy-to-measure criteria which only marginally reflect true program goals. As one example, if I want to assess change in community racial tensions, I want to do more than just count interracial assault cases on the police blotter. But I may not be able to spend too much time in the neighborhood. All-out evaluation may tax my resources beyond their limits. So, I settle.

4. Definitive evaluation often requires considerable professional expertise, if not a full-dress professional research investigation. Tests of proven reliability and validity, unbiased measurements before and after the intervention, sophisticated control group designs, may all be part of the requisite technical apparatus. Bona fide evaluation experts are not often found at the grass-roots level; researchers and program developers are different breeds. And even the highest powered technology may not be sufficient to account for or eliminate all possible sources of measurement error.[14]

5. Highly detailed measurement can itself inhibit or otherwise alter the change you are trying to bring about. Testing makes most people feel defensive. It may raise or lower performance from normal levels. And extensive testing can rupture the personal bond between initiator and recipient that is so important for desired social change to occur.

6. Many natural groups will not sit still for testing in the first place. The audiences in cases one and two were captives, lured to the change agents' home turf. The agent in foreign territory, or without institutional advantages, will generally have a tougher time getting people to reveal themselves. In addition, the institution-based change agent evaluating one's own institutional programs may face internal resistance from one's own colleagues.

7. Evaluative data from questionnaires and interviews may be biased, in that people may protect your feelings (cf. chapter 3). Especially if a personal bond *has* been forged, it's hard to tell someone who has tried so hard to teach you that you haven't learned a thing. It's hard to tell yourself that, too.[15] Instead, we confer some value even when we know deep inside that no value exists. Partly for these reasons, questionnaire and interview responses are called "soft" data; the "hard" data of concrete behavior change may be what we really are after.

8. But behavior change is reclusive and shy. It will not come up and say hello to the evaluator. If change happens, it happens privately, behind closed doors, or on some occasion when the evaluator is absent. The evaluator often fails to find it – the *attempt* to find it was barely made in the examples cited – because it's not known where and when the occasion is going to be, because no one can be everywhere at once, and finally because no invitation has been extended.

9. Social programs frequently aim for long-term effects, since these effects are often the most beneficial. But the longer-term the effect, the greater the difficulty in attributing it to the program. Too many events between the program intervention and the effect will have occurred to permit an unambiguous interpretation. If **B** follows right after **A**, we have reason to believe that **B** was caused by **A**. But if **B** does not surface until next summer, we're much less sure – **A** is a suspect, but so are A_1, A_2, A_3, and anything else that happened in-between. It's not that long-term effects cannot occur, but rather that they are extremely difficult to detect.[16]

10. Even when a program effect can be convincingly demonstrated, the results may apply only to that single case. The evaluator might want to claim that *in general* similar programs will have similar effects. Such motivation is well-grounded, for community work should be cumulative, as in any other discipline, where we can learn from and apply the results of others. But the situational variables will probably be different in the next case, and so may the results. We're not yet far enough along to know for sure which variables count when, and for how much. It's risky to generalize too broadly from a sample size of one.

11. Cost effectiveness, equating conventional inputs and outputs, may not always be an appropriate criterion for measuring overall program worth. For instance, I might think it worth 500 hours of my time to teach one autistic child to speak one word; or I might not want to spend ten minutes writing a letter to get a guaranteed $1,000 donation from an organization that I felt exploited the community. Considerations of ultimate social value are involved; so are personal costs and effects for the people who are doing the work; both resist objective measurement. The "bottom line" has obvious managerial appeal, but is partly illusion. In a given situation, there may be several bottom lines, each computed differently, and each with competing claims.

If evaluation were on trial for fraud, this would be the summary for the prosecution. The defense now gets a chance to state its case.

All the charges in the indictment may be true, the defense

admits. But nevertheless, evaluation is not guilty of fraud. Some of the charges need not apply in a particular instance. And the majority are original sins of *social science inquiry in general* – evaluation should not be singled out for blame.

Evaluation of real-life programs proceeds on the basis of approximations and best guesses. The evaluator is a detective, whose job is detective work. Clues turn up which indicate that such-and-such a program has been functioning well or poorly. The accumulated clues may be suggestive, but rarely are cases open-and-shut. The sum of the evidence is usually circumstantial; the program never "confesses"; most conclusions are accompanied by reasonable doubt. Still, the evaluator has to make best judgments and live with them for the time being.

And, contrary to some opinion, the earth will not tremble if a program is not evaluated at all. Evaluation, which follows actions having some degree of impact, cannot alter the prior impact already felt. Nor should it change how recipients perceive the quality of the program; the program's effects, or lack of effects, on its target population should stay about the same. At some moments, evaluation of results may not even be wise. Evaluation should not occur, for example, until a program has had a sufficient chance to show its stuff. Or in a true time of crisis, the immediate need for service may temporarily outweigh the longer-term need for assessment.

The question is not whether evaluation is imperfect, nor whether one can do good community work without bothering to evaluate. It is, and one can. The real question is whether evaluation as it stands can add enough to program quality to make it worth the formal effort. I believe it can, and that the effort is worthwhile. Assuming your program is truly meant to serve others, and that you want to keep on serving them, then the corrective effects of honest and serious evaluation will ultimately help you serve more people more effectively. I know I can't prove this to you on paper; you will have to go out and see for yourself. But I will suggest that even though your own program evaluations may now be deficient, you can learn enough here to make them one or two cuts better – and therefore more useful to you. If your evaluations have been nonexistent, you now know enough to start. And even if evaluation only helps you to think through your ultimate goals more clearly, and to cast them into measurable form this time or next, that will be of value in itself.

What about the evaluations in the case examples we reviewed? It's a matter of what standard you choose. By a professional research or scientific journal standard, the evaluations are not worth very much. Even as textbook examples of grass-roots evaluation, their quality leaves a great deal to be desired. But for the people executing each of the three programs, the evaluations served a purpose. They gave some tentative indication that the programs were on the right track. They supplied some hints (especially qualitative hints, mostly not emphasized here) about how to improve the programs next time. They boosted staff confidence in starting related programs in the future. I'd expect future rounds of programs – and evaluations – to show demonstrable improvement.

It's true that the deficiencies of method and the tentativeness of findings in our examples – in just about all evaluations, really – force us back to faith as a motivator for carrying on our work. We could be worse off. There's nothing wrong with using faith as a stimulant: Scientific inquiry of all kinds depends upon faith in the underlying lawfulness of the universe, upon the scientist's own belief that meaningful patterns in a jumble of events can be found. Loosely translated, and applied to you, this means that if your program feels like a rose, and smells like a rose, the chances are good that it is a rose, and you should continue to act as if it were. The problem is not with faith, but with blind faith which takes the place of hard data. You also need to look around with your eyes wide open to make sure that a rose is what you have.

A VERDICT, AND SOME RECOMMENDATIONS

Having heard the testimony on both sides, this judge offers a verdict of not guilty as charged. But he also wishes to speak publicly to the defendant before the case is dismissed: (The judge gets a little carried away sometimes, so you will have to excuse him if his rhetoric gets inflated.)

Evaluation, you may be innocent of fraud, but the charges made against you are for the most part true. You are not as powerful a force as you should be in social change work. People are a little scared of you, or they don't regard you highly enough, or both. You must find ways of promoting and maximizing your own benefits, while minimizing your costs to the evaluators you serve. The eight-step model we outlined before is a first move in the right direction. Making the commitment to evaluate, clarifying your purpose, evaluating in terms of measurable goals and criteria, and planning your evaluation carefully in advance should together give most evaluators enough momentum to press forward and complete their missions. But before you leave the courtroom, I'd like to suggest some additional ideas to help you gain more of the power you deserve. Let me speak directly to other evaluators in the audience as well. I'll try to be brief:

1. You may not be able to make your evaluation a full-scale research project, but you should pay attention to what other evaluative researchers in your content area have found. Their findings may advise you of how programs similar to your own are faring, as well as suggest ways in which you could improve both the content and the evaluation of your work.

2. One avenue for learning about these findings is to read. This means you may wish to research the relevant books and journals in your field, and either borrow them, purchase them, or persuade your library to purchase them. Then read them to grasp at least the main points.

3. Or you can talk face to face with others. If you have a specific evaluation problem, you can ask experts, teachers, or simply people more knowledgeable than you, for specific technical advice. The general idea both here and in the preceding paragraphs is to get out far enough from behind your own program to borrow from the experience of others who have encountered and perhaps solved problems similar to yours.

4. Sometimes, especially if you have money to spend or friends in high places, you may be able to arrange for outsiders to come in and do an evaluation for you. Their evaluation will be incomplete, missing your own intimate knowledge of the program. But their viewpoint should be fresh, and their findings free from your biases.

5. Evaluation goes more smoothly when everyone knows it is coming, accepts the methods used, and believes that any recommendations will be fairly and wisely implemented. The moral is clear. Those affected by the evaluation should be able to help form the evaluation plan and influence the evaluation process throughout. An atmosphere of openness and honesty creates trust, which not only reduces evaluative bias, but also links people more closely to the program itself.

6. An elaboration of #5: If you are evaluating an agency or institutional program, take special care to build institutional support for your evaluation, starting from the top. More so than the general public, agency people are inclined to see evaluation as a potential threat (sometimes correctly), and they react accordingly. Your goal is to win their honest support honestly. A challenge, but you can do this by applying the same support-building techniques outlined in chapter 5.

7. If generating enough time to carry out the evaluation is a problem – and possibly even if it isn't – participants in the program can be enlisted and trained to help you. Their sharing of the burden can lighten your load; it may also solidify participant commitment and increase the chances of the results being used.

8. Take advantage of both regular and chance opportunities to evaluate. Some evaluations can be performed as part of regularly scheduled meetings or other events; all you may need is a few minutes on the agenda. Or if you find yourself with an unexpected, one-time-only chance to measure attitudes or behaviors, don't pass it by.

9. Create your own opportunities for collecting ongoing feedback. Evaluative data should be spontaneously coming in all the time, not just solicited on formal occasions. Devices such as suggestion boxes and their kin, feedback forms on publications, comment logs by the phone, and designated critique times at meetings, timeworn and imperfect as they are, are still no-cost sources of potentially valuable information. You may be able to think of other ideas along this line. And again, an open and supportive environment will foster unsolicited and uninhibited commentary.

10. Look for relevant "free" data which already exist, and also for indirect evidence which can be accumulated at a distance, without intervening directly into the situation. Examples: arrival times (a possible indicator of interest); refreshments consumed (a possible indicator of sociability); spontaneous comments overheard at the end of a meeting or session. These partial, unobtrusive measures will supplement data collected by more direct means.[17]

11. Use more than a single criterion measure. Data stemming from several different measures, when they fit together well, strengthen the credibility of any general conclusions reached. When they don't fit well, you can suspect that your program is strong in some dimensions and weaker in others. You don't have to evaluate on every available criterion, though. As elsewhere, evaluation should be kept on a scale proportional to the rest of your work.

12. Collect comparative data. This means data comparing your program to others on measurable criteria, when data are in fact comparable and you can track them down. But it especially means data from your own program collected through time. Time-oriented data – a.k.a. trend data, baseline data, before-and-after data – will help you (a) check on perceived trends in your own operations; (b) spot new trends; (c) assess the effects of specific program interventions; and consequently, (d) increase the prospect of findings being used in practice. Since you can't draw reliable trends from data which aren't comparable with each other, you should use the same evaluation instruments and techniques through time whenever possible.

All of these ideas may help. But they must be *used*, together with the evaluation model previously described, or else all bets are off. Without use in practice, evaluation will soon be back on trial again, rightfully so, and with less hope for leniency.

An effective way of incorporating evaluation, or any new element, into a program routine is to make it a habit. More formally, you can set up organizational structures and procedures to support evaluation and to make sure it occurs. You can build evaluation right into the system, so that it eventually becomes second nature. There are a number of specifics for making this happen. They include:

- securing an advance commitment from top leadership on down to utilize the results of the evaluation
- assigning a specific person or persons the responsibility for conducting evaluations
- providing those responsible with the necessary training
- giving those responsible an evaluation budget, when possible, on a scale with the rest of the program operations
- ensuring that evaluation proceeds according to a predetermined plan
- blocking out a fixed percentage of time for evaluation, or at least enough time to get the job done properly
- printing, posting, or otherwise circulating the results of the evaluation inside the group, especially among its leadership
- discussing the results of the evaluation at program meetings, including special meetings involving those affected if necessary, and deciding what consequences should follow
- distributing the results of the evaluation outside the group, when this is feasible and appropriate, possibly soliciting additional review and comment in the process
- refining or revising objective program goals on the basis of evaluation results, including the publication of revised goals and the possible provision of incentives for meeting them
- responding as specifically, quickly, and personally as possible to all feedback received, whether critical or not, so as to maintain the flow of evaluative data coming in
- implementing program decisions made on the basis of evaluation results, and monitoring those decisions until the next formal evaluation cycle concludes.

The more structured and formal aspects of this entire process must be repeated on a periodic basis. The more informal parts should be going on continuously. Just as you can master soufflés with a little experience, so you can master putting your evaluations into practical use. The key ingredient, I feel, is the first item listed: a commitment to the evaluative results, and a willingness to try something new if that's what the results tell you. The willingness to change on the basis of evidence is a major progressive force in program operations, as in life, a force which maximizes chances for long-run survival.

We close this chapter by placing our discussion in larger perspective. Any personal attempt at self-improvement, any community change activity – any social program, and any national policy – may be viewed as an ongoing experiment. If it works out, fine. If it doesn't, we don't give up on change, but rather try out something else. To know how well we are doing at any endeavor, we have to measure, we have to evaluate. This, in simplified form, is the thesis of an enormously influential article written by the psychologist Donald Campbell at the end of the 1960s. Campbell believed in particular that all social reforms should truly be experiments, in the scientific sense. He opened by stating:

> The United States and other modern nations should be ready for an experimental approach to social reform, an approach in which we try out new programs designed to cure specific social problems, in which we learn whether or not these programs are effective, and in which we retain, imitate, modify, or discard them on the basis of apparent effectiveness on the multiple imperfect criteria available.[18]

A mouthful – simple, tough-minded, rational, compassionate, and radical all at the same time. Perhaps Campbell's timetable was too optimistic, for nations now seem hardly more willing to undertake an experimental approach to social reform than they were then. But we in our own communities need not wait for nations, nor anybody else. Evaluation can begin right now, at home.

7
Personal Qualities

In John Cheever's novel *Falconer*, Jody and Farragut are in jail. Jody, who is doing time for burglary and kidnapping, is telling Farragut what he's learned about human nature:

> Jody ticked off his points on the bars of Farragut's cell. "One. Let the other fellow feel that all the good ideas are his. Two. Throw down a challenge. Three. Open up with praise and honest appreciation. Four. If you're wrong admit it quickly. Five. Get the other person saying yes. Six. Talk about your mistakes. Seven. Let the other man save his face. Eight. Use encouragement. Nine. Make the thing you want to do seem easy. Ten. Make the other person seem happy about doing what you want. Shit, man, any hustler knows that. That's my life, that's the story of my life. I've been doing all this ever since I was a little kid and look where it got me."[1]

Jody knows all the techniques. Technique may not have made him a prisoner, but it's possible to become a prisoner of technique.

THE ROLE OF THE HEART

The material we have discussed in the last four chapters has dealt primarily with general principles of community programming — methods, pointers, thoughts on relating to real-world situations — "technique" in a word. The topics covered and the ideas expressed have hardly been path-breaking or revolutionary. To a degree, the treatment here has been a reminder of what on some level we know already — what is already within us, not too far beneath the surface. All of us have some degree of technique at our disposal right now. And to the extent we do, what has been offered so far is a collection of homilies, dressed up for the occasion. But there is virtue in homilies; we are not so accomplished that we don't need to be reminded.

The technique you may not yet have learned would appear to be learnable. There may be plenty of it, but it sounds like the kind of knowledge you could get from reading or going to school, and surely from practical experience and observation. In other words, you should be able to *learn* technique, to make it a part of yourself, and by doing so to become more effective as a change agent. I believe this is true.

But I also believe that technique or skill alone is insufficient. There is also a person using that technique, whose personality extends into and well beyond the technique itself, and who affects the outcome of most social interventions profoundly. People respond to other people in their fullness, not just to the tools they employ. Success in community work cannot be disassociated from the person who is the community worker. Success is inextricably linked with the personal qualities of the change agent.

Before pursuing this point, let's make sure the role of technique is properly appreciated. Technique is important in all social interventions, probably crucial in many. Application of proper technique can get people interested, bring them together, heal their divisions, maintain their enthusiasm. One who ventures forth without knowing or paying attention to technique is taking on an extra burden which increases the probability of failure. All practitioners need to find the knowledge of technique they have within themselves, to expand it through formal study, then to practice and sharpen it through experience. More than this: community change is far from a completed field of study; there will be new techniques to learn about and master.

But if technique alone ensured success, community workers would be able to accomplish a whole lot more than they do now. Their course of study would be cut-and-dried. Their textbooks would read more like charts or manuals, with no place for homilies. In fact, technique alone can take you only so far. When it's not well blended into the person who is *using* the technique, results don't meet expectations. In the long run, you won't convince your neighbor by using rulebook principles of persuasion unless both those principles and your arguments are a part of you. You won't turn a meeting around with your group dynamics skills if those skills are seen as disembodied from their owner. Technique alone is stiff and inauthentic; it distances people from you, if not also you from them. Overreliance on technique stunts your growth, dries you up inside. Witnessing such examples, others shy away from learning technique, even though the new skills would increase their own impact.

The right personal qualities, on the other hand, can carry you much of the way. They can get through to people, move them, inspire them, as technique cannot. When someone's eyes flash, you pay attention to what is being said. When someone gets up to speak, and you sense that the speech is from the heart, you are affected. Conviction – as one example of a personal quality – counts, and even if you are ignorant of technique, or if you botch up, it may see you through. Perhaps this is because the social norm is one of going through the motions, just doing a job. Those who stand outside the norm are noticed.[2]

Like technique, personal qualities are insufficient by themselves. You may get in to see the director on guts, but your proposal has a snowball's chance unless it is well thought out and keyed to meet a need. Passionate belief will not substitute for dispassionate data. There has to be substance to go along with the style. And as the study of social change matures, the role of substance, of technique, will probably become more important, as it has in every developing discipline. If new techniques can be employed wisely and ethically, this prospect can be welcomed.

A clear conclusion is that we are looking for both technique and style. As in most creative endeavors, the two must be joined together. In fine art, we look for imaginative depth, but not to the exclusion of technical mastery of one's medium. In hard science, we place a premium on technical knowledge, but that knowledge is wasted unless the scientist has the personal vision of how to harness it, plus the inner resources to carry out the required experimentation. Community work, neither pure art nor pure science, can be most properly described as a craft, where the quality of the finished product depends upon the skill and training of the craftsperson, and also upon vision and soul.

So there is heart as well as head in creating change. There is the person who is doing, as well as the things being done. But the heart, and the doer, have been neglected in most formal accounts of social change processes. Technical skills are easier to identify, accumulate, and transmit. Heart qualities seem more elusive, harder to pin down, "unscientific," and therefore easier to ignore. This is all the more reason to explore the role of the heart in more detail, and that is the intent of this chapter. In doing so, we need not leave critical analysis behind, for the role of the heart itself is both a possible and a desirable object of scientific study. On an abstract level, to understand the linkages between specific personal qualities and specific community outcomes is basic to understanding social change. On a personal level, if we want to become more skilled practitioners, then it is essential to develop those parts of our own natures which are most closely associated with intervention success. Admitting the heart into the study of social and community change is an indicator of both personal and professional strength.

One way of proceeding from here is to propose some questions about personal qualities and to see how far we can move toward resolving them within the space of a chapter. Suppose we start with these four:

1. How important are personal qualities in determining the success of social interventions?

2. What personal qualities are most closely associated with successful interventions?

3. Is it possible to acquire those personal qualities desired?

4. If so, how?

If we can make some headway on these questions, we can then consider some implications of our answers.

Regrets are expressed in advance if our answers fall short of being definitive. There's no attempt here at a literature review. Even in a review, we would find that personal qualities as a factor in social interventions have, as noted, received relatively little formal study.[3] The implicit assumptions of most scholars in the field have been either that mastery of technique or possession of controlling power are sufficient conditions for success, and/or that personal qualities, even if important, are too nebulous or too subjective to teach and write about. The balance may be adjusted in time; meanwhile, our efforts here may count as one in a necessary series of successive approximations.[4]

WHAT PERSONAL QUALITIES, AND HOW TO GET THEM?

1. **How important are personal qualities?** We'll assume their importance: but how much? We would like to specify a percentage value, a weighting factor, to make a statement like "personal qualities determine 44 percent of the consequences of the average intervention." Immediately we run into trouble. On what evidence can we specify a percentage value? What methods do we use? If we were researchers, we could theoretically hold personality constant and measure changes in outcome by systematically varying technique; and theoretically we could hold technique constant, while varying personal qualities. But to do this with any degree of rigor in real-life situations is beyond current scientific reach, as well as practical ability. The issue is about as complex as trying to measure

the relative contributions of heredity and environment to human behavior, a completed answer to which has eluded psychologists since psychology began.

Lacking hard experimental data, we fall back on observational evidence – my own, plus that of other practitioners in the field – and on inferential evidence from other psychological research. Summing across this evidence, we can offer two very general propositions. First, personal qualities are important enough to account for much of the success of most social interventions. Their importance is comparable to that of technique and to other variables, though we can rarely specify precise percentages.[5] As a corollary, the appropriate personal qualities are in fact necessary in almost all cases, even if sufficient in relatively few.

Second, the importance of personal qualities relative to technique (and other variables) varies with the situation. Since the number of possible situations is infinite, we cannot attempt a detailed analysis in this space. But personal qualities will usually play a more prominent role when:

a. You are in a situation with few formal role relationships.

b. You are dealing with citizens in the community rather than people in agencies, institutions, or other rule-following bureaucracies.

c. You are a newcomer to the situation. (Cf. the importance of making a good first impression; judgment of your technical skill tends to come after gut-level judgment of you as a person.)

d. You have little formal power in the situation. (With low power, especially in an unstructured situation, it's often easier to get what you want by displays of personal character than of technical skill.)

e. You are in a small-scale setting; there is then more opportunity to exercise personal influence, assuming role relationships are not too rigid.

f. You are in a large-scale setting, in competition for a scarce good with many other persons of approximately equal paper qualifications; here, showing your personal qualities can help you stand out.

g. The situation requires little specialized knowledge or technical skill.

h. Others in your work group are already demonstrating technical skills adequate enough to maintain effective group performance.

i. You need something in a hurry, or you are in a "crisis" (and so become able to "suspend the rules").

j. The situation calls for a quick response, with little time available for deliberation.

k. The situation is ambiguous: the reality of the situation is unclear, or different versions of reality are conflicting.

These somewhat overlapping hypotheses are more amenable to

direct test. Generally, the more person-to-person contact the situation allows, and the less structured it is, the more important personal qualities become. More personal, less structured situations are those most commonly found when developing supportive activities on a community level – the type of activity basic to this book. Hopefully, other writers and researchers will add more variables to this list and refine the above analysis. We must leave it now and move on to the next question.

2. What personal qualities are most closely associated with successful interventions? (By a "successful" intervention, we mean here one which fulfills the stated goals of the change agent.)

This question implies that some general qualities exist, not just qualities specific to a given situation. But is this so? Again, the number of potential intervention situations is immeasurable. Presumably, the exact qualities contributing to success would not always be the same, but would vary with the situation, just as the relative importance of personal qualities and technique themsleves. Scholars in the related field of leadership are inclined to agree.[6]

So how do we find what qualities go with what situation? The community worker would need a table, or scorecard, listing all possible situations (or at least different categories of them) along the rows, and the best-fitting personal qualities for each along the columns. Clearly, the number of potential qualities, like the number of situations, is limited only by the number of descriptive adjectives in one's vocabulary. And each quality may possess a broad range of values. Take a moment to visualize the magnitude of this task. To keep score, to learn what's needed, one must track down and record the optimal mix of personal qualities, their kind and value, for each particular intervention situation. Completing this table would be something like assessing the effects of a limitless number of drugs on a limitless number of subjects, while depriving the researcher of laboratory measuring apparatus.[7]

At this point, it's not too hard to see that we have dug a big hole for oursleves. We had better not climb in. Filling in the blanks of the scorecard is a worthwhile project, but a lifetime project, perhaps several lifetimes for several scholars. As actors in the community, we cannot afford this time investment; we must rather make best guesses rooted in what we know now. We need to look again for general characteristics, cutting across specific situations, even if the present evidence for them is imperfect and indirect.

The primary types of evidence available to us are again observational and inferential. Here, though, the inferential evidence is richer than in question 1. Findings of particular interest to us come from research on attitude change (especially "source variables"), psychotherapy ("therapist variables"), organizational development, and leadership style. The validity of our inferences will depend on how well data collected in smaller-scale, laboratory, or specially manufactured settings will transfer to community situations which are considerably more complex.

To serve up all this evidence would go well beyond the scope of this chapter and would duplicate review work already done.[8] What we can offer instead is a buffet, a summary table of personal qualities associated with successful interventions in general, as gleaned

Table 12
Some Personal Qualities Generally Associated
with Successful Social Interventions

(A successful community worker is . . .)

adaptable	farsighted	nondominating
aggressive	flexible	open
ambitious	focused	organized
assertive	forceful	passionate
(has) belief in others	goal directed	patient
(has) belief in self	(a) good listener	persistent
calm	(a) good planner	powerful
caring	(a) good speaker	pragmatic
catalytic	(a) good teacher	pushy
centered	(a) good writer	righteous
charismatic	graceful	(has a) sense of humor
(has) chutzpah	hard working	sensitive to others
committed	healthy	sincere
compassionate	honest	stable
confident	(a) hustler	strong
creative	idealistic	task oriented
credible	intelligent	thick skinned
demanding	kind	thoughtful
determined	modest	tolerant of ambiguity
diplomatic	motivated	tolerant of others
direct	naive	tough
energetic	noncontrolling	(a) visionary
enthusiastic	nondefensive	(a) wheeler-dealer

from both the observational and inferential sources mentioned. This summary is given in an adjacent table. The table is not guaranteed to be fully comprehensive, and it lacks official certification. But it will serve our present purposes, which are to move several steps closer toward understanding and appreciating the role of personal qualities in community work and to learn from their implications.

Let's bring this discussion a little more down to earth. So, an exercise for you. Get yourself ready, and then evaluate the list of personal qualities in the table for a few minutes. Are there others of your own you would like to add? Now, see if you can pick out those three qualities which you feel in general are most closely associated with the success of social interventions.[9] Determine for yourself how important you think those qualities are in community work. Examine the source(s) of evidence behind your selections. Finally, consider the implications of your own conclusions. For example, if you weight certain personal qualities highly, what actual consequences does this have for bringing about social change in your own community? And what should you do about those consequences?

Right away I want to bend the rules and not restrict myself to three. Just about all of these personal qualities seem important, even though we are unlikely to find all of them well-developed in the same person. We've already talked about some fundamental personal qualities in chapter 2. Beyond those, I know that I value a change agent who is confident, assertive yet a good listener, demanding yet flexible, and one who can leaven underlying seriousness with humor. I also want to put in a good word for a certain kind of naiveté – for I've seen enough cases where people have succeeded partly because they didn't know that what they were doing couldn't be done.

But if I were recruiting an ideal change agent, I would want to look in particular for three related personal qualities which stand out, based on my interpretation of the evidence and my own experience. The first is a sense of direction, a clarity of purpose. Some synonyms: focus, vision, goal orientation. The ideal change agent knows what he wants to do and how he wants to do it.* He puts forth his goals in concrete, objective terms and plots a course of action to reach them. Then he keeps on that course, without distraction, forsaking the seductive side trips along the way.

---

*In this and the next chapter, when the change agent is personified, gender pronouns are occasionally used for clarity of style. All gender references apply equally to both sexes.

The second is motivation to do the work, a drive to reach the goal. The ideal change agent has a powerful ambition, though not necessarily for personal glory. He has what athletic coaches call desire; he is hungry. Better, he sees the work in question as a cause, a calling, a passion, a mission. His motivation comes from deep within, suffuses his whole being, radiates outward to others. He is a soul on fire. As targets of influence, we know how much more difficult it is to resist someone who really cares about what he is doing, not just acting on assignment. The successful change agent really cares, and shows it.

The third is persistence, staying power, the ability to sustain motivation and pursue one's goal relentlessly. Frustration and defeat come with living in the world; they are inevitable some of the time in social change work. The ideal change agent can absorb either one, though not necessarily with ease. He will learn from his mistakes, adjust tactics if necessary, pick himself up, and keep coming back. He will not take a new job, or scatter himself on other projects, or let himself get wound down, until his work reaches a natural end point. He will stay with the task until it is done.

Direction, motivation, and persistence combine. Consider yourself about to pilot your ship on a long-distance voyage through unfamiliar waters; you need to know where you want to go, you need enough of some energy source to get you there, and you need to keep your ship moving through the lonely seas. Or consider yourself carrying a torch, this one acetylene rather than romantic; your requirements are an object to work on, and a flame hot enough and long-lasting enough to complete the job. In navigation, in welding, within the context of many other analogies, these three qualities must fuse together. When one is missing, no task worthy of the name can be completed.

But when all three are present and potent in the same person, you have the makings of community impact. You also have the makings of success in almost any human endeavor. Direction, motivation, and persistence are just as important in getting elected to office, excelling in school, making the basketball team, or winning over one's true love. They are homely, apple-pie virtues, but also perpetual virtues, Western Civilization virtues. Those involved in community change work would do well to acknowledge them openly and seek them out.

The personal qualities necessary for successful community change are not found only in some select members of the species, but are instead qualities present in some degree inside all of us. In successful community work, these qualities must be especially focused, abundant, and durable, for the *scope* of the work – attempting to improve the condition of others – is usually more ambitious and more difficult than simply attempting to better oneself. Yet perhaps we can find ways to refine and strengthen those latent (or not so latent) qualities we already have.[10]

3. Is it possible to acquire those personal qualities desired? The general issue is whether personal characteristics are learned in the first place, as opposed to being inherited. A safe consensus judgment of personality researchers, here adopted, is that such characteristics are in fact largely learned.[11] The specific qualities we may desire should be no less learnable. For our purposes here, we do not have to assign a percentage to "largely," nor to deny potential roles for genetic factors or gene-environment interactions, but only to maintain that personal qualities can be shaped by experience to a substantial degree. With that easy disposition, we can move ahead.

4. If so, how? Presumably, personal qualities are learned according to the same rules as any other social behavior. The principles of reinforcement are dominant; role models are necessary; the learning process starts at birth and continues throughout life; parental influences and early socialization experiences are especially formative. Personal qualities, though not usually taught directly, emerge from the sum of one's learning experiences to date. A skilled and detailed analysis would be able to show how particular past events manifest themselves in present personality.

As community workers, it makes sense to search for intervention situations which call upon the personal qualities we already have. But a key question for us is whether desired but missing personal qualities can be acquired *now*, reshaping the already shaped person standing before us. Probably they can be, to a degree – again, we don't have to specify the exact degree. A basic assumption of behavioral science is that adult behavior is modifiable, by means of the same learning principles operating in childhood. We can study those principles and put them to work. As private citizens, we frequently make active attempts to modify parts of our own personalities, following pathways as diverse as prayer, meditation, running, reading, psychotherapy, or attending the Dale Carnegie school. We may not transform ourselves radically, but we feel a difference. Similarly, as community workers we may design pathways to enhance our own personal and professional effectiveness. The person for whom social change is a career or a mission may in addition want to design pathways that others can follow.

IMPLICATIONS

All this rather sober analysis has brought us around to the following position:

- Personal qualities are important in social change work, and are comparable in importance to technique.
- We can specify, at least tentatively, those personal qualities most closely associated with successful interventions.
- Those qualities to a large extent are learned, through ordinary life experiences, following conventional learning principles.
- To some extent, the desired qualities can be strengthened, through conscious training and effort, starting at any time.

These conclusions are simple and safe, yet timid and dull. If they were the whole story, please believe that we would not be making such a fuss. But there is more. Simple as these conclusions may be, they are also unheeded. Actually paying attention to them, actually dealing with their implications, leads directly to some basic rethinking about doing community work.

What rethinking? What courses of action follow? We'll single out two main areas for now. One has to do with whether changing the self – consciously choosing to strengthen desired personal qualities – is a precondition for changing society. The other involves the issue of "professionalism" in community work. A third area, the possible limits of personal accomplishment, we'll save for the next chapter.

CHANGING THE SELF VS. CHANGING SOCIETY

If desired personal qualities can be strengthened through simple intention and practice, away from the world of social action, it's tempting to keep moving right on down that path. The question is how far down to go.

You can argue: If you do the necessary work on yourself first, when you return to face social problems you return on a higher moral and spiritual plane. Your personal qualities are more developed. What you have to give counts for more. The great social leaders of our time, and historically, are frequently distinguished by their spirituality; many have been active members of the priesthood. Self-development offers you a pure vision that is much more difficult to obtain when you keep grinding away in the pits.

Or you can say: If you spend time "working on yourself," whatever that is, that's so much less clock time you have to work in the world. Striving to perfect oneself is understandable, but essentially self-indulgent. There are so many problems which cry for immediate attention right now. You are needed right now. How can you spend your time in contemplation?

The world has problems precisely because there is too much trafficking in it. Ceaseless maneuvering in the world, manipulating, pushing and shoving, gets you nowhere. Maybe it used to, but traditional approaches to problem solving have failed. The results are plain for all to see. You need to develop your self, keeping above the battle. Your purer vision will not only focus more clearly on what needs to be done, but it will also inspire; and it will surely yield greater eventual impact.

Problems come not from too much maneuvering, but from not enough of the right kind. Traditional approaches work very nicely when they're well executed, but most people fly around by the seat of their pants and pin blame elsewhere when they crash land. And the spiritually developed person coming back into the world may lack the practical skills to get anything done. He may once have had them but let them die out. Or he may still have them, but not care to use them. Either way, without a solid organizational base, sound marketing techniques, and good business sense—attributes not obtainable in isolation—the visionary will have to enjoy his vision alone.

The time you spend with yourself need not be spiritual time as such. But you must get some rest and relaxation, for you can't go on strung out indefinitely. You must grow personally, so that you don't stand still. You have to trust your body, honor your fullness, respect your own sense of pace. At the least, you need time to prepare yourself mentally, to gear yourself up. Time away recharges you and broadens your perspective. When you go back to work, you are calmer and stronger inside, and therefore more effective.

What makes you more effective is not time off, but time on. Doing work in the world is what enhances both your rate of success and your personal qualities as well. Doing work in the world can bring out the best within you. Doesn't this then increase your spirituality, your sense of mission, your connection with the universal? Doesn't all this talk about inner calm and trusting your body smack of rationalization and narcissism? Don't we still believe in salvation through works?

Elsewhere in this book (chapter 1 especially), it's argued forcefully that ordinary people are capable of a great deal more than they think. And the point is repeated that the way to get started is through a stripping-away process, a removal of the mental debris that gets between you and your true self. But debris removal is an internal process, a self-change process, which has to take place (and maybe take place first) in order for good social change work to occur.

True, but self-change is inevitably linked with socioeconomic condi-

tions. If you are poor and desperate – or powerful and overextended – you are going to think less about spiritual renewal than about making it through the day. To achieve the self-change you want, socioeconomic conditions must be changed first, so that people will have both the psychological hope *for an ideal, and the physical* time *to bring that ideal about.*

What's needed is a revolution of the spirit; social change will then follow.

By changing the world, you change the spirit within it.

The debate rages far into the night. As integrators, we can bring the two sides together, at least part way. Changing the self and changing society are not mutually exclusive; neither side really claims they are. One can have both, and one should. No argument is being made for complete self-absorption, any more than for non-stop social immersion. And neither self- nor social change need take priority; instead, both complement and fuel each other. Social commitment can yield spiritual change, which can reinforce social commitment, and so on.

Except that this integration is a little too neat, too glib. Both components are necessary, but that's not saying enough. We who seek guidance on how to run our lives would like specifics. We want recipes. We want to know *how much* inner time, *how much* outer time, whether the two should be whipped together, stirred gently, or kept in separate bowls. Putting it into numbers, if I allow 10 units of energy for self-improvement, will society get back 10 units, or 5, or 0, or 20, or 100? What's the graphical relationship? How can I maximize my impact? If you can't tell me specifically, then what should I do?

I'm sorry, but I can't tell you specifically. I don't have numbers to give you. You're asking me to enclose the art of living in a formula, and I can't do that for you, not in this edition. I can advise you to reflect on and develop the right personal qualities for your own work, and I can argue for balance between changing self and changing society, but not too much more. The balance point will vary from person to person, and for the same person at different times. The correct balancing move for you right now depends on where you are on the rope. Awareness of yourself, of your position in time and space, will help keep you righted, and discussions like these can foster that awareness. After that – "Work out your own salvation with diligence."

PROFESSIONALISM

If the right personal qualities can increase chances for intervention success, we'd like to be sure that the professional change agent has them (though certainly not to the exclusion of other people). What does this mean for the person who has chosen one of the helping professions as a career? Suppose we begin with the aspiring professional, about to make a career choice, and follow his development on through.

Selection in professional training.

How does the aspiring but unformed professional reach his goal? In social service, the preferred credential for most mid-level paying jobs on up is a graduate school degree. To get into graduate school, you need good undergraduate grades, letters of recommendation, sometimes a qualifying score on advanced tests such as the Graduate Record Examination, or certain kinds of life experience. These admission criteria may be weighted differently in different settings, but essentially show little variation from school to school or from discipline to discipline. Detailed personal statements are infrequently called for; personal interviews are rarer still.

An outside observer might expect that graduate programs in community psychology, social work, organizational behavior, adult education — in the helping professions across the board — would want to select their students at least partially on the basis of who they are as people. This would not merely be a "subjective" selection, based on an applicant's compatibility with preset professional school values, but a *pragmatic* one, based on the assumption that applicants ranked highly in certain personal qualities would in fact turn out to be more successful social change agents. To choose on the basis of personal qualities — to meet your prospects and poke at them thoroughly before selecting — does invite personal bias and interpersonal conflict; it is less objective, more time consuming, harder to do. It is more wearing on admissions committees, whose sometimes reluctant members are already hard-pressed to meet their own teaching and research obligations. Yet it is necessary; for in negating personal qualities, the professional school subverts its own professionalism, by diminishing its capacity to train effective workers.

Training itself.

If selection processes should change, so should professional training practices themselves. Professional schools should not only *value* personal qualities, but *embody* them in their own outlooks and methods of instruction. They should cultivate and nourish the desired qualities their students already have. They should also, with equal diligence, work to minimize personal deficits by taking intentional steps to *instill* those personal qualities associated with successful community work. School is an ideal place to do this. Direction, motivation, and persistence, among other qualities, can be taught. Professional faculties – exemplars, not just one-dimensional lecturers – should *themselves* be chosen in part upon their ability to teach them. They should *teach* about personal style, and *exemplify* desired personal qualities, so that at the very least students will come to appreciate their importance. Students can then take the next step of internalizing those attributes taught and observed, gradually adjusting their behavior accordingly.[12]

None of this need occur at the expense of training content. There is no substitute for rigorous academic instruction, understanding of the relevant literature, translation of key findings into practice, and research projects well conceived and executed. It is a matter of balance. We don't wish to preside over a cheerleading school, or a community of saints. But for the community worker, technical training must be supplemented by active study and understanding of the personal context in which it will be utilized. Otherwise, it is bloodless.[13]

Hiring.

When training is completed, our student is certified as a "professional" and cast out on the job market. Job hiring is a selection process, in some ways similar to the one which yielded professional school admission in the first place. If personal qualities were important then, they should be important now. And they are. Unlike graduate training situations, in hiring the personal interview is essential; the employer will frequently make a point of selecting for personal attributes. Except that the attributes selected for may not be those associated with successful interventions, but rather those associated with blending into the present operation, with keeping the organization on its present track, whatever that happens to be.

Still, the wise and socially conscious interviewer with freedom to choose will break any chain that perpetuates mediocrity. The interviewer will realize that you need to make some waves to move the boat along. Applicants will be hired who back up their formal credentials with the personal stuff to do good works, and their progress in the organization will be monitored to keep tabs on judgment.

The professional on the job.

If an aspiring professional should first be admitted to school, then trained, and finally hired on the basis of his personal qualities, what consequences follow when he is at last on the job? More broadly, even if his position is gained by other means, what are the defining characteristics of a "professional" in a world where the cream does not always rise to the top?

The professional is traditionally thought of as possessing specialized knowledge, a specific body of technique or skill beyond the current grasp of the common person. Usually he does, even though there are those of us who can design our own houses, defend ourselves in court, or play in the town symphony. The less resemblance the task has to everyday life events, or the less frequently the task has to be performed, then the greater the usual degree of task specialization, and the further removed from lay duplication. The medical specialist and the trapeze artist are two diverse cases in point.

The human service professional has his complement of specialized knowledge; but his specialty consists of a collection of helping methodologies, attitudes, and concrete behaviors which are neither completely foreign to nor unduplicated by his clients in their daily lives. Put more simply, you or I might try to counsel a depressed relative, or rally the neighbors together – sometimes with success – where we would not attempt a brain operation or a triple somersault in mid-air. Though no less useful, the specialized knowledge of the human service professional is in this sense less "special" – not necessarily an undesirable state of affairs. Even if it were "more special," we have stressed earlier on that knowledge of technique in the human service field does not by itself lead to success.

Then is it the personal qualities of the professional that set him apart? Maybe they should, but it's doubtful they do. The professional may have no more of the desired personal qualities then the nonprofessional. For any given piece of work, he may have less. He may be less goal-oriented, less enthusiastic, less directly concerned. He may not be able to stay with a project because he changes jobs, or gets a new assignment, or simply runs out of steam. It's not *his* kid who is brain-damaged, not *his* mother who can't cope any more. It's not his project, frequently not his community; he will not suffer personally if nothing much happens.

The professional (the paraprofessional too) in a formal helping organization is particularly exposed to occupational hazards which may wear him down. Living in an insulated climate where organizational survival, limited expectations, and direct or indirect promotion of client dependence are the norms, he sees so many innovative ideas get ground to dust. Worse, the residues of despair may enter his bloodstream, poisoning his ambitions for social change, leaving him jaded, cynical, and beaten. It hurts too much to fight. His negativism is contagious, ready to infect others, both inside and outside his own organization. He becomes a role model for little hope. In a more advanced form of this disease, the professional, himself lacking hope, comes to think that only he is qualified to give community service, that others proposing to do so are unfit, foolish, or even dangerous. Complications of elitism, arrogance, and blaming the victim are likely to set in. The prognosis is then poor.

The distinguishing marks of the human service professional, of the professional change agent in general, need to be redrawn. Technique often, personal qualities sometimes, but that's far from all. First, on a dollars-and-cents level, the professional gets paid for his work. Some funding source has chosen to subsidize him for services that some others already perform, perhaps less well, for free. Next, the professional has the time to work. His pay buys his time, as part of his contract; he doesn't have to squeeze spare hours out of evenings and weekends. Together with pay and time come status. Some status may have been previously achieved, through award of degree or license, or completion of some other recognized training. Other elements of status are ascribed: either self-ascribed, through use of a professional title and trappings, and/or ascribed by the community – if he is being paid for this kind of work, he must know more than I. Pay and time and status are components of community credibility, and credibility brings the power to influence. Credibility, blended together with technique and style, and sometimes even without them, can cure; the placebo effect is as alive in the helping professions as in medicine. The new professional comes already installed with high credibility, even if it's not fully tested. He spends his first day on the job conferred with assets that many never earn in an lifetime.

What defines someone as a human service professional, then, are chiefly characteristics of his position rather than technical skills or personal qualities. Let us provisionally concede to the professional some superiority in knowledge and technique (though not without mentioning an extensive literature documenting the equal or nearly equal effectiveness of nonprofessionals in, for example, counseling situations).[14] Let us not yet concede to the professional any advantage in desired personal qualities, in the absence of convincing evidence that professionals possess any more of them. When the dust has cleared, though, both these factors are secondary. The primary distinguishing marks of the professional are external, not internal. One may become a "professional" simply by accepting a job, and remain one simply by accepting a check.

SOME MORALS FOR COMMUNITY WORK

If this analysis comes close to the truth, there are lessons for both the professional and the nonprofessional in doing community work.

1. To the extent that impact depends on proper techniques, the professional should teach those techniques to all that don't have them and want them. The skilled nonprofessional can do some formal or informal teaching too. Both groups should seek to learn those effective techniques not already in place. We've discussed this before, in the opening chapter.

2. To the extent that impact depends upon proper personal qualities, both the professional and the nonprofessional need to develop and refine them. This is easier for the professional in some respects. Simply moving out of one's office into the community and being with people there can help. So can carefully chosen inservice training. Alternatively, training others, especially outside the organization, sharing with them his knowledge and his person, can be energizing. And sometimes a different assignment, or a different job altogether, can be negotiated.

But the nonprofessional has advantages of his own. He carries none of the professional baggage that tires one out. He can come into a situation fresher, with more personal spark. Often he has more time to improve himself, and fewer constraints. For both the nonprofessional and the professional, some source of personal support – better yet, of inspiration – should be sought out and cultivated. Both should also seek some form of personal renewal and growth in their work. One person may grow more by looking outside the job, another by looking within it, but the underlying need is the same.

3. To the extent that impact depends on one's position, over and above both technique and personal qualities, both the professional and the nonprofessional should realize that: (a) *Any* nonprofessional working for community change could become more effective by being invested with a professional position, thereby acquiring more time, money, status, credibility, and influence; and, conversely, (b) Any professional stripped of his professional perquisites would probably become significantly less effective. Since position, unlike technique, cannot easily be shared, the professional inherits an obligation, leading us to the next point.

4. The professional has a social responsibility, which comes with his position – this is one other distinctive professional attribute, as yet unmentioned. Regardless of his technical or personal limitations, no matter how he got to where he is, he is the one with

society's mandate to provide service, to give power to others, and to promote necessary change. He is a surrogate for what others could be if they had the same professional fittings; and so he needs to get the maximum leverage from his position, as well as from whatever special skills and qualities he may have. Where the accountability of the nonprofessional is chiefly to himself, perhaps extending to a few others around him, the professional's accountability is to the entire community which supports him. It's a formal obligation, a special responsibility, and not one to be worn lightly.

Our discussion of personal qualities has drifted into a discussion of professionalism, but the drift has not been random. The connection must be understood. On a national level, possibly the majority of total person-hours put into community service work comes from professionals; yet it is professionals who have seriously neglected the importance of personal qualities in determining the success of their efforts, and who have misperceived the sources of their own power. They must begin to correct these deficiencies.

I hope what I've written, though, is not interpreted as an all-out attack on human service professionals or as demeaning their accomplishments. I am a human service professional myself; I know the special role they can play. I would not want to argue that all, or even most, nonprofessionals would equal the professional's effectiveness if placed in a professional's position. Most professionals know more, and many care more. The concept of professionalism should surely be retained, for there is social wisdom in granting a legitimate, formal, and subsidized role to the social change agent.

Yet I do believe that most professionals could do with added humility—not an abject or kick-me humility, but a humility which sets them not quite so far apart from the people they are supposed to be serving, which acts against feelings of personal superiority which establishes them as partners rather than quiet adversaries and which promotes public service in the best literal sense of the word. This is the gist of the message here.

The message for the "ordinary" person, the nonprofessional, is no less significant. Appreciation of the importance of personal qualities in success can free up a good deal of trapped energy for community work. You as a concerned citizen can properly value your own personal strengths, using them freely, honing them and building on them at the same time. You can move out from under the shadow of any professional on a pedestal. In fact, you can take him off the pedestal entirely, for the higher the pedestal you place him on, the greater the distance between him and you, both physically and psychologically. By perceiving him as knowing more than he does, or being more than he is, you really demean your own abilities and your confidence to change things. More than that, you absolve yourself of your personal responsibility for taking social action when action is necessary. This absolution is less affordable than it used to be.

PERSONAL COSTS AND LIMITS

We could end here, except that such an ending would be a bit too slick and a shade too righteous. At least two nagging problems remain.

First, the personal qualities we desire can get us into trouble when present in great amounts. At some ill-defined point, goal direction becomes tunnel vision, motivation becomes mania, persistence becomes obsession. High doses can have side effects, or personal costs. They can get you into personal fixes with yourself, and into interpersonal fixes with others. The existential question, then, is one of where you draw your own line and proclaim "no more."

Second, if it were true that a perfectly developed person endowed with perfect technical skills and "perfect" personal qualities could solve any social problem, we could all merely aim for perfection and rest a little easier. Unfortunately, even for the perfect there are limits on personal accomplishment, or at least there seem to be. This problem is important enough to deserve special treatment of its own. We will look at the issue of limits in the next chapter and try to figure out how to deal with them.

8

Limits

DRIVING THROUGH TEWKSBURY

I remember very well the experience which brought the limits of community work home to me.

A soft and fragrant Friday evening in June. I'd been working late in Lowell, finishing up the week. Sometime before seven o'clock I left, and not being in a hurry thought I would take a back road home. Driving slowly, unwinding, I passed twin rows of cars parked alongside the road, signaling some kind of event. I had the time to be curious, so I stopped and got out.

A Little League baseball game, the Tewksbury American League versus the National League champions. A good-sized crowd spread out behind the baselines – parents, brothers, sisters, a few others attracted to baseball regardless of uniform. People seemed at ease; they gathered in clusters, camped on aluminum chairs, dipped into picnic baskets, traded casual conversation while taking in the real excitement of the game. Despite the on-field drama, the scene was peaceful, relaxed, quintessentially American.

I love public events, and I was brought up on baseball, so it was easy for me to stay and blend into the crowd. Only after a few innings did I realize that I didn't know anybody there, and that as far as I could tell nobody knew me. My mind left the game. When I had begun work in the Lowell area, I would tell myself – sometimes even my friends – that I was responsible for improving the mental health of a quarter of a million people. I was going to blaze a trail, raise the quality of life, make people's lives better in tangible, meaningful, and lasting ways. To do this, I had gone above and beyond reasonable job expectations, had poured my heart and soul into my work for the past several years. Here was a testimony to my efforts: were they worth more than a clutch hit down the line?

Tewksbury was my territory, but I was unknown. All the meetings, hallway conversations, phone calls, letters, homework sessions, extra attentions, closely worked strategies – had they touched anyone in the crowd? I knew the problems of evaluating effects; I knew that effects were hard to feel; still, I couldn't feel any. The people watching the game seemed unconcerned with mental health issues, either in the narrow sense or the broad. Watching the game itself was mentally healthy. I was an outsider there, permitted to watch and to share their experience, but they didn't need me to intervene in their lives. I would leave the game and their lives would go on, manageably, without my help. I would leave my job, and they would not know, much less care.

So given the length and the intensity of my involvement, what was the outcome? Did my work – and the work of others I had helped to employ – enter into people's lives at all? Looking beyond that crowd, could I show that I had had *any* impact worth speaking of on the life of the community in general? The Lowell area still seemed the same; or if it were different, I couldn't say it was because of me. I had collided with Lowell, but I couldn't detect any damage. I wasn't even sure about nicks or scratches. Well, maybe over here there was this dirt spot which looked like it would wash off with the first rain.

It was at that moment the limits of change reached over to shake my hand. At times, I can still feel the imprint.

You may have received a different handshake, or perhaps no handshake at all. But everyone who becomes involved in social change work must at some point run up against the issue of the limits of change. How one deals with this issue – not defining possible limits themselves at this point, but the *issue* of limits – will determine the basic relationship of self to work; it will also bear on work accomplishment and satisfaction. Accordingly, to think about and resolve the issue of limits is a first-magnitude task. The task may not be easy, for at least two distinct voices make two distinct appeals.

TWO VOICES

First Voice

Without any question at all, there are limits on what one person, or any group of people, can do. The wisest course of action is to define and understand your own limits, then to plan your activities within them.

How can you argue any other position seriously? Even the giants of our age are bounded in their accomplishments. No political leader has eliminated the prospect of war, no religious leader has reshaped collective morality, no scientist has ultimately forestalled human pain and suffering. The activist heroes of our time – the Cesar Chavezes, the Ralph Naders, the Martin Luther Kings – trade a lifetime of struggle for what in the long run are a few scuff marks on the machinery.

As for you, you are neither Chavez, nor Nader, nor King, nor whoever your heroes are. You will do well enough to make the local papers a couple of times a year. To speak, for example, of "improving the mental health of a quarter of a million people" is a seriously misguided fantasy. Misguided, in the first place, because it is out-and-out unrealistic. Then, it is arrogant – who are *you* to bring about this transformation? Finally, it can be destructive, draining time and energy away from the concrete tasks you in fact could be working on.

Not to be too tough on you, but you'd be best off to put your messiah complex to rest. Relax a little and enjoy the game. It takes maturity and courage to accept one's limits. More than that, since you are rightly concerned with the impact of your work, there are practical reasons to accept your limits as well:

1. Limits give structure and direction to your work, so that you are not scattered all over the place. They provide boundary-points for action, a means for accomplishing more, not less. If a particular piece does not fit within the boundaries, then you can in good conscience set it aside. The boundaries can enclose only so much space. In order to do anything, you have to give up the idea of doing everything.[1]

2. Limits can stop you from expecting too much of yourself, from feeling perpetually disappointed or guilt-ridden or wildly driven in your own work. Like children, if we test for limits and find none, we are insecure and fearful. You own *feelings* about your work are important too, not just its effect on society.

3. And your feelings about work will inevitably spill over into your work itself. If you always expect too much, if nothing is good enough, you tend to become worn down, soured on the outside, scarred on the inside, less of a role model for others, less able to gain their help. In extreme cases, your unwillingness to accept limits can lead to programmatic despair. Limits are a natural corrective for extremes; they allow you to maintain the persistence, the steady pace we have agreed is so important for community work.

4. Limits help you keep your life in balance. Other parts of your life need attention; their claim is legitimate. When you set clear

limits on all your involvements, you shape what others can expect from you as well as what to expect from yourself. You control your life. You didn't sign a contract to spend all your waking hours on the job. You can take your share of life's other pleasures; when you return to your task, you will find that your time spent elsewhere will if anything increase your productivity.

In your work, you do what you can, and take satisfaction in doing that much. This is really a life lesson, certainly a required lesson for anyone who is serious about social change.

Second Voice

To talk in terms of limits, even to raise the question, is counter-productive. To speak of creating social change and in the next ᴄreath to place limits on what is possible – then to urge *acceptance* of those limits – defeats your own purpose. It is like putting on racing shoes, tying your feet together, and telling yourself how well you can run if you don't stretch your bonds too far apart. You might as well quit the race before you start.

Setting up limits means that *by that very process* your thoughts and actions are restricted. Limits exert a braking force, either directly, or merely by their presence in the background. Limits stifle ambition; they make you content with less than what you could do. You expect less, not only from yourself, but from others as well. You establish a negative climate for those who would act unbounded. Instead of supporting them, you inhibit them, or put them down. They are threatening to you, for their successes would highlight your deficiencies. And so you perpetuate a subculture of diminished possibilities.

Limit setters are older, more conservative, stuck within the existing system. They are no longer the doers of change, but rather the writers, the supervisors, the teachers, now retired from the action. They guide your work now not so much because of their victories, but rather more because their fatigue, the pain of their defeats has forced them to the sidelines. They hand over to you not their inspiration, but rather their resignation to fate. In presuming to protect you, they really protect themselves. They too perpetuate the diminished subculture.

But to operate without limits is to be free, to live and cheat death. You feel charged up, energized, you shift into a different gear. You inspire others, are a hero. You can let your talents play all over the field. You need to do so, because to create social change, or any-thing else, *means* to move beyond prior boundaries. Without being bound by limits, you will in fact accomplish more. Whether or not limits "really" exist does not matter; the point is that you have to work *as if* they do not.

If the ceiling is only four feet high, then men can be only four feet tall.[2] In your efforts, you must burst through the ceiling altogether. Community work, as we have noted, is both art and science; both the artist and the scientist need a vision which is completely free and clear, unfettered by prior constraints. Would you define for either one the limits of creation? And if not, how can you define them for the community worker?

A RESOLUTION

We look to resolve these two classic positions. If the two voices cannot be made to harmonize with each other, perhaps they can at least reach a negotiated settlement. A middle ground would avoid the sometimes jaded paternalism of the first voice, but would also keep the modern-day Icarus from breaking his neck. A resolution, a possible synthesis, might sound like this:

Social change work, like any other kind of work, has to coexist with the other demands of your life. Someone in any household of one or more has to shop for food, pay the bills, clean the house, watch the kids, shovel the walk, fix the leak, and carry out all the other well-known support missions that make maneuvers in the working world possible at all. That someone, of course, is the present or future you. Whether we like it or not, and often we do not, we can't get entirely out from under these demands. They have to limit the time and energy available to you.

Then, many of us are obligated to make a living doing something other than social change work. The number of paid social change agents is relatively small. When the rest of us come home, our physical if not emotional state is likely to range from fatigue on down. Community work then gets assigned to evenings or weekends, when economic survival has been assured, when other routine demands have been met, when the physical and mental effort can be made, and when it is chosen over other social, recreational, or educational opportunities. These forces impose limits as well.

There are exceptions, besides the paid professionals. A few of us have the money or the power to screen off many obligations of daily living; they can delegate to their secretaries, their housekeepers, or other subordinates. A few more reduce their obligations by choosing a scaled-down lifestyle, with fewer attachments to partners, children, or possessions. Some of us have daytime hours to volunteer. Some are students, not yet saddled with conventional adult responsibilities. Some are retired. Those falling into any of these categories find themselves with more time to improve the social environment. Those who happen to be adult members of nuclear families usually find themselves with less. But in any category, time and energy limits are a condition of living in the world, whether they are openly acknowledged or not.

A second reality factor is that most people simply do not aspire to transform the world by themselves, even if their time and energy were unrestricted. Their goals are more for personal or family fulfillment, perhaps for making the world close around them a little bit better, and that is about as far as they want to go. If I helped make the church fair a success, or helped get a stop sign put up on my street, then I have contributed. If I have run for school committee, or paved the way for the new recycling center, then I have done more than most of my neighbors. I am willing to do my share, but I hope someone else will lead the drive next year. . . .

Most people have no problem accepting limits for themselves; many actively seek them out. Those who chafe at limits, who will go nonstop at full steam, are rare blood types, a small minority, who may be encouraged if they are not tearing themselves apart in the process. But for far greater numbers, taking on more than they are ready to handle can be personally overwhelming. What you can do as an agent of social change is to raise their (or your) sights a notch or two, maybe more – or at least to make them more skilled and more confident in operating within the limits they have chosen. Their contributions, or yours, should not be discounted. They can add up.

So, this resolution continues, in daily life as we live it limits are inevitable for all and acceptable for most. But it doesn't follow that you as a social change agent need to be resigned to whatever your present limits might be, or unchallenged by actions you have not yet dared to take. If you are motivated and even minimally skilled, you can set modest goals for yourself, reach them, and fix your level of aspiration a bit higher the next time around. You can gradually stretch your own limits, just as an athlete in training. You may learn new techniques for doing so. As you grow stronger, your performance will improve and you can push your expectations further and further forward. Your ultimate limits may exist in some abstract sense, but they are elusive, always a step out of reach. You can start this stretching process or not, as you wish; and if you start, you may continue it indefinitely, or choose to stop at any time.

In any case, at any given point, you can make sure to use your time well, to prioritize, to hunt down impact, to focus in completely on what you are doing. You can pick your spots and take your victories wherever you can. You can mobilize all your technical and personal resources to bear on the task at hand. You can teach others to do the same. You can try to do the best you can with the time you have – that is, if you want to, and you don't have to, for you may wish to make a less demanding commitment or no commitment at all. But if you want to try, and are also willing to stretch your limits, what more can others realistically ask of you, or you from yourself? And what other response to the issue of limits can make more sense?

PROBLEMS WITH THE RESOLUTION

Whatever you may think about this resolution, something about it makes me uncomfortable. It feels too easy, too pat, almost smug. The primary criterion for judgment, I know, should be pragmatic rather than aesthetic, and perhaps pragmatics are the source of my real concern. If this resolution really holds, then why aren't more of us living in cohesive, tightly knit, supportive surroundings? Why instead does the social fabric seem to be unravelling at every turn? Why is the world so close to the abyss? Why is it, in the words of one of America's leading sociologists:

> If we observe a society faced with a problem – poverty, riots, unsafe cars – and formulating a program to deal with it, we can be sure that nine times out of ten the problem will not be solved.[3]

Are we confronting here a failure of individual responsibility and will; or a simple absence of right leadership; or social forces truly beyond our control; or are the limitations we have set up for ourselves, even when reformulated and "enlightened," in some way helping to maintain a situation where we expect less from our life in society, and we get it?

The socially concerned citizen may stop here without prejudice accepting either first or second voice or their proposed resolution as part of the human condition. The more impassioned change agent, for whom changing the world is reason for being in it, looks for a way to beat the system. Even though he seems to be operating at or near peak capability, he pushes on. You can follow him, if you will risk the outcome.

EXTRA EFFORT, AND ITS POSSIBLE REWARDS

In chapter 5, we talked about getting your message across as a precondition for successful outcomes. This is often hard to do, for countless bits of information compete for attention. As information consumers, we must protect against sensory overload. Droves of persuasive messages come pounding at the gates, and we construct solid barriers to keep them from entering our own limited-capacity nervous systems. As information dispensers—change agents—our job is to hurdle past those barriers, to march into awareness, and to convert awareness into response.

The impact potential of any stimulus, of any message, increases as a function of its magnitude and frequency. A thunderclap, for example, compels our attention; a series of thunderclaps may prompt us to action. Because everyday social behavior is in part determined by fundamental laws of perception, the same general principle applies. To get past the barriers, our message needs a competitive advantage. To gain an advantage, our message should be powerful and insistent. It should approximate thunder.

A clear inference is that one way to push back prior limits is to put more energy into disseminating your persuasive message. In other words, you work harder. The more energy, the more intensity and duration, the more program success. As obvious as this seems, we can probably absorb at least one reminder that people who work harder tend to accomplish more. Putting in the extra effort may bring you both intrinsic and extrinsic rewards.

But extra effort may also bring problems. The gist of the problem is that input and output are imperfectly related. That is, the correlation between either magnitude or frequency and impact is variable. More effort does not *necessarily* yield more results; even when it does, the results may or may not have been worth the added work. Let us consider two common types of community situations, where the graphical forms of the input-output relationships appear to be quite different, but where the consequences in several key respects may be quite similar.

1. Suppose you are putting on an educational program—a talk, a training event, whatever the format. While your ultimate goal may be to have that program produce specific behavioral and/or attitudinal changes among its audience, a necessary subgoal is to get people to attend the program in the first place. This takes work; specifically, publicity. Assume the outlines of the publicity package are agreed on. Then, with (say) five hours of concentrated effort— writing news releases, duplicating flyers, sending out mailings, etc.—20 people may come to the event. If you put in 10 hours, other factors being equal, the chances are you will not draw as many as 40. If you put in 100 hours, you will almost certainly not draw as many as 400.

In marketing situations, like this one, you reach the most responsive segment of your audience with the first publicity wave. After that, with your primary market exhausted, a law of diminishing returns comes into play. The relationship between input and output, effort and results, is negatively accelerating, as shown in Figure 8.[4]

Figure 8
Relationship between Effort and Results in Community
Situations where Results are Defined by Total Number of Actors

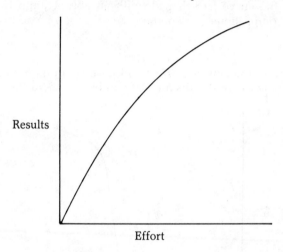

Results

Effort

From a strict cost-benefit standpoint, the extra effort is hard to justify by the extra results. After a point, leftover energy might better have been directed toward another task. This relationship, and this conclusion, generally hold true for instances where the primary concern is with *total numbers* of people who choose a particular action, such as attending an event, or enrolling, signing, voting, contributing, volunteering – and this covers perhaps the majority of community situations.[5]

But the community worker, the publicist in this case, is motivated by considerations which go beyond pure program economics. If 20 people came to a similar event last year, 20 coming this time might not be a personal success; five hours of publicity might not be enough. Only (say) 50 attendees, or 20 hours of work, may satisfy personal pride. The cultural value that more is better is well internalized. Extra effort here can push back prior limits, while lowering cost effectiveness. And as it happens, the people most likely to make the extra effort, to lower their overall efficiency, tend to be the most dedicated and conscientious workers.

2. Suppose you are applying for funding to a nearby foundation. This time your goal is to write a winning proposal. You know in advance that the foundation can make only a small number of awards from the many applications it receives; so your proposal will need to stand out from the rest. Not surprisingly, most other applicants share your thinking.

In cases like this, the relationship between effort and results seems very different compared to the educational program example. Here, the curve is S-shaped, with an abrupt jump from one level of accomplishment to another. (See Figure 9.) You may have

Figure 9
Relationship between Effort and Results in Community
Situations where Results are Defined by Yes-or-No Decision

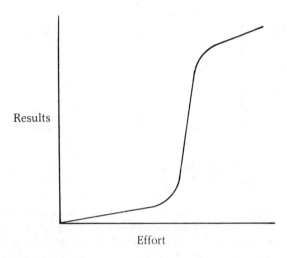

Results

Effort

nothing at all to show for 10, 20, even 50 hours of effort. Up to a point, increases in input have virtually no apparent effect on output. But with 60, or 55, or even 51 hours of work, accomplishment may suddenly jump to maximum value. That is, your proposal wins.

This is because many decisions in community work, as in life, are of the yes-no variety. Results in these cases do not fall on a continuum, as in the previous example. The foundation either awards you money, or it does not. The city council either endorses your project, or it does not. The V. F. W. either loans you its meeting hall, or it does not. To change a "no" into a "yes" means crossing over a decision threshold. What does it take to get you over the threshold?

Often, extra effort. The extra effort may very clearly be responsible for your success.

Often, but not always. It could be your proposal would fail regardless of how many hours you put into it, or that you could get by with a lot less than you thought. Other variables – political, procedural, personal – may be operating for or against you. What makes matters more tantalizing, sometimes to the point of pain, is that you can rarely tell how much extra effort, if any at all, you will need to push you over the top. The decision makers may not know themselves. So, pursuing your goal in a partial vacuum, and being highly motivated to succeed, you may expend considerably more effort than the situation calls for. And, as in the last example, if you are additionally motivated by personal pride, you may well put further effort into your own work even though you may have already crossed the threshold and won your prize.[6]

Let's review our argument up to now. Real-life limits on accomplishment exist, but more change is necessary than has so far been achieved. The serious community worker, whose time, job, or inner nature allows for a deeper commitment than the average person's, bridles at limits. He may be using all of his intelligence, he may be working at technical and personal capacity, yet he is rarely content with what he has done. He seeks a way to accomplish more. How? The open option is to buckle down and work harder, to lower his head and plow forward like a fullback going for the extra yard. Some community situations are structured so that the extra effort pays off. Sometimes that effort is *necessary* for success. Even when the payoff is negligible, there may still have been some measurable gain; and even when the payoff is nil, there remains the personal satisfaction from having done one's best, plus the social approval of others who place positive value on raw, gritty, slogging work. The attempt to push back limits may succeed, at least enough of the time to reinforce that behavior pattern.

BURNOUT, AND ITS NEAR-RELATIONS

Unfortunately, there is a price tag on extra effort. Personal energy, unlike its physical counterpart, may be able to be created or destroyed, but only so much of it can be available at a given place. If you put extra effort into one project, you take it away from another. If you are only involved in one project, perhaps you *should* be involved in another. Your special investment in one activity may get you the results you want, but in terms of *your overall potential impact*, perhaps you would be better advised to spread your energies around. When the waiting room is overflowing, you may not be wise, or even responsible, in spending an hour with each patient. Your extra effort itself limits you.

A social change agent, we may argue, should function as a catalyst, a Johnny Appleseed, sowing the seeds of change where-ever he goes. By doing so, he musters followers, gathers a rep·itation, at least as easily as if he cultivated one garden. And more seeds are likely to germinate. Others will nourish them, and learn to prize their growth. Impact, germination, the number of flowers blooming throughout the countryside, is what social change work is about. Is it preferable to do one task with excellence than several with competence?[7] Values collide. Our quality standards tell us yes. Our practical concerns with total impact tell us maybe not.

The deep-down committed, limit-busting social change agent has a hard time accepting the price tag. He wants slices of all the cakes in the bakery and to eat them too. On his good days, he feels he can put the same extra effort into many projects at once. He cites the maxim, "If you want something done, ask a busy person." On his good days, he may be right. But most of the time, for himself and most of his colleagues, he is wrong.

The human machine is skilled, often marvelously skilled, at responding to demands on it. All of us can put sleep aside when the occasion really warrants, or go for quite some time with the throttle wide open. The more rugged among us always seem able to take an extra load, juggle it around their packs, and keep moving on. Elasticity and resiliency are built into all living systems. But all systems, when sufficiently overloaded, begin to break down. There comes a time when the social change agent cannot cope adequately with all the demands on him.

The symptoms of overload are relatively uniform, and easy to recognize—though less easy to acknowledge from the inside. They include neglect of other social obligations, such as friends, family, spouse;[8] neglect of personal obligations, such as sleep, exercise, diet; first-time feelings of staleness at work; disillusionment, irritability, reduced ability to focus on the task at hand; and increases in internal levels of anxiety, depression, guilt, and insecurity. In more advanced stages, previous quality standards are not met, and symptoms become recognizable to others. In serious cases, the change agent may become physically or emotionally ill.[9] These symptoms may occur even when the work itself is going well; their likelihood increases when work is going poorly or when expectations are not being met. The entire constellation of symptoms goes under the popular heading of "burnout."

Whether or not burnout is actually on the rise, discussions about it certainly are.[10] Current social concern with burnout itself points to the limits of accomplishment, for the very recognition of burnout is an indirect admission that ideal goals are not being met. In fact, though, true burnout is considerably less common than two related phenomena, both less extreme but also damaging to the chosen cause.

One is "pullout," where outside life events collar the change agent and pull him out of action. His boss reassigns him; his mate dumps him; his creditors sue him; his reports are overdue. Alternatively, the big promotion comes. Alternatively again, some of us being more fickle than others, another project simply becomes more appealing. Energy levels may remain the same, but less energy, or no energy, is available to invest in the original activity.

The other phenomenon is "burndown," where outside conditions stay roughly the same, but where the change agent simply operates at a much reduced rate. To turn all burners on full blast is self-destructive, so he knows or has been told. To shut down completely risks losing previous rewards, possibly even one's job. So the onetime activist keeps his pilot light on, heats up maybe enough to cause a simmer, but stays away from the rolling boil. For human service professionals, unwilling to risk burnout, but unable at least for the moment to pull out into a new job, burndown is frequently the response of choice. Nonprofessionals probably burn down at least as frequently; some look at the process in positive terms, and take pride in their having "mellowed."

But if the social change agent burns out or pulls out or burns down, what is the likelihood of meaningful social change over the long haul? And if the full-time professional is no more immune than the lay person, who will lead the future struggles and teach the rest of us?

The additional and sad irony is that the best among us are the most susceptible to overload. Specifically, the change agent who possesses those personal qualities most closely associated with successful social interventions — direction, motivation, persistence, and others — is precisely the person who will bear the extra burden, or have it thrust upon him. His own commitment motivates him to stretch his capacities as far as they can go. His own standards impel him to put in the extra effort. And if he is even modestly successful, others will come to him with new requests, new projects to take on. Success in any enterprise brings clients to the door. How can he now turn them down, when prodded by his own social conscience, by his hard-won reputation, and also by the expressed needs of others, which he took pains to solicit in the first place?

He will not find it easy to turn them down. The chances are good that he will become overloaded, that his work will suffer, that he will lose his edge. Quality contains the seeds of its own destruction. The best change agents may not burn down any more frequently than the rest of us, for their personal qualities will work to counteract the external and internal pressures on them. But they will tend to burn down just the same. Good community work requires a steady, high, though adjustable flame. Those who can sustain that flame over many years are truly noble spirits, persons to learn from and emulate, even though they may have their own price to pay. Most of us instead settle for our pilot lights. The road to reaction or repression, take your pick, is paved with ex-activists who have mellowed out, who have chosen to put their own personal lives in order, who have damped down their fires to conserve fuel.

IS THERE A WAY OUT?

So our discussion of limits comes down to this: for the social change agent, for you or anyone involved in a community cause, working at less than peak capacity is to undercut the responsibility you took on to make life better in your own setting. Working even at your peak does not get enough done, relative to all the changes that need to be made. Working beyond normal capacity, stretching the limits, runs the risk of overload, burndown, or worse. Those most desirous of pushing back limits are the most likely to find them. And at whatever level you work, you may fail to reach your goal. You may fail time after time. The more ambitious and visionary the goal, the greater your likelihood of failure. In a world of limits and failures, you may opt for smaller achievements; but those content with less will accomplish less. You may work primarily from a sense of moral obligation, or from a satisfaction in the process of working, the joy of striving; but however legitimate and praiseworthy those motivations, by themselves they do not yield social impact.

First Voice

You acknowledge your limits and work within them. Excessive concern with accomplishment is unbecoming. It is breast beating. It violates the essential Tao of the universe.

> Gravity is the root of grace
> The mainstay of all speed . . .
>
> Those who would take over the earth
> And shape it to their will
> Never, I notice, succeed.[11]

Second Voice

You free yourself of limits, and you live with the consequences. Is it more becoming to sit calmly in the midst of injustice and suffering, while the world around you verges on collapse?

> Ask, and it will be given you;
> seek, and you will find;
> knock, and it will be opened to you.[12]

We look again for a resolution, to get beyond this impasse. We can accept that the issue of limits is an issue of human existence, going beyond the particular problems of the social change agent. But that is cold comfort; we need to know what course of action to follow.

Our birthright, however, does not include the promise of a solution for every problem of living. In this case, I don't believe there is a uniform solution as such. There are individual solutions, ranging all across the spectrum of alternatives we have been discussing. For each one of the solutions, you essentially get what you pay for and you pay for what you get. You can choose to do little or nothing from the start, and disqualify yourself from personal involvement in the analysis. Or you can set firm limits on your own time and energy, narrow your range of aspirations, and do an outstanding job within those constraints. Or you can stretch all the fibers of your being as far as they will go and keep them stretched out as long as they will hold up. Or you can aim somewhere in-between. The more you push beyond your accustomed limits, the greater the possibility of social impact, and the greater the personal cost. The truly inflamed activist, the addict, the lifer, hands back a customary existence; he sacrifices many of life's small pleasures; he watches parts of himself wither and die; consciously or unconsciously, he is willing to pay the price, at least for the while. The ordinary concerned citizen will manage his life routines more skillfully, will develop into a more conventionally balanced person, and will accept the judgment that his social contribution was less than it might have been.

Advantage may lie in respecting the practical and moral value of different individual solutions. We hesitate to specify what level of involvement each of us must have toward helping others and creating social change. The level of involvement chosen may well be the level of one's most feasible contribution at this time. To ask for more may be asking for what one is not yet personally nor practically ready to give. We are on safer ground in portraying the alternative possibilities vividly, and in stimulating intentional rather than unanalyzed choice. We can encourage increased social awareness and action. We can seek ways of maximizing overall impact while minimizing personal cost. We can work smarter, if not also harder. We can lead by example. And we can also be gentle with others and with ourselves, welcoming whatever contribution is given, hoping very hard that that gentleness will remain an adaptive social value. The next time, not too far along, we may expect more.

This conclusion would be less accepting and more judgmental if the linkages between action and accomplishment were stronger. Instead, they are shaky. The most impassioned actions sometimes fail, while the most casual can succeed. And in the longer view, the view above the battle, so few of our actions change people's lives forever. A comment of the American essayist and social critic Vivian Gornick has stayed with me:

> At the center of it all is the social malaise and the American longing for magic. Change, growth, self-realization—these are all large and painful abstractions. They become real only through a lifetime of hard, lonely, serious work during which the same inch of ground is fought for over and over again. True wisdom lies with the recognition and acceptance of this bitter truth.[13]

I know that I have not fully accepted the bitter truth Gornick offers, but neither have I been able to dismiss it. Perhaps this is why I feel that the universe of social action has room for the supernova and the steady star, the light source hurtling past former limits, and the one holding closer to home. I can appreciate each light shining today, and look for ways to make each one burn more brightly tomorrow.

9

Future Prospects

PROPHECY

Most of the material we have presented till now has been independent of the current social context. Assessment, planning, execution, and evaluation skills relate to any time or place; so do issues of personal style and limits. These and related concepts are content-free, for we can plan destruction just as we plan cooperation. Personality too can deceive as well as inspire. While our intent throughout has been to strengthen ability and desire, this in no way guarantees that either quality will be put to proper use.

Proper use depends on understanding of where our society is headed, so that we can align the resources we have with the challenges we will face. We need to know more precisely where to plug in. We need, therefore, to anticipate the future, pitting our best guesses against everyone else's. The community worker, already fully saddled with responsibilities, may balk at adding prophecy to the list of required skills. But this is necessary for any change agent, as well as for anyone wishing to shape one's own destiny. It may help to think of prophecy as a needs assessment of the future. Assessment of the general future and of the specific present can complement each other and jointly determine social action.

The purposes of this concluding chapter, then, are to offer some thoughts about where we are heading and some ideas about how we might respond on a community level. Our chapter plan follows accordingly: first, some assumptions about our current course; next, some derivations based on those assumptions; then, some specific support-building responses and initiatives we might take; finally, some underlying strategies for building those supports. The

221

argument is directed both to lay citizens and to members of professional service agencies, since both groups will be called upon to act – separately, and also together, along the lines of the partnership proposed in chapter 1.

I believe that with proper action it's possible to approximate an ideal network of social and economic supports in our neighborhoods and communities that will brighten and deepen the quality of our lives. I think this can be done in fat times or lean. In what follows, I hope you will judge this for yourself.

ASSUMPTIONS

1. The standard of living for most Americans will decline over the next several decades. "Standard of living" is understood here in conventional economic terms, particularly in terms of real purchasing power, measured in constant dollars. More bluntly, most people will be able to buy less.

An analysis and documentation of expected decline goes well beyond the scope of this book. However, the key causal factors are already in place and have by now become familiar. The depletion of natural resources, the rising costs of energy, the expense of an arms buildup, the precariousness of anti-inflation policies, the instability of the dollar, the flattening out of productivity, the political resistance to American influence abroad – all of them contribute to the prognosis, and few of them show any signs of near-term reversal. The decline may be variously described in terms of "inflation," "stagflation," "recession," or "depression." It may be confined to the United States, or it may extend through the Western world and beyond. It may occur slower or faster, either smoothly or with fits and starts. It may eventually turn around. But the belief here is that decline will happen.

The behavior of people who gradually have less money to spend is reasonably well known. The outer rings of their lives get stripped away. When affluence increases, most people expand the breadth and depth of their outside concerns – they add social, recreational, educational involvements onto their personal cores, and spread them over a progressively wider geographic area. But as affluence declines, these involvements come off in approximately the same order they came on, while the geographic range narrows. Out-of-town friendships become harder to maintain, vacations are fewer, school away from home is a dimmer prospect.

As the standard of living decreases further, more layers of life are jettisoned. Membership in clubs and professional associations, continuing education courses, magazine subscriptions, tickets to cultural and sporting events, shopping trips to the big city are post-poned, curtailed, or ended outright. The exact order of sloughing off will vary from person to person (some may have little to slough off to begin with), and expenses for basic necessities may be cut back too, but the outermost layers will almost always be those most seriously affected. People will move back toward their core in-volvements, which for most persons consist of self, family, friends, the immediate community around them. In other words, a major social consequence of economic decline will be an increased concern with events closer to home.

2. Private automobile travel will decrease, whether because of insufficient gasoline supply, accelerating price, or legal restrictions on availability. This assumption overlaps with the one preceding, but deserves special mention here.

Most energy experts are united in believing that the eventual trend for gasoline prices is up. Continued price rises, if unac-companied by rises in real purchasing power, will inevitably reduce gasoline consumption. Both consumption and highway travel in fact show recent absolute declines; and though cars are right arms to many, poll data suggest that with further price surges many drivers would leave their right arms at home.[1] What is more, the long-term outlook is for reduced domestic oil production, while dependence on foreign oil, recent conservation efforts and import reductions notwithstanding, is still high.[2] The total oil supply will remain as uncertain as it is essential. Any significant shutoff or shutdown will surely make gasoline less available, cause prices to rise still higher, and increase pressures for rationing.

The social significance of gasoline is what concerns us here. Decreases in consumption will mean less travel outside the immediate home area. Any rationing system will of course reduce consumption and travel still further. The geographic range again narrows. Whether by preference or default, people will spend more time in their own neighborhoods.

3. Public funding of human service programs will decrease, in constant dollar terms. This is one more aspect of economic down-turn, isolated for particular attention.

Recall that government financial support of human services is comparatively new. In 1930, only 4.2 percent of the gross national product was devoted to public social welfare expenditures, com-pared to 8.9 percent in 1950 and 15.3 percent in 1970.[3] But our memories are short, and once a service starts we quickly get used to having it around. Without some memory (or library) search, we are not likely to remember that anti-poverty agencies, community mental health centers, low-income legal services, neighborhood health clinics, special education and court diversion programs, Foster Grandparents and Senior Companions, Head Start, meals on wheels, consumer advisory commissions, and transportation services for the disabled did not exist, at least in nowhere near their present form, before the 1960s or later. With economic growth, as in the postwar generation, governments have more money to invest in quality of life.

But with decline, governments and other institutions have less. Like individuals, they strip away their outer rings. Those rings stripped away again tend to be those most recently added on (such as programs of the 1960s), those which are most difficult to evaluate (such as preventive, or health-promoting programs), and those which are not targeted toward a specific or vocal constituency (such as programs aimed at the community as a whole). In another era, we might expect the government eventually to prime the pump, to inject new federal dollars into employment and public service programs to revive the economy. But this downturn is unlike those in the past. The ideological climate is anti big government, anti government spending, pro tax relief, pro defense expenditure, pro balanced budget, pro holding on to my share. It will be hard to manage the economy while reducing taxes and increasing military spending. It will be harder to return political power to those who believe in widening the pump's flow.

There will be less government money for social programs. Some existing programs will be terminated, others trimmed, and all but the most alluring new projects will stay on the shelf. Programs providing broadly targeted community support will be among the first casualties. Advocacy, even militancy, will at best be able to preserve the status quo. Human service activists may squeeze, but will find government a spent orange. Proposal writing and other chasing after government money will gradually become a less productive use of time. The federal example will be echoed, if not amplified, on state and local levels. Those wishing to improve community life and needing dollars to do so will be increasingly obliged to turn to private sources, to revise their financial requirements, or to question their starting premises.

These interrelated assumptions aren't exactly news. Quite the contrary, they are conventional wisdom by now. With theme and variations having saturated the popular media and scholarly press, the old assumptions—that the public would willingly subsidize services for all, and that government would lead in their implementation—are cold-frozen if not actually buried. But the new assumptions are still new enough, the scene has changed fast enough, that we haven't yet fully absorbed their consequences. Suppose we pass beyond abstract understanding and *believe* these assumptions, internalize them, take them personally, treat them as if they will really change our daily lives; we then enter a new dimension of thought. This is as good a time to explore that dimension as any.

Suppose you do believe these assumptions; if you don't, or are unsure, pretend you do for the time being. There are derivations which follow for community life in the future. Suppose further that we try to flesh out those derivations and to experience them vicariously. Then we can see what further consequences follow for community action.

DERIVATIONS

• Less money, less travel, less government all suggest that the neighborhood will be a dominant force in future social life.[4] People will spend more of their time near where they live. They will initially do so not so much out of choice as out of necessity, for increasingly they will need each other simply to get by. Economic pressures will foster local interdependence. Society will decentralize, with all the pluses and minuses any decentralization brings. The neighborhood will be insulated, circumscribed, claustrophobic to some, but also an arena where people can test themselves out, show off their power, get things done, and rekindle a feeling of community.

The neighborhood will provide an increasing amount of social as well as economic support. Coping is more difficult, and more support is necessary, when times are harder. But at just those times social supports outside the neighborhood begin to disappear. The problem with outside supports is that they cost money. If you can't afford them, or can't afford to get to them, then you can't use them. If you can't use them, then you have to find support nearer to home. Neighbors, shopkeepers, acquaintances, people you know only by name or by nod become more valued as actual or potential sources of support. So do existing organizations and institutions in the community—clubs, churches, taverns, schools, all manner of voluntary associations. These groupings will grow in size and strength, while others will arise to fill needs created by previous sources drying up. The actual support given will not necessarily have to involve sacrifice, commitment, or overt help. The social value even of hellos and smiles should not be underestimated. Many of us will not have to travel quite so far to find them.

• The primary source of support will be the living unit, the ring closest to the core. The family or household is in the best position to give support which is most personal, most substantive, and most frequent. More time will be spent with living unit members, and that time will be more highly valued. The future of the nuclear family looks bright, and only partly because of the economic and social costs of divorce. More than this, the extended family may enjoy a revival. Elderly people in good health but unable to live on retirement incomes may have few options other than moving back in with their children. Nursing home or other institutional placements for the infirm elderly will be progressively less affordable. Grandparents and grandchildren will care for each other. Adolescents leaving their teens will have strong economic incentives to keep living at home. Boarders will fill empty rooms. At the same time, shared living arrangements among unrelated persons will continue to grow in number and variety. Household life in general will be denser, harder, more conflictful, more rewarding, and gradually more stable.

• Work, another major source of support, will also be located closer by. Increasing energy costs will motivate expansion of small-scale, labor-intensive, community-based businesses which will compete successfully with larger enterprises. Big corporations will take advantage of computer technology to locate more jobs at local centers or inside the home itself. More business transactions – and social services too – will take place over the telephone or video display rather than in person. Jobs may be scarcer, and the number of homebound unemployed may increase. In any case, commuting long distances to work will be less viable – and the shorter the commute, the more time available for one's community.[5]

• People will broaden their range of domestic skills. The behavioral content of self-sufficiency will change. If income no longer covers expenses, calling in the plumber becomes a luxury. Self-sufficiency will come to mean knowing how to stop leaks, can tomatoes, wire circuits, and patch roofs. Gardening, baking, sewing, home repair of all kinds may become economic obligations as well as avocations. Having these skills will reduce household costs and conceivably produce a little extra income on the side. Those possessing domestic skills will call upon them more frequently; those lacking them will be prodded to learn. The generalist will be better adapted to the environment than the narrowly-trained but otherwise unskilled specialist.

• Recreational time, like domestic maintenance time, will also be spent in the neighborhood. The high-motion, high-stimulation, high-expense recreations many of us are used to may be cut back by economic pressures. The focus will instead be on slower-paced, lower-cost activities. Some of these will take place inside the home – reading, TV-watching, listening to music, visiting, talking on the telephone, playing games, just sitting around. Other recreations will involve neighborhood people coming together in local sporting events or church suppers, or simply sitting on the stoop or walking in the park.

• Local cultural activities will expand as commercial culture becomes less affordable. Theater, dance, and concert performances, even movie tickets, will be priced beyond a larger percentage of their current audiences. Magazine, record, and trade book sales will begin to fall off. Cable and pay-as-you-watch programming will control a greater share of both the television market and remaining cultural dollars. With fewer national outlets for artists, and with fewer subsidies and fewer consumer dollars for the arts, home-grown culture will take up some of the slack. Locally produced performances and library book borrowing should both increase. The local library will in addition become a natural cultural center, a focal point for information about community events, and a possible source of program sponsorship.

• Traditions will be rediscovered and revalued, both inside and outside the home. The role of tradition in supplying meaning to life, in providing continuity, stability, and emotional release, is well known. Historically, the place of tradition in American society lessened with the development of social supports outside the community. But in economic hard times, traditions should revive. A special role for traditions will be the strengthening of community life by bringing residents together in festivals or commemorations.

• Concern with physical security inside the community will increase. Strong and cohesive communities will attract outsiders hoping to join them or exploit them. But the carrying capacities of those communities will be limited, and measures will be taken to keep outsiders out. Even poor and struggling communities will act to protect the limited resources they have. Both crime and the fear of crime will grow. Community patrols, block watches, semi- and self-appointed law enforcement groups will grow as well. Joining together to protect one's assets heightens the awareness of outgroups and sharpens the sense of being an ingroup member. Mutual protection will thus build community solidarity while at the same time isolating the community from the outside.

• Concern with events outside the community will decline. The number of concerns we can deal with is finite, and if more attention is paid to the neighborhood, something has to give. The most expendable something will be the outside world—both involvements in it and attention to it. Psychological life space will compress along with the physical. Boundaries will be more sharply and narrowly drawn, with perceived power to influence events inside the community proportionally higher, and perceived outside power proportionally lower. Less life energy will be available for events beyond the system—for international developments, for national issues, for the plight of the poor in the next county. This redistribution of energy will in one sense be adaptive, reflecting rational limit setting. But in another sense it may lead to rigidity, moral shrinkage, and distrust of imported ideas.

All of these derivations are adaptations to economic hard times. A common theme among them is a pulling in, a relocation of the geographic center of life space closer in to the self. The new center will for many be the immediate community; the world beyond the community will be seen to be of decreasing help; and with a reduction in institutional supports, people will cope by attempting to create more local supports of their own.

If all or most of these adaptations are made, will we be better for them? What will be their effects on life satisfaction? This is uncertain. It's possible that a simplified and stripped-down existence will bring happiness only dreamed about. It's possible that new satisfactions and new deprivations will trade off about evenly. It's also possible that lives for most people will become solitary, poor, nasty, brutish, and short, for real poverty eats at body and soul, leaving little energy for community support building. Economics does determine social existence, and there are powerful economic forces beyond our immediate control. But the determinism is not complete. In perhaps all but the most crushing economic conditions, we can select from a variety of social responses. And life satisfaction in the future will hinge on which of two basic responses we make.

One is individualistic. Tough times mean that you look out for yourself and your loved ones. You hold on to what you've got; you defend your property assertively, aggressively if necessary. You make sure you have at least your share, and play things safe from there. You scapegoat deviants and blame outsiders. You resist outside authority and fight external interference. You welcome inside authority and support internal crackdowns (as long as you and the authorities see eye to eye). Your predominant motives are self-preservation and security. Others will have to manage as best they can. You live by the ethics you can afford.[6]

The other response is cooperative. Tough times mean that social and economic security will depend more upon one's neighbors; with each helping the other, all can pull through. Bartering, loaning, sharing, merging of resources will supplement monetary exchange. And all kinds of cooperative arrangements will spring up, varying greatly in content, membership, formality, and sophistication. A key determinant of cooperative success will be trust. Trust in turn will be nourished by some history of credibility, of compliance with expected role behaviors. So the chances for success will improve if the foundations for collective action, cooperative prototypes, are built up sooner rather than later, while the social substructure is still strong enough to bear their weight.

These alternatives are overly polarized; one needn't choose all one or all another. However, I believe the cooperative choice incorporates mutual self-interest, is more adaptive biologically and socially, and is therefore generally preferable.[7] For those agreeing, a major task for the future is the creation of a network of social and economic supports on a local level that will raise life satisfaction while lowering stress.

If the individual is the hub, the community is the rim, and supports are the connecting spokes. And if the wheel is to spin smoothly, many new supports will have to be added to those already in place. Some can be reconnected from past models, while others will have to be made to order. There's enough time to do this, since the rhythm of life moves slowly and gives us a margin. The little, stabilizing tasks of daily existence – reading the Sunday paper, washing the car, picking up a six-pack – will not disappear. If we start now, we may create something better than what we had before.

In the next sections, we outline some components of an idealized community support network of the future, based on the assumptions already described, and capitalizing on the energy stored within their derivations. Economic supports are outlined first, then social, though the two overlap. In some cases, the natural leaders in developing these supports will be present-day social agencies and institutions; in others, the initiative may stem from individual citizens and citizen groups. In all cases, support building will require a joint effort; agencies, institutions, individuals, and citizen groups will have to share their resources and work in alignment rather than at cross purposes. The time to do this is now, while there are still sufficient agency and institutional resources to share. While the rhythm moves slowly, it moves inexorably, and continuing on our present course may leave us caught unprepared on a chilly day in November.

RESPONSES: (1) ECONOMIC SUPPORTS

If purchasing power will decrease, but heads are to remain above water, then people must spend less. Community-based economic supports contain spending primarily by improving existing resource utilization and secondarily by expanding the potential for local resource generation. They divide roughly into categories of skills, services, and goods.

Skills

People will need to acquire more technical skills, skills in working with materials rather than people. Producing one's own goods, or repairing the goods one has, or preserving function by routine maintenance, or improvising something from materials on hand are all ways of increasing self-sufficiency and mastery over one's environment. More practically, application of technical skill will also cut expenses; it is an economic coping strategy.

The kind of skills we are talking about are mostly traditional, those described in most any book on home repair or course in home economics—plumbing, wiring, masonry, carpentry, refinishing, insulating, canning, pruning, painting, small engine repair, simple auto mechanics. Most of us have plenty yet to learn. Traditional skills also extend beyond domestic maintenance. Learning the basics of a trade, shoemaking for example, or metalworking, or landscaping, will further increase individual self-sufficiency as well as provide a source of backup income. Possessing either skill or trade can also improve community self-sufficiency if that knowledge can be shared.

A step beyond is to combine these traditional skills with mostly new, mostly small, mostly low-budget technology. Some community groups, for example, teach courses on adapting automobile engines to run on alcohol; others have begun to generate electric power from wind and water, or to plant fruit and nut trees on public land for public use. In his pathbreaking book *Community Technology*, Karl Hess tells of growing vegetables hydroponically on row-house rooftops while raising rainbow trout in basement tanks below. Hess is a New Age materialist. He argues:

> If there was to be a free society . . . there would have to be a supporting material base. . . . The material base, we felt, would have to be one in which people generally could develop, deploy, and maintain the tools

of everyday life and production, directing them democratically rather than being directed by them.[8]

Neighborhood skills should be technical as well as managerial. There's a Whole Earth Catalog full of possibilities; one can find several innovative ideas each month simply by leafing through the *Mother Earth News, CoEvolution Quarterly,* or one of their sister publications. The technology is there; it's largely a question of motivation.

Technical education.

How should technical skills be taught? There's nothing wrong with traditional methods. Many of them can be self-taught, by reading a column or book, by watching, or by trial and error. Many of them can be handed down, from parent to child, or handed across, from neighbor to neighbor. Some vocationally oriented agencies can offer skills training programs, and institutions like technical schools can provide certificates or degrees. These traditional methods, already in place, are essential; but it's possible to enlarge upon and supplement them. For example:

Agencies can do more to meet economic problems head-on. Those agencies with broad or flexible mandates can become more involved in areas such as consumer information, nutritional education, or financial counseling. Much learning here can take place in group meetings at the central or neighborhood office. Some agencies may also be able to make house calls to educate or demonstrate, just as county agricultural agents visit local farms.

Schools can start technical (versus vocational) education in the elementary grades. It's easy enough to bring simple tools and machines from home into class, to take them apart, and to show how they work. Class trips can include visits to the public works and natural resources departments as well as to police and fire stations.

Students from junior high school years on up, possibly even younger, can apprentice themselves to tradespersons in their own communities. No student should be too young to find a job, or have no alternative but to hang out during a long summer.

Public vocational schools can expand their avocational course offerings and assist in job retraining for adults.

Hardware stores and building supply outlets can run demonstrations and clinics on Saturday mornings. (A combined public service and sales-boosting device.)

The media can likewise enlarge and systematize its skill-building role. My local newspaper, for example, has run a clip-and-save series on topics ranging from cleaning up storm damage to shopping for credit. It also sits its Home and Garden editor next to a phone one afternoon a week: anyone getting through receives free technical advice.

Skill sharing.

The discussion so far has focused on individual skill acquisition. But few of us will have the skills necessary to solve every technical problem we face. Even when the skills are there, the inclination to use them sometimes is not. To extend the economic (and social) reach of individual skills possessed, local sharing arrangements can be set up to utilize the skills of the larger group.

On the simplest level, skill sharing means that I will help you insulate your attic if you will help me with my income taxes. Reciprocity is present, and the recipients of service can also be learners or co-participants. Even the smallest and least formal of these barter arrangements can be valuable. But there can be much greater value in broadening the range of skills available and in systematizing access to them. Consider the desirability of finding someone to fix your brakes, or to teach you guitar, or to type your manuscripts, all free of direct charge, just by looking in a special directory and placing a call. These formal skill-sharing arrangements work like banks, with time replacing money. When you draw on an available service, you incur a debit; when you give your own skills to others, you receive a credit. Your "bank balance" may not remain below zero for an extended time, and you must abide by other house rules.[9]

Services

Economic supports, exchanges in particular, don't have to center around technical skills. Not everyone can rebuild a motor or repair fine china, but just about anyone can handle a sinkful of dishes or a sleeping baby. Exchanges can also focus on everyday, relatively unskilled services, and groups of people can organize around specific services they need. These exchanges can operate informally, or through the same debit-credit system described above.

Child care is a common need, and child care cooperatives – parents taking care of each other's children – are a common result. The same service-exchange concept can branch outward to:

Vacation care (for example, exchanges of children for a week or two at a time, so that parents can take some vacation time alone)

Cooking (for example, one member cooks a meal or main course for other members once in a specified number of nights, and receives a meal on other nights)

Travel (for example, car-pooling, with alternating cars and drivers)

"Manual labor" (As one example, the solar energy organization in my community has been sponsoring "solar barnraisings," where people get together over the weekend to help each other install solar equipment. Technical advice is supplied; members are asked only to bring their own muscles.)

These service exchanges in many ways are extensions of the division of labor that already takes place in existing households. And they can extend still further, as in cases when a group decides to purchase a service that no one member is able to or wishes to provide. For example, a group can contract with nonmembers to collect trash, to supply 24-hour transportation, to provide legal services, or to lead activities for children after school. The group, here operating as a formal organization (or corporation), sets the terms, pays the price, and monitors the performance.

Goods

Not paying cash for skills and services will cut costs significantly, but a household also needs material goods. The cooperative principles discussed before can be modified to apply here as well. Among the possible models:

1. Direct exchange. Most of us have had experience buying second-hand goods at thrift shops, flea markets, and yard sales. Direct exchange simply takes the money out of the transaction and replaces it with goods of equivalent value to the seller. Private-party direct exchanges can be fostered by community organizations and particularly by local media. Newspapers, for instance, can publish swap ads free; radio stations can make broadcast time available for listeners to call in with goods to trade or sell cheaply.

The swap shop extends the direct exchange principle to larger groups. Here, people bring in goods of a certain type to a common location, and trade them for goods of similar type and value. The goods accepted can be unrestricted, or limited to certain categories—clothing (especially children's clothing), sporting goods (especially rapidly-outgrown items like bicycles and skates), toys, books, records, magazines, tapes, cooking utensils, and hardware are common candidates. Swap shop organizers need space, staffing (usually volunteer) and local ground rules. Ground rules vary; sometimes, one may take what one needs when it's needed, and bring in goods of replacement value when and if one can.

2. Cooperative buying. The principle here is that individuals combine their buying power to purchase goods in quantity, and therefore at a reduced price. Fuel oil, for example, can be bought in bulk if there is a safe and convenient place to store it; so can items like food, insulating materials, and building supplies. These buying arrangements are like commercial buying clubs, but cheaper, being community controlled, without the middleman. And they can extend to services as well, as in credit unions.

3. Cooperative ownership. When cooperative buying power is joined with a physical location, one possible outcome is a cooperatively owned store. The store solicits members, acquires goods in quantity, and sells to its members at a discount. Food cooperatives are perhaps the most successful example, in large part because food is a daily necessity and high-volume potential is built in. But collective ownership can apply to any of the goods mentioned above under "direct exchange," and also to higher priced items not as easily divisible. Cars, for example—a group of people which has only occasional need for private transportation can band together and purchase an automobile. Or recreational equipment, or tools—it's much cheaper and may be almost as rewarding to buy a one-tenth share of an extension ladder, or sailboat, or rototiller than to buy it outright, especially when you can use it just about whenever you need it. Or (expanding the vision) houses; or (expanding it further) land; or (shifting the focus) other local businesses.

This listing of economic supports hasn't been exhaustive, and the division into skills, services, and goods has been only one way of classifying them. If space permitted, we could do more than mention such variations as farmers' markets and crafts co-ops; larger-scale agricultural cooperatives; food banks, of surplus or slightly bruised goods; time-shared ownership, where each member has sole use of an item for a specified period per year; cooperative repair shops, particularly for bicycles and cars, which provide low-cost work space, tools, and instruction for do-it-yourselfers; cooperative "junk" shops, with spare parts, scrap pieces, and other items too down-and-out to sell directly, but still useful to somebody—a sort of perpetual community yard sale; and tool-rental arrangements operated by local libraries, where tools are considered instruments of knowledge and are borrowed just like books.

The way is clear for all levels in a community to establish these and other economic supports. An individual can begin on a block level; a citizen group can organize a larger constituency; an agency can sponsor, train, and provide technical assistance; a town government can encourage and perhaps supply in-kind services; better yet, these different levels can come together and work as one. Superficially, organizing these arrangements seems easy: their basic principle – barter – and their underlying dynamic – trust – date back to the beginnings of civilization. After thousands of years, we ought to have learned how to make them work well.

But though the economic benefits of skill and service sharing are obvious, and the strengthening of community cohesion only slightly less so, long-lasting sharing networks of any size are still relatively rare. The slippage between ideal and real has three primary causes. One is our ingrained consumer orientation, paired with the lack of widely established alternatives; when we need something, we've been well-conditioned to flash a credit card or write a check. Two is the slowness of trust to develop, specifically the trust that one will receive fair value for value given. Three is the lack of defined and continuous leadership. Skill- or service-sharing networks are not conventional agency responsibilities, and for community residents to construct them themselves takes vision, time, and energy. Someone has to be the dreamer, organizer, canvasser, compiler, distributor, bookkeeper, collection agent, and all-around trouble-shooter. Just as important, all these roles have to be maintained, for eternal vigilance is the price of program success.

To create these and any other kind of supports, the implementation guidelines discussed in chapter 5 apply. Planning in advance, generating awareness and community backing, providing a concrete benefit, allowing enough time, building a bridge from intention to action are program principles as universal as anything we have. Yet it will also be beneficial to nurture those seedlings of cooperation already visible in the community. And it will always be essential to keep program energy going. Even though more people will be attracted to new economic supports, attraction will fade unless leadership continuously recruits new participants and continuously ensures that economic benefits outweigh personal costs. The less the cooperative tradition in a given community – I'm thinking of poor and worn down communities – the harder this is to do, and the more important it is to do it. Cooperatives must not be allowed to become playthings for the educated and socially concerned.

When cooperatives and exchanges do work well, they can be powerful social as well as economic forces. If nothing else, they are natural places for people to meet, talk, and form new linkages on their own. Cooperatives are also excellent launching pads for other community activities. The food co-op I belong to, despite its own organizational problems, has at various times spun off a cross-country ski group, a chorus, a garden, a delivery service for elders, men's and women's softball teams, and a coffee shop with live music, next to the bananas. Members can also become involved in other local economic or political issues. In general, cooperatives strengthen community bonds, as well as personal feelings of achievement, control, and responsibility. And cooperatives, exchanges, economic supports in general illustrate another basic law of social action: One thing leads to another.

RESPONSES: (2) SOCIAL SUPPORTS

Even though economic conditions have decisive social consequences, we must also concentrate on the more purely social side of the ledger. In many ways, social supports fall more easily within helping agency and individual citizen spheres of action. What does this mean concretely?

First of all, existing social supports provided by agencies, institutions, individuals, and other groups must hold as steady as possible. Agencies and institutions must continue to serve the destitute and the dispossessed, the seriously impaired, and those needing specialized attention. Individuals and citizen groups must take responsibilty for preserving and fortifying the network of personal supports around them. People will be obliged to give at least as much emotional sustenance to families, friends, neighbors, colleagues, maybe more; and they will need to receive at least as much support in return.

We must then build on the existing support base. The material following outlines two complementary approaches for doing this. The first examines the physical location where social support is given. The second partially redefines the support-giving relationship between individual and agency. The value of either approach (or any other one) will turn largely on its ability to strengthen available supports while reducing or at least stabilizing costs. We'll try not to lose sight of this criterion as we proceed.

Physical Location

The starting principle here is that there should be many ways to get help. The corollary is that there ought to be many places which give it. Most helping services stay still: they would do better to move around. In this section, we explore four different service settings—the neighborhood, the larger community, the home, and the outdoors—with an eye toward increasing utilization of each.

The neighborhood.

One way agencies can expand their impact without expanding staffing is by delivering more of their services in neighborhood settings. This has multiple advantages. First, it gets agency staff out of the home office and makes them more sensitive to the problems of the community. Second, it increases the community's appreciation of the agency's services. Third, it helps the agency's services become more personal and less bureaucratic. Fourth, it opens up more possibilities for training neighborhood residents as paraprofessionals, volunteers, or individual helpers. Fifth, it allows potential clients who cannot or will not travel to take advantage of services. Sixth, it is usually less expensive for clients, since travel costs as well as travel time are lowered. Seventh, it can reduce both average length of client contact and long-run agency costs by treating problems early, by making better in-community referrals, and so by making visits to the main facility less necessary. And eighth, it improves the overall responsiveness and accountability of the agency to the community it serves.

Neighborhood-based services can operate out of school, church, storefront, mobile van, whatever is available. Sometimes they can be delivered right out in the street. Full-time services may not be necessary. Agency staff can rotate from neighborhood to neighborhood, spending several scheduled hours a week in each one. If many agencies join together in this model and work out of a common location, then each neighborhood can distribute schedules of agency "office hours." The full range of human services – in health, education, rehabilitation, law, welfare, employment (and also in art, music, virtually anything else) – can be given at least part of the time directly in neighborhoods, and residents will be better off for it.

The citizen counterpart of agency-sponsored service delivery is the neighborhood association. With increasing time spent inside the neighborhood, it's logical to expect that these associations will continue to emerge and grow in power. Their general function will be to improve neighborhood life by helping to shape local economic, social, and physical developments. Because they are usually closer to the residents and freer to choose their issues, neighborhood groups are often more effective than professional agencies; in any case, they are necessary adjuncts to them. Even though specific issues will vary widely across groups and may shift over time, neighborhood associations can ensure that necesssary services are delivered one way or another.

For the community, neighborhood associations supply self-determination. For people within it, they are social cement, bonding the individual to a larger supportive group. For both these reasons, their growth should be encouraged. There's room for associations of different sizes. The smallest should be small enough so that the average resident can go to a meeting and know most of the people there. These may be block associations, for many the most valued of all. Block associations can confederate within larger neighborhood groups. Even larger groups may profit from meeting together occasionally to exchange strategies and program ideas, and to unite on common concerns.

There are hazards. Neighborhood associations tend to get caught up in nonessentials, and their day-to-day operations often border on chaos. Agency consultants can sometimes help here, working with neighborhood leaders to establish basic structures and ways for sticking to them. A different danger is that an organization can turn sour with success. Especially in larger cities, associations sometimes represent "neighborhoods" of 25,000, 50,000 and up. These organizations can grow so big, so partisan, sometimes so politically powerful, that they become as bureaucratized, as self-perpetuating, as out of touch as the institutions they formed to fight against. This is when division into autonomous but allied smaller units makes sense.

Not all social services or supports need to be provided within the neighborhood. Some persons will prefer to travel outside, and this option should be open. But the services given in central locations can change, too.

The larger community.

In most communities, agencies are separately located and scattered around town; instead, they could be based in one or more centralized facilities, serving a larger population. A person desiring services could check on employment benefits, get a blood pressure readout, attend a marriage counseling session, and pick up adult education literature, all under one roof. Such multi-service centers should improve overall client care through the proximity of service providers; would reduce individual agency outlays through shared rent, utility, switchboard, and secretarial costs; and would lower travel time and expense for many clients. These centers could also catalyze citizen-initiated programs by providing community meeting space. In a multi-service center, each agency would retain its own identity; but interagency cooperation, coordination, and planning should all be advanced.

The community center is the grass-roots analogue of the multi-service center. Block associations can operate from kitchens or front steps, but larger community organizations will gain from having an identifiable and semi-permanent home. Sometimes a church hall, club, agency-sponsored center, or even private residence will serve very well; but on other occasions, for reasons of cost, geography, sectarianism, tradition, or square footage, none of these will do. If a larger community (or smaller neighborhood within a community) has no widely accepted and flexible meeting place available to all, then the time may be right to create one.

"Community center" may sometimes be too fancy a term. A center need not have too much more than comfortable tables and chairs, rudimentary office equipment, room enough to relax, and a cheerful appearance. A rented street-level storefront may do nicely, as may a donated space, as long as it's well-located, visible from the outside, and easily accessible to most community residents. A few thousand dollars a year, raised locally, with possible municipal or corporate assistance, can cover the costs. A rotating volunteer staff can coordinate operations.

Some community groups may not be content with the stripped-down center model and may look to add options. Recreational facilities are one, though these can run into money. Agency services directly in the center are another, which has the added advantage of bringing agency and community closer together. Separate centers for different segments of the population are perhaps the most ambitious option of the three. Yet with clever planning, there's no inherent reason why a single location could not accommodate mothers and toddlers in the morning, senior citizens in the afternoon, and teen-agers at night. Space is sometimes a precious asset, but community support means sharing the assets one has.

Community centers serve multiple functions and pay multiple dividends. They are meeting places for community groups of all stripes, but more than that. A physical center properly set up will encourage people to drop in and find out what is going on; to post notices and copy down phone numbers; to take part in activities they never knew existed (or which never did); to meet by chance and become friends. It's the subtle, incidental, coincidental effects of a community center which may be the most important. When people are given the opportunity to rub together on an informal basis, all kinds of sparks will fly. Some of those sparks are going to ignite.

The home.

Multi-service and community centers are a step outward from the immediate neighborhood. We can also take some steps closer in. What added supports can be provided within the home itself, over and above the built-in supports of family and friends?

Consider first the telephone. Service by phone is cheaper for both agency and client, at least as fast, frequently just as appropriate, and absolutely necessary in severe cold weather or when physical distances are great. And as travel costs rise, communication by telephone will become increasingly essential. Social service agencies already use the phone to handle informational requests. But most agencies are geared more toward face-to-face contact; incoming phone calls are often regarded as interruptions of normal routine, something like the baby crying. The phone call, though, can easily get a status lift. Staff persons other than the telephone operator can be specially trained to give information, make referrals, and provide as much direct service over the phone as possible. With a little public education, service volume could rise while cost declines. ·

There are other ways to use the phone. Telephone follow-ups could in some cases replace personal follow-up visits. Organizations serving the elderly could set up "telecare" programs, where check-in calls are made to each program member at a designated time each day, or "phone-mate" programs, where pairs of older people provide the same service for each other. Agency services in general could be supplemented by tape-recorded educational messages, perhaps several minutes in length, available around the clock, on frequently-asked-about topics.[10] State or regional agencies could serve as informational clearinghouses in specific content areas, and make services available over toll-free numbers.

A particularly useful support for many communities would be a 24-hour multi-service hotline. It's a commonplace that many service needs and most emergencies occur after agency staff have gone home for the day. A knowledgeable and comforting voice over the phone could go a long way toward resolving a weekend conflict or easing a midnight crisis. That same voice might be part of a community information bank, able to tell you where to find a dentist with evening hours, how to thaw out a frozen pipe, or what band might be available for a last-minute party engagement. In true emergencies, when neither police nor hospitals are appropriate, designated agency staff could be called or paged by beeper. Staffing for such hotline services could be assumed by a single community agency, by a rotating group of agencies, or by trained volunteers. In some cases, this one-channel, central-intake service system could operate during the day as well. A well-conceived hotline could extend the hours of available services to the community, reduce costs through the elimination of duplication, and improve interagency cooperation at the same time.[11]

Cable television may never become as universal as the telephone, but most American homes may still get hooked into it. Cable marketers must provide "community access" channels for their subscribers, and this opens the front door to community support-building opportunities. Neighborhood news, forums, debates, meetings, call-in shows, editorials, announcements, requests, exhibits, cultural presentations, sports events, lectures, and demonstrations can all be presented over the screen. Community members can be producers, directors, moderators, participants, or unadorned viewers. Through two-way communication channels, even the sick and homebound will be able to register their input on community issues. Cable can evolve into a mere entertainment device and can draw people away from community life; but it can also be a bulletin board, a skills exchange, a master teacher, and a help-giver of the air. Farsighted community groups, while not neglecting existing local media outlets, will already be planning how they can use cable to meet community needs.

The same analysis applies to the next technology wave, whether it takes the form of multi-person video conference calls, or of home computers linked up with neighborhood data bases, or of something else as yet unforeseen. All these applications share the same dual promise. They can help. But whatever their form, no electronic or printed device will substitute for face-to-face conversation; the home will not substitute for the community. The intent of this section is not to make contacts any less personal, but rather to enlarge the total support network by enlarging the range of choices available. Someone desiring services ought to be able to get them in the neighborhood or at a central facility, in person or anonymously, from an agency or from friends.

Let's clarify this last point: home-based supports don't have to be initiated by public service agencies, and they don't have to be delivered by impersonal communications media. Individual citizens and groups can certainly organize newsletters, radio broadcasts, voluntary phone systems for checking on each other's welfare, and phone trees for communicating necessary information. And of course they can do one thing that many agencies can't do efficiently – pay home visits. Neighborhoods where visiting traditions are well-established, where people sit outside in the evening, where dropping in is not a privacy invasion, are likely to be the most cohesive and supportive. Even if they are declining in number, the decline can be reversed. Reversal starts with getting to know one's neighbors, something possible to do even in the most archetypal bedroom community or high-rise apartment complex.[12] Along a different line, citizens can pay informal visits to, or organize structured programs for, the sick, the convalescing, the newcomers, the new mothers, the elderly, the otherwise shut in, similar to the visitation plans outlined in chapter 4. And agencies can help train them.

The outdoors.

"The real education of the Athenian, and of many another Greek, was given in the places of assembly."[13] The social supports discussed so far all take place behind closed doors. But in his account of Greek civilization, the historian H. D. F. Kitto notes how the Greeks paid special attention to what went on outside, in the open air. There are still lessons for us in the Greek legacy.

Street life in many American communities is conspicuous by its absence. In downtowns, people zip by, eyes straight ahead to avoid collisions. Small-town centers, in contrast, are sometimes literally bare. And who spends time outside on residential streets but children at play? But street life is community yeast. The street is a place for people to make contact with each other – to meet, to converse, to share information, to plan future encounters, or just to affirm by physical presence that they belong to the community and are entitled to a basic human regard. The street is a community center without a roof.

Support from street and other outdoor contacts depends first of all upon the outdoors being an attractive place to be. A temperate climate helps, but so does intelligent city planning, starting with an economically viable town or neighborhood center. Social and economic factors dovetail again. City planners, too infrequently trained in sociology or psychology, need to understand that if shopping centers are designed to satisfy more than purely retail needs, retail trade is likely to flourish.

Shopping areas should have benches and plazas, flowers and fountains, wide sidewalks and attractive streetlights. There should be spaces free from traffic noise, for it's so much easier to communicate when nothing speaks louder than words. New residential developments as well should be planned with common social space in mind. Many of these amenities cost money; but since much federal and state aid to cities and towns is already targeted for bricks-and-mortar projects, they might as well be planned to bring out feelings of community. So much unstructured but supportive social contact rests on intelligent physical design.[14]

Beyond the purely physical, there are smaller, lower-cost initiatives more within the capacity of individuals and community groups. Street art, for one: art exhibits, murals, sculptures, side-

walk painting; street music, and street dancing; street theater, and story telling; "speaker's corners" for discussions, arguments, debates; street vendors and pushcart peddlers; sidewalk sales; maps and directories; town bulletin boards, with space for posting the town or neighborhood newspaper; graffiti walls, where anyone's creation can go on temporary public view; neighborhood play spaces; block-level socials and barbecues. And I have a recurring fantasy of a town employee (or agency staff member? or volunteer?) whose job is simply to walk the streets and give information, make referrals, engage in friendly conversation, and respond to specific requests within broad limits. In some communities, the police still fill this role; where they don't anymore, or never did, perhaps someone else can.

These informal and often spontaneous activities can be supplemented by more formal and structured ones. Clean-ups, for example; or contests and competitions, perhaps sponsored by local merchants. Competitions between neighborhoods, as in athletic leagues, double as recreational outlets and builders of neighborhood pride. Then there are community wide fairs, parades, exhibits, founder's days, traditional events, all boosters of the spirit as well as of the local economy. Where traditions don't exist, they can be begun. Several years ago, my own community hit upon an annual Town Day. The main street is closed off, and people stroll about, stop at booths, eat home cooking, climb onto the hay wagon, or watch the hot air balloon go up. It's not spectacular, but it's honest fun, it draws a crowd, and, as the publicity poster illustrates, it's done with zest and spirit.

Support from outdoor contacts may be neither as powerful nor as focused as that from more personalized attention, but it can be enough to reinforce connections between individual and community, and to increase the chances of more contacts occurring. Street life can be supportive without resembling Mardi gras. Streets, after all, must still get people from one place to another. But too often our outdoor environment is sterile and bleak; when it is, we need to find ways of brightening it up.

Individual and Agency

We shift perspectives now, away from location. A theme cross-cutting the previous discussion and the entire book has been the relationship between the individual and the helping agency. In the opening chapter, we spoke of a partnership; in this chapter, we alluded to a redefinition of roles. How can we redefine roles so as to expand social supports while holding the line on costs?

Part of the answer may lie in examining how (as contrasted with where) social support is given and received in our society. Individuals can take the lead in initiating support for themselves; so can helping agencies.[15] That same support can be received either in an individual or a group context. The alternatives for initiation and receipt intersect each other and make it possible to classify support four ways:[16]

Table 13
Some Examples of Initiating and Receiving Social Support

RECEIVING CONTEXT

	Individual	*Group*
	1	2
Individual	talking	*"Traditional" groups*
	reading	clubs
		churches
	listening	athletic teams
		classroom groups
	observation	discussion groups
		workplace groups
	reflection	political groups
		"New" groups
		exchanges
		cooperatives
		neighborhood and
		block associations
		support groups

INITIATOR

	3	4
	individual counseling (or other one-on-one client contact)	group counseling (including support groups)
•*Agency*	individual consultation	group consultation
	educational outreach (via printed material or mass media)	educational outreach (via public talks and discussions)
		training
		program skills
		counseling
		conflict resolution
		support group
		leadership

In cell 1 of the table, an individual seeks out and receives support independently, by oneself. A person may talk to a family member, neighbor, or friend, formally or in passing. Or that same person may read, listen, observe, or reflect. These venerable ways of seeking support will persist indefinitely. But the chances of getting what one needs – and of choosing to seek it in the first place – will be greatly improved if the social fabric in the family and the neighborhood is tight. And getting support tightens the fabric in turn; the process is self-reinforcing.

In cell 2, an individual initiates, and receives support within a group. That group may already exist, be it club, church, committee, classroom, card game, coffeeklatsch, or other community organization. But without denying the range and power of existing groups, they alone are probably not sufficient to provide the personal support needed in stressful times. More community groups are necessary, and new types of groups may be called for.

The cooperatives and neighborhood associations we've mentioned are two such types; a third is the support group, whose proliferation has been well under way. There are groups for the separated, divorced, widowed, bereaved, victims of all major diseases, family members of those victims, teen-agers, retirees, women, men, couples, parents, single parents, parents of handicapped children, parents who have abused their children, children with aging parents, over- and undereaters, the un- and overemployed, the battered and the batterer, gay persons, gamblers, smokers, drinkers, drug addicts, mental patients, prisoners, ex-members of the last six categories, executives, office workers, career changers, the lonely, the dissatisfied, and the growth-seekers, just to skim off the top of the list. These groups may be big or small, open or closed, formal or casual, time-limited or semi-permanent, authoritarian or anarchic, planned or coincidental. But if you have a common life problem or concern, and if you live in or near a metropolitan area, the chances are good that you can find a support group to discuss it with.

All these groups are designed to help people who share a particular kind of life circumstance. One person talks; the others respond with concern, empathy, suggestions; the focus eventually shifts to someone else, and the process repeats. In virtually every case, nonprofessionals have been shown capable of handling all aspects of group organization and operations. Though the effects of these self-help groups are not easily evaluated, it's a safe judgment that on balance they provide useful support of a kind often hard to find elsewhere.

There is plenty of room for support group expansion – if only 5 percent of the American population had interest in joining a new group, that is upwards of 10,000,000 new members, or 1,000,000 groups at 10 persons per group.[17] For those interested, but not finding what they want, starting one's own group is definitely possible (see references in bibliography). Support groups are too structured and artificial for some, too middle-class for others. They are certainly neither magical nor sufficient solutions to social problems – no single ideas are. But they do represent an effective way for individuals to help themselves without agency intervention, and they figure prominently in the network of supports that ought to be available.

The remaining two cells bring social agencies into play. In Cell 3, the agency initiates support-building attempts directed toward single individuals. This is already done routinely via one-to-one transactions between helping professional and client. It's done a lot less routinely via well-planned educational outreach. Every agency in town can step up its output of information geared to help the individual recognize and deal with life problems. While a good deal of this information is already in circulation, it brushes much too lightly against many too few.

Consider one oversimplified but cogent example, a mental health clinic wishing to educate about coping with stress. It can hire an experienced clinician for about $10.00 an hour ($20,000 a year, not counting overhead), during which hour the clinician may see one client. Or it can hire a mental health educator for the same rate or less, who during the same hour may compose a flyer sent to 200 people, or write a press release read by 5,000, or design a transit ad seen by 500 riders per day for a month. Which approach is more cost effective? Do we offer a lot to a little, or a little to a lot? With limited eggs, how many baskets? Which choice is best?

It's difficult to say, in the absence of hard information on the effects of the therapy session or outreach activity. Agencies usually opt for both approaches, and the question then becomes one of the proper mix. My experience is that the mix commonly chosen is 90 percent or more "direct service" (counseling) and 10 percent or less "indirect service" (education, plus consultation and training). But clearly this choice is based on tradition or service mandate rather than factual evidence, and traditions and mandates can change. Would the agency be wiser to set its mix at 80–20, or 60–40, or 50–50? I'd vote for more equal shares. I'd like to see more confirming evidence (though evidence can be collected). But if our goal is community empowerment, isn't change worth the try?

The mass media and other social institutions, though not normally considered service agencies, also have a central role in this category of support. The media in particular are conduits for self-help information. Media staff, with community encouragement, can initiate locally written advice columns, reader/listener forums, guest editorials, suggestion contests, and resource directories, and promote community support-building opportunities vigorously—any or all of this at negligible cost. A given media outlet may have some of these possibilities already in place; but they can be expanded, and others added. An hour's thought should yield a host of other ideas worth checking out with your local audience.

Agencies can also initiate supportive programs in group contexts, as in cell 4. They can do more group counseling, probably improving their cost effectiveness in the process. They can give more one-shot educational programs to schools, clubs, and other community groups. They can consult to community groups on group problems and work with them to develop new program ideas. (Some consultation can be given to individuals, too.) But if I headed a helping agency myself, I'd want to set aside a healthy budget line for community group training. There are four types of training I have particularly in mind.

One is training in the skills and attitudes conveyed in this book. Every person ought to have a firm grasp of program skills that make for effectiveness in the local setting. And every person ought to develop those stylistic qualities associated with success in social action. If these skills and attitudes are not taught in school, then they should be taught in adult life. Agency professionals are logical teachers.[18] The ideal goal may be to make community activists of everyone; the realistic goal will be to raise the skill and confidence levels of the greatest possible number by the greatest number of degrees.

A second is volunteer counselor training. Agencies which do counseling ought to train groups of volunteers to listen to problems, to explore background reasons, to raise alternative solutions, and to intervene supportively and empoweringly in the client's behalf; then they ought to put them to work. There has to be something in this for the volunteer—school credits, agency privileges, a paying job possibility. But motivated and well-trained volunteers can handle a significant percentage of the counseling load. Research evidence consistently indicates that "paraprofessionals achieve clinical outcomes equal to or significantly better than those obtained by professionals."[19] And the more counseling volunteers can do, the more educational outreach and training can be done.

A third type is training in conflict resolution techniques. This is because stress heightens interpersonal conflict, pitting neighbor against neighbor and group against group. Bitter, screaming, fist-waving, openly violent conflicts are almost always a waste of valuable social energy. Rational problem-solving techniques can reduce their frequency of occurrence. It would be an advantage if every community had its own conflict resolution specialist, or local mediation center (some of which are already in operation), but better still if community people could become their own specialists. They could receive training in basic listening skills (again), restating another's position, finding shared viewpoints, specifying existing differences, disagreeing without provoking, negotiating livable agreements, and keeping them in force. They would then be able to substitute these tools for verbal or physical attack.

A fourth type emphasizes the support groups we have already discussed. Agencies can run support groups themselves, perhaps as adjuncts to group counseling sessions. Alternatively, they can start groups out, bring them along for a while, train one or more group members in leadership skills, and gradually withdraw as the group develops a life of its own. As yet another option, agency staff can provide formal training programs for potential group leaders, along the lines of the support group leadership program described in chapter 6. They can help the graduate trainees get started in using their skills, monitor their progress, and remain available for consultation as necessary. All three options are attractive, but in terms of social and economic payback, the last one is the contest winner.

Not all agencies are professionally capable of doing all these things, but each can do more than it's doing now. To maximize effects, they can pool resources in training collaboratives; they can customize training to stated community needs; and besides teaching volunteers, they can market their training to those with the most natural opportunities to use it—local officials, other agency staff, teachers, ministers, funeral directors, hospital workers, barbers, beauticians, bartenders, receptionists, others whose work is serving the general public. This is partnership and role redefinition near its best: the greater the citizen participation, the greater the diffusion of skills, the greater the proportion of agency time spent in training than in direct provision of services, the more long-run impact agency efforts will have.

The social and economic supports listed here should not be taken as blanket prescriptions for all settings, but rather as potentially useful ideas which may apply to your own. They need to be adapted to local conditions. In your setting, some very basic services and supports not mentioned here may be missing or deficient, and these may require priority effort. Or some which are mentioned may already be operating quite effectively. Or again, a proposed service or support may need to be retooled to mesh with a unique set of local circumstances. You as a community worker will, as always, have to look around, figure out what needs to be done, and decide on how to do it.

STRATEGIES

Reorientation.

Examining individual and agency roles edges us toward a general discussion of strategies. If the supports previously suggested are useful, a next question is what underlying strategies will be necessary to make them real. It's of course possible to accomplish a great deal with no guiding strategy at all. But an understanding of broader strategies should lessen our reliance on packaged solutions and should improve flexibility and responsiveness all around. Most strategies desired have already been introduced, implicitly or explicitly, in prior discussion. And sometimes the lines between "strategy," "service," and "orienting concept" are blurry. But we can make a summarizing attempt. What follows is a working draft, open to further refinement.

Table 14
Support-building Strategies for Communities of the Future

Neighborhood/community focus
Decentralization: community control

Strengthening of existing natural support networks
Creation of new networks

Sharing of existing resources
Generation of new resources

Multiple service options
−in terms of place (multiple locations)
−in terms of time (24-hour availability)

Maximization of informal contact opportunities

Self-sufficiency
Self-empowerment
Self-help

Consultation
Education
Prevention
Training

Volunteerism and paraprofessional services
Leveraging of other institutions

Interagency cooperation
Cooperation between agencies and citizens

Taken individually, none of these strategies is shiny and new. If anything, the opposite; most of them are well embedded in the professional and how-to literature, and few informed observers would discount the value of any one. But taken collectively, these strategies compel a major reorientation, a "paradigm shift," in the way human services are conceived and delivered. The present-day service system is fragmented, immobile, dependency oriented, overprofessionalized, externally controlled, and disconnected from the people it is meant to serve. The system proposed is integrated, flexible, empowering, broadly based, locally controlled, and accountable. There's some poetic license here. But in their extreme forms, the two systems are night and day.

Much of this reorientation – the emphasis on natural support systems, volunteerism, self-sufficiency, decentralization – is consciously traditional, harking back to helping systems of yesterday. What makes it progressive instead of regressive is that people will not simply be left to take care of their own needs, but will strategically and deliberately be empowered to do so. If social science has taught us anything, we should know more about how to establish community support systems than we did several generations ago. The question is whether we will keep this knowledge to ourselves or set it free.

Difficulties.

If reorientation occurs, it won't occur without tears. Neighborhoods and small communities, however important they are, aren't lands of milk and honey. Smallness can mean small-minded leadership, or an inadequate resource base from which to adapt and innovate. Smallness can mean reinventing common program ideas from scratch, or doing without them altogether. Role relationships in small communities solidify, and are hard to escape from. Meanwhile, inbred strains, hostile to new ideas and to new idea bearers, are alive and well. Small isn't beautiful, it's only small. And if these advisories are not sobering enough, remember that many people live where there is little local organization or no sense of community – in downtown rooming houses, in rural areas, in wealthy suburbs. Services and strategies based on local self-determination and involvement will not work unless community roots have already taken hold; but to establish them from the outset requires a massive investment of time and energy.

Reorientation won't come easily for helping agencies either. Many agencies supply most of their help in one-on-one counseling situations, for that is how professional schools instruct. Since the need for such counseling will not decrease, neither will the pressure to maintain it. Consultation, education, and training, preventive services in general – which ultimately are most cost-effective – are less familiar, less evaluable, and less utilized; moreover, from a hard economic standpoint, there's less money in them. Agencies, like other organisms, have a will to live. They will cling to existence by reinforcing client dependence, by invoking special wisdom, by guarding skills zealously, by hanging aloof, by unionization, or by knifing other agencies if that's what it takes. To change agency attitudes and service emphases will require vigorous leadership from the top and vigorous pressure from lower agency echelons, as well as vigorous influence from the community itself.

One more stumbling block for all concerned is finding the time to put these strategies into practice. More involvement may be solicited, but there are only so many hours in the day. The basic routines just by themselves are voracious consumers of free time. Most of us finish work ready for a nap, a paper, a drink, some loving words, anything but another whole set of demands and responsibilities. To expect the weary and footsore now to wash up and charge out into the night may be expecting too much.

Counter-pressures.

These points are real, but must be weighed against some counter-pressures. Less commuting to work and fewer investments outside the community will free up more time. Actions inside the community will be socially reinforced, and this will be energizing; seeing one's community actions bear fruit will be more reinforcing and energizing still. Helping agencies which become parts *of* the community, rather than just inhabitants *in* it, will become more responsive and productive. Agencies may even realize that they *need* citizens to lobby for them, and citizens may find that agency staff sometimes really do possess special wisdom. In any case, the expectation is less for overnight transformation than for incremental change. There is room enough for more involvement without running the risk of personal or institutional collapse.

What's more, the burden need not fall exclusively on the full-time working person. Not everyone is out straight for eight hours a day. A demographic glance reveals several other classes of people potentially able to take on more community responsibility and to become empowered in the process – the voluntarily unemployed; the retired; the physically disabled; college students; teachers on summer vacation; teen-agers; older children; part-time and temporary workers; people between jobs or careers; the welfare recipient; the comfortably wealthy; women at home; and especially adult men, who amidst the surge of recent female accomplishments have become almost forgotten as a community resource.

Nor should involvement be limited to private citizens, or even to citizens and helping agencies working together. Other social institutions can review, reconceptualize, and expand their own community linkages. Businesses, hospitals, the mass media, schools, police departments, universities, municipal governments, churches – all can provide at least as much community support as helping agencies themselves, even though their primary concerns may lie elsewhere. The specific possibilities for broadening institutional involvement range virtually without limit. No effort here will be made to list them, but rather to stress the desirability of agencies and individuals exerting joint pressure on institutions that have more power than they do. A slight but well-applied force can set enormous amounts of positive energy into motion. Institutional leveraging can multiply resources and effectiveness many times over.

If the starting assumptions of this chapter prove correct, the chances are good that some of the services and strategies proposed here will take hold without consciously imposed direction. Economic struggle will encourage cooperation and change. Social stress will eventually be treated by home remedies. We don't always need books to tell us what to do. Yet this argument is not an excuse to sit back while nature takes its course. Hard times will bring out ruthlessness in people as well as protectiveness, hoarding as well as sharing, meanness as well as nobility. Some dislocation and suffering are bound to result. A carefully thought out transition will minimize the material and psychic damage. A community able to anticipate the future, and willing to plan for it, will be far better off than one obliged to improvise responses on the spot.

UTOPIAN VISIONS

Suppose that reorientation does occur, with some success. What kind of community might emerge? Community life will be determined by more than its support systems, but in sunnier moments I believe that people in communities of the future may:

• feel closer to people around them

- gain more security through mutual support
- show more concern and compassion for others
- cooperate more with their neighbors
- acquire more personal coping skills
- have more attachment for their communities
- hold more power to shape community direction
- take more responsibility for community life
- participate more in community affairs
- fulfill more of their individual potentials

In short, they will live in communities that you, and I, and utopian dreamers throughout the centuries have been longing for.

This vision is only one of several possible outcomes. To realize it will mean digging deeply into our personal stockpiles of skill and will. But for me the vision follows naturally from the reorientation suggested. And it can happen without uncommon knowledge, depleting cost, partisan politics, revolutionary change, or much dependence on government altogether. Up to a point, economic retrenchment can be a stimulus for social and moral growth. Any material losses may be more than compensated for by social and moral gains.

Suppose, though, that our starting assumptions are wrong. Suppose that alternative energy sources become commercially available sooner than we think, that the world monetary system stops its rumbling, and that linkages between rightful development and global survival become more keenly perceived. Suppose that around the corner is not more downturn, but an age of affluence equalling or surpassing any in our past. What differences should this make to the services and strategies recommended? The answer depends on how much importance you place on the values we have alluded to before. If you believe that tangible possessions and leisure time are life's main goals, then the quality of community life may take a back seat to the quest for personal fulfillment. But if you prize cooperativeness, self-sufficiency, participation, and responsibility highly, as I do, then there should be little difference in the supports we seek. There might be one less spur on the boot. But within a broad range, the ideal community should be independent of how materially wealthy its members are.

Suppose instead that our starting assumptions are too rosy, not too grim. Suppose that the future holds widespread hardship and suffering on a scale not yet seriously imagined. Suppose there is nuclear war, and some survive. In such case, the ideas and values discussed carry that much more weight. Self-sufficiency and cooperativeness, for example, will not be based just on moral preference, but will be required for self-preservation. So will the services and strategies that go with them. The worse the prospect, the more necessary the reliance on economic rather than purely social supports. But if there is to be a community at all, community values must be fostered; the same attention to the nurturance and empowerment of community members must be paid.

The exact shape of the future will forever elude us, but one prediction is reasonably sure: the skills discussed in this book will be essential for community fulfillment. Whether living in affluence, in poverty, or somewhere in between, people will need to know how to assess, to plan, to execute, to evaluate, to make things happen in the most efficient and supporting ways. They will need to sharpen the skills they already have, and to acquire those they do not. And just as important, they will need to believe in their own personal power and want to use it for the common good. These points apply equally to liberals and conservatives, radicals and reactionaries. They are ideological common ground.

Technique and personal qualities, skill and will, are universal donors, capable of pumping life into almost any situation. They are portable, transferable, renewable, invaluable resources in infinite supply. Everyone should posses as much of them as wanted, and, not to discount well-maintained socioeconomic barriers, most of us can. No single source can tell you all you need to know, but many can contribute. Books can help. So can the experience of others. So can your own experiences, your own day-to-day inquiry into what works for you where you are. And so can helping agencies, which must continue to strengthen the disenfranchised while also assuming the more general responsibility of spreading their own power as far as it will go. You as readers must share that responsibility by absorbing as much of that power as you can; it belongs to you; and you will need it.

What I have been describing in this last chapter is part of a personal utopia. By utopia, I don't mean paradise on earth, but rather a community I would like to belong to, where most human aspirations can be fulfilled in harmony and grace. Utopian thinking is brushed aside in our society, perhaps a reflection of the cynical and constricted temper of our times. But I believe this utopia is within our grasp. It's certainly within our reach. True, it won't come about through community actions alone, even at the highest pinnacles of achievement. The battle for economic justice must continue to be fought, with victory hardly assured. And political activism will be necessary to ensure our very survival. These are other arenas for action, and topics for other books.

You may equate utopias with castles in the air, or your utopian vision may be quite different from mine. Yet most of us, regardless of ideology, can agree that we can do something to make community life better than it is now. This is one place to begin, whether through an action complete in itself, or as part of a grander design. Your skill may be imperfectly developed and your ambition limited, but you are not yet aspiring to sainthood. There's no expectation that you rescue the world on your first try. The important decisions are first to start, and then to keep going – thoughtfully, forcefully, unceasingly, using all the internal and external resources you can muster. And enjoy the journey along the way. Here is a good place for me to end this work, as you prepare to carry on with your own.

Notes

CHAPTER 1

1. For social welfare expenditures, see U.S. Bureau of the Census, *Statistical Abstract of the United States*, 101st ed. (Washington, D.C.: Government Printing Office, 1980), p. 329, Table 530; see also Executive Office of the President, Office of Management and Budget, *The United States Budget in Brief: Fiscal Year 1982* (Washington, D.C.: Government Printing Office, 1981), pp. 79 and 82. For charitable contributions, see U.S. Bureau of the Census, *Statistical Abstract*, p. 363, Table 589; see also Carl Bakal, *Charity U.S.A.* (New York: Times Books, 1979), pp. 13, 56, and 63 ff. For attitudes on taxation, see Everett Carll Ladd, Jr. et al., "The Polls: Taxing and Spending," *Public Opinion Quarterly* 43 (1979):126-135, though Ladd's data also indicate that most Americans want most of the services that tax dollars pay for. For conservatism, see *ISR Newsletter* (Institute for Social Research, University of Michigan) 9, no. 1 (1981):3, although somewhat contrasting statistics are found in *Public Opinion*, 4, no. 1 (1981):20. For spendable income, see *Monthly Labor Review*, 104, no. 1 (1981):86 (data updated monthly). For national expectations, see note 22.

2. The argument here draws from the hierarchical theory of motivation posited by Abraham H. Maslow, *Motivation and Personality* (New York: Harper & Row, 1954).

3. "By 79-17%, Americans say it is more important to teach people to live with basic essentials than to reach higher standards of living." This is one of many similar Harris poll statistics cited in Louis Harris, "Our Changing Structure of Values," in C. Stewart Sheppard and Donald C. Carroll, eds., *Working in the Twenty-First Century* (New York: John Wiley & Sons, 1980), pp. 123-130. Quote from p. 124. For related findings, see Angus Campbell, *The Sense of Well-Being in America* (New York: McGraw-Hill, 1981); Jonathan L. Freedman, *Happy People* (New York: Harcourt Brace Jovanovich, 1978); and U.S. Bureau of the Census, *Social Indicators III* (Washington, D.C.: Government Printing Office, 1981).

4. Lewis Mumford, *The City in History* (New York: Harcourt, Brace & World, 1961), chap. 1 ff.

5. Kirkpatrick Sale, *Human Scale* (New York: Coward, McCann & Geoghegan, 1980), pp. 185-186, 181, and 179 respectively. Quote from p. 179.

6. For an historical account of "community" in America, see Thomas Bender, *Community and Social Change in America* (New Brunswick, N.J.:

Rutgers University Press, 1978). For a less abstract treatment of small-town life, see Richard Lingeman, *Small Town America* (New York: G. P. Putnam's Sons, 1980).

7. Support and help are treated here as overlappping concepts, support being the more general term and more central to our purposes. Helping behaviors are supportive, but not all supports involve overt helping. They *could* help, though; they are latent helping sources.

8. Documentation substantiating these four conclusions is scattered across the psychological literature. A seminal article is Sidney Cobb, "Social Support as a Moderator of Life Stress," *Psychosomatic Medicine* 38 (1976): 300-314. A good overview is Task Panel on Community Support Systems, "Report of the Task Panel on Community Support Systems," in *Task Panel Reports Submitted to the President's Commission on Mental Health*, Vol. 2, Appendix (Washington: Government Printing Office, 1978), pp. 139-235. The anxiety-affiliation relationship traces back to Stanley Schachter, *The Psychology of Affiliation* (Stanford, Calif.: Stanford University Press, 1959). Biological data are presented in James J. Lynch, *The Broken Heart* (New York: Basic Books, 1979). Some recent reviews, each giving additional references, are David Dooley and Ralph Catalano, "Economic Change as a Cause of Behavioral Disorder," *Psychological Bulletin* 87 (1980):450-468; Michael S. Goldstein, "The Sociology of Mental Health and Illness," in *Annual Review of Sociology*, Vol. 5 (Palo Alto, Calif.: Annual Reviews, Inc., 1979), pp. 381-409; and John S. Strauss, "Social and Cultural Influences on Psychopathology," in *Annual Review of Psychology*, Vol. 30 (Palo Alto, Calif.: Annual Reviews, Inc., 1979), pp. 397-415.

9. The percentage of the population experiencing a "hungering for community" increased from 32% in 1973 to 47% in 1980. These poll data collected by Daniel Yankelovich are cited on pp. 60 and 85 of his article "New Rules in American Life: Searching for Self-Fulfillment in a World Turned Upside Down," in *Psychology Today* 15, no. 4 (1981):35-91.

10. This section can be no more than a brief sketch, with necessary oversimplification. For further detail, see Willard Gaylin et al., *Doing Good* (New York: Pantheon, 1978); Sheila B. Kamerman and Alfred J. Kahn, *Social Services in the United States* (Philadelphia: Temple University Press, 1976); Walter A. Friedlander, *Introduction to Social Welfare*, 3rd ed. (Englewood Cliffs, N.J.: Prentice-Hall, 1968); and Bakal, *Charity U.S.A.*, chap. 2 ff.

11. A less charitable analysis is that the economically powerful in American society supported limited social services in order to maintain control over the working classes and to forestall worker revolts.

12. U.S. Bureau of the Census, *Statistical Abstract* p. 329, Table 530. However, see also U.S. Bureau of the Census, *Historical Statistics of the United States, Colonial Times to 1970*, Bicentennial Edition, Part 1 (Washington, D.C.: Government Printing Office, 1975), p. 340, which indicates that social welfare expenditures as a percentage of GNP also rose significantly during the 1929-1950 period.

13. Elliot Richardson, cited in Kamerman and Kahn, *Social Services*, p. 441.

14. Sar A. Levitan, *Programs in Aid of the Poor for the 1980s*, 4th ed. (Baltimore: Johns Hopkins University Press, 1980), p. 19.

15. Executive Office of the President, Office of Management and Budget, *The United States Budget in Brief*, pp. 79 and 82. Federal contributions appear to peak in the late 1970s and show a plateau lasting through 1980. See also Levitan, *Programs in Aid of the Poor*, p. 144.

16. Wilbur J. Cohen, "Foreword," in Yeheskel Hasenfeld and Richard A. English, eds., *Human Service Organizations* (Ann Arbor, Mich.: University of Michigan Press, 1974), p. x.

17. Merlin A. Taber, *The Social Context of Helping* (Rockville, Md.: National Institute of Mental Health, 1980), p. 95 ff.

18. Cf. the discussion of the Professional-Managerial Class in Barbara Ehrenreich and John Ehrenreich, "The Professional-Managerial Class," *Radical America* 11, no. 2 (1977):7-31.

19. Cuts proposed by the Reagan administration and trends projected through 1986 are summarized in Executive Office of the President, Office of Management and Budget, *Fiscal Year 1982 Budget Revisions* (Washington, D.C.: Government Printing Office, 1981), pp. 126-129, 144-159 ff.

20. From Reagan's State of the Union Message on Economic Recovery, February 18, 1981. Reprinted in *Vital Speeches of the Day* 47, no. 11 (15 March 1981):326.

21. At this writing such programs include the Office of Neighborhood Self-Help Development, the National Consumer Cooperative Bank, "Operation Outreach" (self-help programs for Vietnam veterans), VISTA, the Community Services Administration, and much nonmilitary foreign aid. Even if these programs survive, the attempt to eliminate them itself points to a dramatically altered view of federal responsibility.

22. Data cited in Paul Blumberg, *Inequality in an Age of Decline* (New York: Oxford University Press, 1980), pp. 255-256. See also additional pessimistic data on expectations presented in *Public Opinion* 3, no. 1 (1980):32 and 33, and 3, no. 3:30 and 31.

23. Governments and other social institutions can help too, though that's not our emphasis here, and it may not be wise to rely too heavily on governments in the near-term future.

24. George A. Miller, "Psychology as a Means of Promoting Human Welfare," *American Psychologist* 24 (1969):1063-1075. Quotes from pp. 1070 and 1071.

25. Miller, "Psychology as a Means of Promoting Human Welfare," p. 1073.

CHAPTER 3

1. Note again that by "community needs" we more accurately mean the needs of your target group, the people you wish to serve. Since this group will often be smaller than the entire community, assessment will be proportionally simpler.

2. The last-named method is the basis of "nominal-group" or "Delbecq"

technique. Collection of thoughts from a variety of persons and reaction to them can also be done at a distance (e.g., by mail), without the "group" members ever having to meet each other (Delphi technique). For more extended descriptions, see André L. Delbecq et al., *Group Techniques for Program Planning* (Glenview, Ill.: Scott, Foresman, 1975).

3. The exact phrasing of questions takes delicate care, since what is crystal-clear to you may be cloudy to someone else, and since a minor shift in language can produce a major variation in response. If you are an inexperienced person doing a serious needs assessment, your best bets are to: (a) do some more background reading; (b) find some professionally conducted assessments, and look at how questions are worded there; (c) get some professional consultation, or at least feedback from colleagues; and (d) test the questions for clarity and appropriateness on a few people similar to the people in your target group, and revise as necessary. Pretesting is wise no matter how experienced you are. Most texts on social research methods cover questionnaire construction in considerable detail. References on needs assessment in the bibliography are also good background sources and contain many sample items.

4. The qualifier "from the standpoint of sampling alone" needs elaboration, since "sampling alone" may not be the only consideration. It may not be best to assess *too* many people if your overall project time is limited and if 100 percent or high-percentage assessment would seriously cut down on service delivery. And assessing a larger, unrepresentative sample *could* prove more useful than assessing a smaller, representative one if such assessment targeted the most likely participants, spurred more overall enthusiasm, and bound larger numbers of people to the eventual program.

5. Three other questions similar in format, plus age, sex, and length-of-membership data, a closing thank-you, and a request for volunteers are omitted here. I am indebted to Marion Yonge for supplying the survey form, survey results, and follow-up information.

6. The sample was unrepresentative, and the questionnaire actually turned out to assess the needs of the more concerned parishioners. However, the assessment committee could justifiably argue that in this case to trace down the other 2000 would not have been cost-effective, and also that the most likely participants in suggested activities (visitation program, etc.) would come from those who did respond.

7. But the assessment process did not work perfectly. The 5 percent of respondents who volunteered to contribute some time were apparently not recontacted; nor did the assessment committee become involved in subsequent planning or decision making.

8. This form was devised by Kathy Desilets. In this case, many of the specific ideas on the form were our own.

9. Several months after the meeting, I noticed that a long-dormant neighborhood group was starting up again in Centralville. I called its chairperson, told him about our interests, and offered our services. He replied: "Well, we'll call you if we need you." I wasn't entirely surprised, and I know I shouldn't have felt hurt.

10. Better (Case 1): "Would you prefer to see music lessons offered in the elementary schools, or do you feel the present music program should remain as it is?" Better (Case 2) "What hours do you think our agency ought to be open for services?" Or (more direct need): "If you needed our services for some reason, what hours would be most convenient for you to visit our agency?"

11. There may sometimes be good reason to design an assessment to maximize the chances of eliciting support for your pre-existing ideas; in any case, it's certainly permissible to embed your own ideas in the assessment to get feedback on them. Nevertheless, loaded questions cannot give you an objective or comprehensive view. And if you are planning to execute a specific program virtually regardless of what needs are expressed, you might as well make that clear to yourself and others from the beginning. You are then not finding out what is needed, but instead "asking permission," "testing the waters," verifying minimum acceptance levels, and/or building support.

12. If you are performing an assessment for some group, even if it's your own, be aware of how easy it is for others to discount or forget about assessment results that make their lives difficult. Assessment in all cases should start with a firm commitment, even a written commitment, to use the results.

13. When drumming up support, you are not assessing a need, but trying to create one. This can be legitimate as long as you don't get the two confused. Ethical issues arise, and reasonable persons disagree, regarding how loudly the drum may be beaten. There are "purists," who interpret community *service* strictly, and who out of conscience would never attempt to impose personal views. And there are "ideologues," committed to converting every last heathen on the block. I believe that it's ethically justified to try to stimulate a community need as long as you work openly, believe that benefits clearly outweigh costs, communicate both, and are willing to accept "no" as a possible answer.

14. A good alternative to the term "resource costs" is "obstacles." Obstacles describe the actual barrier rather than the resource costs necessary to surmount it. Overall cost or feasibility would then be measured by the potency of resources on hand as versus obstacles. We use the term "obstacles" when discussing planning in the next chapter. The precise "obstacles" or "resource costs," whichever term is used, should be specified in advance, before decisions are made.

15. In different terms, a sensible match between the resources you have and the obstacles to be overcome.

16. Letter from Franklin to Joseph Priestley (the discoverer of oxygen), September 19, 1772. In Albert Henry Smyth, ed., *The Writings of Benjamin Franklin*, Vol. 5 (New York: The Macmillan Company, 1906), p. 437.

17. Several conventions are adopted for this example. Benefits here are assumed to take user costs into account. To achieve symmetry with other values, feasibility is computed by subtracting the "current resources" scale value from the "needed resources" scale value, and then subtracting this dif-

ference from 10. Costs and feasibility are assumed equal. Total value is computed by summing columns (1), (2), (3), and (6).

18. Sometimes in practice you may not be limited to one choice. A creative community worker will always be looking for opportunities to address two or more needs at the same time, or sequentially, or to refer some needs elsewhere, or to combine them in some fashion. Even so, priorities must still be set.

19. A good introductory text is Bruce F. Baird, *Introduction to Decision Analysis* (North Scituate, Mass.: Duxbury Press, 1978). For a recent review, see Hillel J. Einhorn and Robin M. Hogarth, "Behavioral Decision Theory: Processes of Judgment and Choice," in *Annual Review of Psychology*, Vol. 32 (Palo Alto, Calif.: Annual Reviews, Inc., 1981), pp. 53-88.

CHAPTER 4

1. The difference is rivalled only by the difference between belief and practice in program evaluation, as we shall note later on.

2. Cf. a more formal statement of this principle in a planning manual based on research evidence: "Practitioners wishing to promote an innovation in a general target system should develop it initially in a partial segment of that target system." In Jack Rothman et al., *Promoting Innovation and Change in Organizations and Communities* (New York: John Wiley & Sons, 1976), p. 25.

3. But there are differences. The chart format used here packs a lot of detail into a small space. The time-bar format provides a clearer visual overview. The critical-path format, sometimes called PERT (for Program Evaluation and Review Technique), depicts more visual interrelationships than either of the others and deserves the attention of the intermediate-to-advanced planner. Neither time-bar nor PERT, however, defines individual responsibilities, though these can be initialled in. It's also possible to combine a pictorial review with written charts. For further discussion, see Duane Dale and Nancy Mitiguy, *Planning, for a Change* (Amherst, Mass.: University of Massachusetts [Citizen Involvement Training Project], 1978), pp. 65-71.

CHAPTER 5

1. But if people don't like you, or if you are locked into an unflattering role, they may be very hard to influence. This is one built-in disadvantage of working in small settings.

2. What may be harder to grasp is why anyone would want to work in an unfamiliar setting in the first place. There are convincing arguments for not doing so, implied in the text. But there are also exceptions: if you work for an agency, it may be part of your mandate to break new ground; if you are known and well-regarded by some members of a setting, you may be invited in for specific help. But with neither mandate nor request, it is wise on both practical and ethical grounds to think carefully before venturing too far from home base.

3. This means less preparation time relative to other action stages and in absolute terms as well. One additional program variable affecting distribution of energy is estimated program length. Short-term programs involve less total preparation time, but a greater percentage of that time may need to be invested in developing initial awareness and support. Longer-term programs usually go with longer preparation periods, but awareness and support-building may fill a smaller percentage of overall time, since these programs often need to place more emphasis on continued participation and eventual responsibility-sharing.

4. Many citizen and nonprofit groups are all for "publicity," but hesitate at "promotion," and shy away from "marketing." Publicity and promotion are used as rough synonyms here. "Marketing" suggests more high-powered and comprehensive techniques, but these may be precisely what your group needs. For an elaboration and defense of marketing concepts, see Philip Kotler, *Marketing for Nonprofit Organizations* (Englewood Cliffs, N.J.: Prentice-Hall, 1975), chap. 1 ff.

5. "Support" has a more restrictive meaning here, compared to its use in chapter 1. There, the term was used more generally to apply to a variety of functions ordering and sustaining individual social life. Here, "support" refers more specifically to agreement with and backing of certain values and ideas. "Support" here is passive, while "participation" involves a more active, behavioral commitment.

6. To supplement the points listed in the text, see Philip G. Zimbardo et al., *Influencing Attitudes and Changing Behavior*, 2nd ed. (Reading, Mass.: Addison-Wesley, 1977), especially Postscript C, for an excellent summary of principles applying to one-on-one persuasion situations. See also Saul Alinsky, *Rules for Radicals* (New York: Vintage, 1972), chap. 7 ("Tactics") ff. for a parallel summary of principles applying to larger-scale community organization situations. The principles listed here fall somewhere in between in scale.

7. As Alinsky put it: "An organizer can communicate only within the areas of experience of his audience; otherwise there is no communication." In Alinsky, *Rules for Radicals*, pp. 69-70.

8. Jonathan L. Freedman and Scott C. Fraser, "Compliance without Pressure: The Foot-in-the-Door Technique," *Journal of Personality and Social Psychology* 4 (1966):195-202.

9. Originally reported by Robert B. Zajonc, "Attitudinal Effects of Mere Exposure," *Journal of Personality and Social Psychology*, Monograph Supplement, Part 2, June, 1968, 1-27, and confirmed in other contexts. Repetition apparently increases attraction even for initially disliked stimuli: see Allen Bukoff and Donald Elman, "Repeated Exposure to Liked and Disliked Social Stimuli," *Journal of Social Psychology* 107 (1979):133-134.

10. To reassure yourself that you can do the job, look at some of the books and magazines on management in your local library. As I read them, their essential advice comes straight from the cracker barrel. For one notable case in point, see Marshall Loeb, "A Guide to Taking Charge," in *Time*, February 25, 1980, p. 82, and compare with the Cheever quotation opening

chapter 7. On the other hand, it's sobering to realize that those who wield massive corporate power may pound-for-pound be no wiser than anyone else.

11. But it's not wise to overbudget deliberately either. This is because work spreads to fill the time available for its completion (Parkinson's Law); because if you think you can reach your goal in less time, you are more likely to; and because if you really convinced yourself that the work would take double or triple your original time estimate to complete, you might not get involved in the first place.

12. In another category of overdelegation, somewhat less common in community change work, group meeting time is actually rare; job assignments are clearly spelled out and distributed, but there is a lack of centralized coordination or authority to monitor progress.

13. For example, see A. Paul Hare, *Handbook of Small Group Research*, 2nd ed. (New York: Free Press, 1976), chaps. 14 and 15 ff.

14. Use of the mail has its own professional literature (see bibliography). But what works generally may not work in your particular situation; that's why it may repay you to experiment.

CHAPTER 6

1. Not just community activities either, but change programs on virtually any scale. Cf. ". . . Most ameliorative programs end up with *no* interpretable evaluation." In Donald T. Campbell, "Reforms as Experiments," *American Psychologist* 24 (1969):409-429. Quote from p. 409 (emphasis in original).

2. A fixed percentage, or even a rule of thumb, is hard to assign. Yet 5 percent of total time for formal evaluation should not be an excessive figure for most established programs, while a higher figure might be more appropriate for new ones.

3. "Almost always" instead of "always," since some activities are intended to right an undesirable intervention or preserve the status quo (cf. the discussion of "reactive programs" in chapter 5). But even these activities need to be evaluated, their general goal being the absence of change or the reversion to an original situation.

4. On a broader level, cf. B. F. Skinner, "Survival is the only value according to which a culture is eventually to be judged . . ." *Beyond Freedom and Dignity* (New York: Alfred A. Knopf, 1972), p. 136.

5. We can add several more layers of complexity. In general, support in any subcategory can be (a) either spontaneous, or solicited by the program; (b) either assessed in terms of the number or the percentage of supportive references from a specified population; or (c) assessed in terms of the references' estimated degree of favorability.

6. The distinction between product and process is not always sharp. For example, awareness, support, attendance, or participation (#2-5 in text) could be treated as processes rather than as products if the program had only a narrowly defined external goal. In hard-science projects, where a typical goal is the creation or alteration of a certain substance, that line of

thinking holds up well. But in community work, awareness, support, and the like are often hoped-for end-states of an intervention, and so can appropriately be viewed as products.

7. As a corollary, evaluation data collected at different time periods should be collected in the same way, using the same techniques, so that fair comparisons can be made. Often, however, no prior evaluation data exist, and your comparison base may then be implicit. If you start a new program which generates 50 participants, and if you know that no one had participated before, then you may legitimately describe a change from zero to 50. Participation data should then continue to be monitored in the future.

8. This is a general form. It's deliberately complex, almost outlandishly so, yet it's still oversimplified in some ways. In practice, only the smallest percentage of community workers or organizations even attempt evaluation in such a systematic way. The chapter thesis is that they should—really. The form here is intended more as an illustration than as a proposed model. For any program you engage in, a customized form could be designed, very possibly a simpler one, but one which would have genuine practicality for you.

9. The program descriptions and evaluations in this and the following two case examples come from experiences within my own prior work unit. The people who put these programs together, and who deserve credit for program successes, were Kathy Desilets, Ann Donnelly, Lauren Flewelling, Gayle Lagana, Rick Schmid, and Kay Shamp.

10. As for the evaluation form itself, it was a justifiable if unremarkable start for a one-page form, and it shouldn't have been much longer. It could have had a space for course name and date, brief instructions and a thank you, and some more quantitative questions with more response alternatives. But this is an adequate first approximation.

11. The *concept* of the support group leader training program, the idea of training people to train other people and to join in self-help networks is in my opinion an excellent one, a prime example of what social agencies should be doing across the board. But this of course is a separate issue from the evaluation of the actual program as given.

12. Ideally, training and control groups should have been randomly assigned. Also, the control group might have received the training at a later point in time, to give it the opportunity of possible benefit from the program.

13. Questions paraphrased and responses combined over all presentations. Seventy-four, or 83 percent of the evaluation forms were returned. Blank answers not included. Repeat attenders answered the same questions more than once.

14. A fully adequate treatment of research designs in evaluations, with their associated pitfalls, is beyond the scope of this chapter. The interested reader is referred to any current text on social research methods. See also bibliography.

15. Bias affects the evaluator as well. It's even harder to tell yourself that, based on your evaluation, your own program is no good. Yet bias can

cut another way; if you as participant falsely tell an evaluator that the program was helpful to you, it's possible that you might come to believe that it was.

16. Those placing great store in long-term "ripple effects" of interventions ought to be aware of the problems in measuring physical ripples.

17. For a catalog of types of indirect evidence and a discussion of their use, see Eugene L. Webb et al., *Nonreactive Measures in the Social Sciences*, 2nd. ed. (Boston: Houghton Mifflin, 1981).

18. Donald Campbell, "Reforms as Experiments," p. 409.

CHAPTER 7

1. John Cheever, *Falconer* (New York: Alfred A. Knopf, 1977), pp. 95-96. Reprinted by permission.

2. One may employ technique to give the *appearance* of conviction, or other personal qualities, often quite successfully. This fact itself points to the desirability of the personal quality in question. Moreover, with practice, the "apparent" quality may become real, embedded in the person.

3. This may be in part because behavioral scientists of the past generation have placed more emphasis on studying social determinants of social phenomena, having previously failed to find personality-trait explanations. The role of personal factors in events as complex as social interventions accordingly became downplayed.

4. A definitional note: "Personal qualities" as used here refers to personality traits or dimensions, deep-seated characteristics of the person. Personal qualities appear across the full range of life situations, as contrasted with technique, whose display is generally more restricted. A closely related term is "style," or "personal style," which has somewhat more verve, but which suggests a grafted-on behavior, as distinct from one's "natural self."

5. "Other variables" also determine intervention success. These include the credibility of the change agent and a battery of environmental factors outside the change agent's direct control. "Credibility" is mentioned later on in this chapter, but no effort is made here to list, much less to weight, all factors which influence outcome.

6. See for example Edwin P. Hollander, *Leadership Dynamics* (New York: The Free Press, 1978). Hollander expresses the popular "interactionist" position: Behavior is a joint function of the person and the situation.

7. Of course, a similar argument could be traced out for technique, substituting "techniques" for personal qualities in the table. For that matter, the argument applies to any field of social science. We introduce the argument in the first place to remind the reader that community change work cannot be reduced entirely to formulas. Continued research investigations are essential. But in the absence of hard information, the change agent needs to act on the best information available, however imperfect.

8. Some entry points to this work are review chapters in the *Annual Review of Psychology*. On source variables in attitude change, see for

example Alice H. Eagly and Samuel Himmelfarb, "Attitudes and Opinions," in *Annual Review of Psychology*, Vol. 29 (Palo Alto, Calif.: Annual Reviews, Inc., 1978), pp. 517-554. On therapist variables in psychotherapy, see Beverly Gomes-Schwartz et al., "Individual Psychotherapy and Behavior Therapy," 29 (1978): 435-471. On organizational development, see Terence R. Mitchell, "Organizational Behavior," 30 (1979):243-281. And on leadership style, see Alvin Zander, "The Psychology of Group Processes," 30 (1979):417-451.

9. Be aware that these qualities are not necessarily the same as qualities of leadership. The change agent may seek to lead, but will often actively avoid that role. In any case, success at interventions requires more than simple leadership ability.

10. Another option, of course, is to join persons of different but complementary qualities together into the same work group. This is often highly desirable, and sometimes necessary. But it's not always feasible, or cost-effective, and it's not a substitute for developing personal qualities on an individual level.

11. For a recent review of research trends, see John C. Masters, "Developmental Psychology," in *Annual Review of Psychology*, Vol. 32 (Palo Alto, Calif.: Annual Reviews, Inc., 1981), pp. 117-151.

12. It would be interesting and not inordinately difficult to test such a training model in practice, within an experimental framework, and to assess the results.

13. A parallel aim of the professional school should be to extend part of its instruction to the community it serves. Community people could then *also* learn about those technical skills and personal qualities which might make them better parents, neighbors, and sources of support for each other.

14. This finding is persistent in the literature; for obvious reasons, professionals have not accepted it with full seriousness. For a sample review, see Joseph A. Durlak, "Comparative Effectiveness of Paraprofessional and Professional Helpers," *Psychological Bulletin* 86 (1979):80-92.

CHAPTER 8

1. Cf. "In order to know anything, we must somehow give up the aspiration of knowing everything . . ." From Robert Oppenheimer, cited by Jerome S. Bruner, "Social Psychology and Perception," in Eleanor E. Maccoby et al., eds., *Readings in Social Psychology* (New York: Henry Holt, 1958), pp. 85-94. Quote from p. 86.

2. Paraphrased from p. 358 of Maslow, *Motivation and Personality*.

3. Amitai Etzioni, "Toward a Theory of Guided Societal Change," *Social Science Quarterly* 50 (1969):749-754. Quote from p. 749.

4. Psychologists will recognize this relationship as taking the form of the classical psychophysical curve, $S = k \log R$, where the response is a logarithmic function of the stimulus. Strictly speaking, in this example the first few

hours of effort yield no direct return at all, since they are spent in preparation rather than contact. But the principle of diminishing returns still holds.

5. Some interesting extensions of this principle, bearing on this example, are found in Alan Lakein's *How To Get Control of Your Time and Your Life* (New York: New American Library, 1974). For example, "80 percent of the value is often gained during the first 20 percent of your work time on a certain task" (p. 98). See also Lakein on the "80/20 Rule," in his chapter 10.

6. These two examples are oversimplified for purposes of illustration. We assume here that total production (or quality of product) increases proportionately with effort expended, and also that effort can be adequately represented by time on the job. Moreover, though the situations described by Figures 8 and 9 are among the most common, other graphical relationships—for example, linear, or bell-shaped—are possible. In those cases, the underlying question of whether the extra effort is justified by the results would still apply. Only if the relationship were positively accelerating, with an extra unit of effort yielding increasingly greater units of results, would reservation about "extra effort" be difficult. But I'm not aware of any realistic community situation which fits this description.

7. Or in more quantitative terms, how do you maximize your total number of "impact points"? And what evidence will you use to support your answer?

8. Cf. Alinsky, *Rules for Radicals*, "The marriage record of organizers is with rare exception disastrous" (p. 65).

9. And in extreme cases the change agent may die an early death. Meyer Friedman and Ray H. Rosenman, in *Type A Behavior and Your Heart* (New York: Alfred A. Knopf, 1974), were among the first to report that people who feel an overpowering and unrelenting need to keep accomplishing more in less time are more likely to experience cardiac disease and shortened life expectancy.

10. For example, Cary Cherniss, *Professional Burnout in Human Service Organizations* (New York: Praeger, 1980); Jerry Edelwich, with Archie Brodsky, *Burn-Out: Stages of Disillusionment in the Helping Professions* (New York: Human Sciences Press, 1980); Herbert J. Freudenberger, with Geraldine Richelson, *Burn-Out: The High Cost of High Achievement* (Garden City, N.Y.: Anchor Press, 1980); and Ayala Pines and Elliot Aronson, with Ditsa Kafry, *Burnout: From Tedium to Personal Growth* (New York: The Free Press, 1980)—all published in 1980 alone. Cf. also the recently burgeoning popular and professional literature on managerial stress in both men and women.

The causes of burnout, stress, and related phenomena can go beyond simple overwork. Poor working conditions, especially lack of social support on the job, can be another major contributing factor. The fundamental misalignment of many helping organizations vis-à-vis actual community needs can also topple many professionals' faith in meaningful social change.

11. *The Way of Life According to Laotzu* (New York: Capricorn Books, 1962), pp. 41 and 43 (from sayings 26 and 29).

12. Luke 11:9.

13. *New York Times Book Review,* April 4, 1976, p. 5. Here Gornick is reviewing a biography of Werner Erhard, the founder of est.

CHAPTER 9

1. For gasoline price and consumption data, see *Monthly Energy Review,* February, 1981, pp. 77 and 36 respectively. For highway travel, see Paul V. Svercl, "Highway Travel Trends during the 1970's," Office of Highway Planning, Federal Highway Administration, U.S. Department of Transportation, July, 1980, pp. 3-6 ff. (though with temporary price stabilization, vehicle travel began to rise in 1981, as noted in the Federal Highway Administration's *Traffic Volume Trends,* February, 1981). For poll data, see *Gallup Opinion Index,* September, 1979, pp. 25-26.

2. On domestic production outlooks, see for example Robert Stobaugh and Daniel Yergin, eds., *Energy Future* (New York: Ballantine Books, 1980), pp. 287 ff. See also National Research Council, National Academy of Sciences, *Energy in Transition 1985-2010* (San Francisco: W. H. Freeman and Company, 1980), pp. 2 ff.

3. U.S. Bureau of the Census, *Historical Statistics,* p. 340. However, social welfare expenditures as a percent of all government expenditures (a different indicator) began their steepest climb only after 1960. See chapter 1, note 12, and other data cited in chapter 1.

4. Not all people live in conventionally-defined neighborhoods, particularly people in rural areas. However, over 70% of the population does live within metropolitan areas (see U.S. Bureau of the Census, *Statistical Abstract,* p. 17, Table 20). And people living in small towns qualify under a broad definition.

5. In addition, more jobs will be part-time and at flexible hours. However, this and other community-based trends may be partially offset by a greater percentage of people attempting to enter the paid labor force, or to secure an additional paying job.

6. This analysis again draws on Maslow, *Motivation and Personality.* Maslow viewed motive patterns as a series of concentric circles, basic physiological motives such as eating and sleeping at the center, surrounded by motives (circles) representing safety/security, love, esteem, and self-actualization, moving successively from center to periphery. Each new motive pattern emerges only after the motive one step closer in has been largely satisfied. Consequently, when safety and security motives are predominant, less life energy is available for investment in "love" and other areas farther from the center.

7. The idea that cooperation is biologically adaptive has Darwinian roots, amplified and elaborated by the Russian naturalist and political philosopher Peter Kropotkin in *Mutual Aid* (1902).

8. Karl Hess, *Community Technology* (New York: Harper & Row, 1979), p. 42.

9. A less structured variation of this concept is the skills file. Here, parti-

cipants simply register their skills in a central location. While they should be responsive to requests, they have less skill-sharing obligation than in a more formal membership organization.

10. One example here is the Tel-Med Program, where any person may call to hear one of several hundred medically approved tapes on health-related topics ranging from headaches to heart attacks. Similar programs supply tape-recorded mental health and legal information.

11. A central-intake hotline could also make it easier for a potential client to call. Many people needing services don't know where to turn: one well-publicized, stigma-free phone number would make searching around less necessary and should weaken some of the obstacles to seeking help.

12. We have a long way to go toward knowing our neighbors, according to data presented by Angus Campbell, *The Sense of Well-Being in America*, p. 244.

13. H. D. F. Kitto, *The Greeks* (Baltimore: Penguin Books, 1951), p. 37.

14. The design principles described by Jane Jacobs in *The Death and Life of Great American Cities* (New York: Vintage, 1961) are still cogent. See also any of several recent books on environmental or urban psychology.

15. There are more partners and roles than just these two. But to simplify subsequent discussion, "individuals" will include community groups, ad hoc coalitions, private citizens in general; "agencies" will include professional organizations and other institutions charged with serving the public.

16. The same classification can be applied to economic supports. In addition, each of the four classifications can be subdivided by each of the four physical locations previously discussed, thus generating 16 possibilities.

17. In one survey I helped conduct in the Lowell area, 6 percent of 500 randomly-sampled residents said they presently belonged to a support or self-help group; 11 percent expressed interest in joining one.

18. Professionals themselves should get this training in their own schooling. Specifically, human service administrators are too often forced to learn planning and management skills on the job. More administratively oriented professional-school training would have definite positive effects on agency service efficiency.

19. Durlak, "Comparative Effectiveness of Paraprofessional and Professional Helpers," p. 80. This quotation summarizes a review of 42 outcome studies.

Bibliography

This bibliography aims to help the community worker become more effective. It's organized around sometimes-overlapping topic areas, including most of the main chapter headings in this book, plus some others. Each topic area has several annotated entries. The topic areas are:

Agencies/Helping Services   Needs Assessment
Attitude/Behavior Change   Neighborhoods/Communities
Community Organizing   Planning
Ethics   Printing/Graphics
Evaluation   Publicity/Marketing
Fund Raising/Grant Writing   Research Methods/Statistics
Future Prospects   Self-help
General Sourcebooks   Series
Groups and Group Dynamics   Specialized Programs
Leadership   Support Systems
Management   Teaching/Training
Miscellaneous

A section on Organizations follows these topic area listings.

The emphasis here is on materials with the greatest potential value to the small-scale, nonprofessional community worker. Generally speaking, the bibliography places more stress on practical utility, on "how-to," than the text. Good scholarship and factual accuracy remain as important criteria for inclusion, but special attention is also paid here to general availability, easy readability, artful style, and reasonable price. For these reasons, journal articles, advanced textbooks, and other technical materials written primarily for the specialist are normally not cited. The entries are obviously selective, since a complete listing would fill a book at least this size. So keep in mind that personal bias has undoubtedly influenced choice as well.

Literature on community change will probably continue to accumulate at an accelerating rate. Even now, there are dozens of good sources for most topics listed here. And especially in this field, much good literature is written by hometown activists for local use; it's produced cheaply, is distributed narrowly, goes out of print quickly, and never reaches a national audience. You may therefore know some excellent sources the rest of us have never heard of. That is fine. Exactly where you start is not crucial; the main point is to get started.

Materials listed below are at this writing in print and available in paperback unless otherwise noted. A few of them should be ordered directly from the publisher; the publisher's address is then given under the "Organizations" heading following the bibliography. In these cases, it's wise to write first for price and availability information, since both are subject to change. The following symbols also accompany some entries:

B = includes an extensive bibliography particularly relevant to community change
F = single copies are currently free on request
H =currently available in hardcover only
O =currently out of print (may be found in good libraries)
P = should be ordered directly from publisher
* = especially recommended for utility, presentation, or both

AGENCIES/HELPING SERVICES

Dugger, James G. *The New Professional: An Introduction for Human Service Workers.* 2nd ed. Monterey, Calif.: Brooks/Cole, 1980. (H)
   One of several general introductory-level texts for the potential human service worker.

Ehrenreich, Barbara, and John Ehrenreich. "The Professional-Managerial Class." *Radical America*, 11, no. 2 (1977): 7-31.
   A journal article, notable here for its thesis postulating a "Professional-Managerial Class" which exists only through the expropriation of the skills and culture once belonging to the working class.

Freudenberger, Herbert J., with Geraldine Richelson. *Burn-Out: The High Cost of High Achievement.* Garden City, N.Y.: Anchor Press, 1980. (H)
   One of many recent books outlining causes and proposing cures. This nonscholarly account, written by a psychoanalyst, features a variety of case histories.

†Gaylin, Willard, Ira Glasser, Steven Marcus, and David J. Rothman. *Doing Good: The Limits of Benevolence.* New York: Pantheon, 1978.
   Four diverse historical and philosophical essays focusing on the limits of government social intervention, the gray areas between benevolence and coerciveness, and the rights and obligations of the individual vs. the state.

Kamerman, Sheila B., and Alfred J. Kahn. *Social Services in the United States: Policies and Programs.* Philadelphia: Temple University Press, 1976.
   A traditional text, not overly lively, but giving a good overview of the

---

†For paperback books, dates given are those of the most recent paperback edition.

American social service system in the mid-1970s. Has considerable detail on services for children and the aged.

Ryan, William. *Blaming the Victim.* New York: Random House, 1976.

Blaming the victim is an alternative (and cheaper) response to social problems, as compared to removing adverse social conditions. Ryan documents this thesis with special reference to black poverty.

ATTITUDE/BEHAVIOR CHANGE

Carnegie, Dale. *How to Win Friends and Influence People.* New York: Simon and Schuster, 1977.

"Six Ways to Make People Like You." "Twelve Ways to Win People to Your Way of Thinking." A classic (1936), dated, hokey, and Horatio-Alger to an extreme; but when all is said and done, the wisdom of the ages.

Fisher, Roger, and William Ury. *Getting to Yes: Negotiating Agreement without Giving In.* Boston: Houghton Mifflin, 1981.

A practical, evidence-based manual, describing easily-understood negotiating techniques and giving case examples.

Mehrabian, Albert. *Tactics of Social Influence.* Englewood Cliffs, N.J.: Prentice-Hall, 1970.

A simple and elegant presentation of how to change behavior through social reinforcement principles. Argues that if behavior is changed first, attitude change will follow. Numerous applications to everyday situations.

*Zimbardo, Philip G., Ebbe G. Ebbesen, and Christina Maslach. *Influencing Attitudes and Changing Behavior: An Introduction to Method, Theory, and Applications of Social Control and Personal Power.* 2nd ed. Reading, Mass.: Addison-Wesley, 1977. (B)

A particularly well-written book, full of principles and real-life examples. Stresses applications of laboratory research. Postscript C, "On Becoming a Social Change Agent," is outstanding.

COMMUNITY ORGANIZING

Alderson, George, and Everett Sentman. *How You Can Influence Congress: The Complete Handbook for the Citizen Lobbyist.* New York: E. P. Dutton, 1979.

A very thorough book on one specialized form of organizing. Especially comprehensive on legislative campaigns and on working with one's congressman. Largely national emphasis, but much transferability to local situations.

*Alinsky, Saul D. *Rules for Radicals: A Pragmatic Primer for Realistic Radicals.* New York: Vintage, 1972.

A brash, irreverent, provocative book by a nationally known organizer. Not just for "radicals," but for anyone interested in community change.

Emphasizes large-scale organizing of the poor. Strong on power acquisition and on confrontational techniques.

Kahn, Si. *Organizing: A Guide for Grassroots Leaders.* New York: McGraw-Hill, 1982.
A comprehensive, nuts-and-bolts organizing guide with a political-economic focus.

Neighborhood Development and Conservation Center. *Organize and Work Together: A Handbook for Block Captains.* Oklahoma City, Okla.: Author, no date. (P)
A short mimeographed publication on how to organize and operate a block club. Emphasis on crime prevention.

Simpson, Dick, and George Beam. *Strategies for Change: How to Make the American Political Dream Work.* Chicago: Swallow Press, 1976.   .
Local-level politics, Chicago-style. Specific ideas for developing ward organizations and executing campaigns. A nice complement to the Alderson and Sentman book above.

Strauss, Bert, and Mary E. Stowe. *How to Get Things Changed: A Handbook for Tackling Community Problems.* Garden City, N.Y.: Doubleday, 1974. (H, O)
Detailed and instructive case examples on a variety of community topics. Good appendices, with checklists and outlines.

Warren, Rachelle B., and Donald I. Warren. *The Neighborhood Organizer's Handbook.* Notre Dame, Ind.: University of Notre Dame Press, 1977.
Combination theory and practice book, with self-study exercises. Good on the neighborhood as a social entity and on diagnosis and classification of different neighborhood types.

ETHICS

Bok, Sissela. *Lying: Moral Choice in Public and Private Life.* New York: Vintage, 1979.
Discusses different types of lies and their consequences. Proposes strategies for increasing truth-telling. Plentiful, though indirect applications to community work.

Dyck, Arthur J. *On Human Care: An Introduction to Ethics.* Nashville, Tenn.: Abingdon, 1977.
A basic survey of contemporary ethical issues. Dyck's chapter on the moral requisites of community is especially relevant to concerns in this book.

London, Perry. *Behavior Control.* 2nd ed. New York: New American Library, 1977. (B)
Covers the history of behavior control, current control technology (e.g., psychotherapy, electronic techniques), the ethics of control, and prospects for future control.

EVALUATION

Posavac, Emil J., and Raymond G. Carey. *Program Evaluation: Method and Case Studies.* Englewood Cliffs, N.J.: Prentice-Hall, 1980. (H)
A comprehensive textbook which details evaluation designs for larger-scale programs. Also devotes space to the social climate of evaluation.

Weiss, Carol H. *Evaluation Research: Methods of Assessing Program Effectiveness.* Englewood Cliffs, N.J.: Prentice-Hall, 1972.
A shorter and simpler alternative to the Posavac and Carey book.

Weiss, Carol H., ed. *Evaluating Action Programs: Readings in Social Action and Education.* Boston: Allyn and Bacon, 1972. (B)
This book of readings is notable both for its perceptiveness and its intellectual honesty in treating the difficulties of evaluating social programs. Deals mostly with large-scale programs, but has easy application to smaller ones.

FUND RAISING/GRANT WRITING

Ardman, Perry, and Harvey Ardman. *The Women's Day Book of Fund Raising.* New York: St. Martin's Press, 1980. (B, H)
A general-audience book describing specific fund-raising events and including sections on mail and phone solicitation.

Donahue, Dan, Don Levitan, George McDowell, and Christine Newell. *The Federal Granting System: A Guide for Local Governments in Massachusetts.* Amherst, Mass.: Cooperative Extension Service, University of Massachusetts, 1978. (Order from Bulletin Center, Cottage A, Thatcher Way, University of Massachusetts, Amherst, Mass. 01003.) (B, P)
Excellent short summary on proposal writing, written by experts. Gives many grant information resources, and indicates how a proposal is reviewed. Single copies free to Massachusetts residents. Applicable to out-of-state users.

*Flanagan, Joan. *The Grass Roots Fundraising Book.* 2nd ed. Chicago: Contemporary Books, 1982. (B)
Describes low-budget community fund-raising events. Divided into beginners, intermediate, and "big-time" categories. Many specific examples.

Hillman, Howard. *The Art of Winning Corporate Grants.* New York: Vanguard Press, 1980. (H)
Approaching the private sector – an area neglected in many fund-raising books, but one slated for increased attention.

Smith, Craig W., and Eric W. Skjei. *Getting Grants.* New York: Harper & Row, 1981. (B)
A good general book with an encouraging tone and many specimen examples.

*U.S. Department of Housing and Urban Development, Office of Neighborhoods, Voluntary Associations, and Consumer Protection. *Funding*

Sources for Neighborhood Groups. Washington, D.C.: Author, 1980. (B, F, P)

Community development focus. Includes much how-to-organize as well as thorough funding information. Lists specific funding sources in both public and private sectors. Contains many references not easily found elsewhere.

*U.S. Department of Housing and Urban Development, Office of Neighborhoods, Voluntary Associations, and Consumer Protection. *Neighborhood Oriented Programs of the Federal Government: A Compendium of Funding and Technical Assistance Resources for Neighborhood Organizations*. 2d ed. Washington, D.C.: Author, 1980. (F, P)

A catalog of relevant federal programs as of 1980, with a brief description of each. Keyed mostly to larger-scale community programs.

Warner, Irving R. *The Art of Fund Raising*. New York: Harper & Row, 1975. (H)

A more reflective book, with much general wisdom, but fewer how-to's. Geared more toward larger fund-raising drives. Has a nice event checklist at end of book.

FUTURE PROSPECTS

*Barnet, Richard J. *The Lean Years: Politics in the Age of Scarcity*. New York: Simon and Schuster, 1982.

Since our economic and social future will depend on adequate physical resources, the community worker should be acquainted with projected resource outlooks. Barnet's outlook – bleak and well-argued – documents projected scarcities in energy, water, minerals, and food, and their anticipated effects on political, economic, and social life.

*Johnson, Warren. *Muddling toward Frugality: A Blueprint for Survival in the 1980s*. Boulder, Colo.: Shambala, 1979.

A probing analysis of the future from an environmentalist point of view. Much discussion of the economic and social consequences of modern technology. Optimistic despite its call for a more frugal (more resource-conscious) lifestyle. A beautifully written book; highly recommended.

Sale, Kirkpatrick. *Human Scale*. New York: Coward, McCann & Geoghegan, 1980. (H)

An expansion of Schumacher's small-is-beautiful thesis into all avenues of society. A large book, original, dense, and well-documented.

Schumacher, E. F. *Small is Beautiful: Economics as if People Mattered*. New York: Harper & Row, 1975.

An eloquent call for an economic order starting with what's best for people, not for larger institutions. This highly influential book argues for smaller, more decentralized, more self-sufficient economic units.

Skinner, B. F. *Walden Two*. New York: Macmillan, 1948. (O)

Skinner's utopian novel of a small community guided by behavioristic principles. Makes for an interesting comparison with the communities described elsewhere in this bibliography by Sidel and Zablocki. Which comes closest to where you would want to live?

Stobaugh, Robert, and Daniel Yergin, eds. *Energy Future: Report of the Energy Project at the Harvard Business School.* New York: Ballantine Books, 1980.

A comprehensive, detailed, but accessible overview of the energy outlook, with strong recommendations for conservation and the development of solar energy.

GENERAL SOURCEBOOKS

*Brand, Stewart, ed. *The Next Whole Earth Catalog.* 2nd ed. New York: Random House, 1981. (B)

A true catalog of tools, physical and otherwise, for self-sufficiency and personal power. The emphasis is on soft technology, but sections on Community, Politics, and Communications also repay close reading. Cf. also *CoEvolution Quarterly,* a journal covering much the same territory, published by the same group.

*Carlson, Karin. *New York Self Help Handbook: A Step by Step Guide to Neighborhood Improvement Projects.* New York: The Citizens Committee for New York City, Inc., 1977. (P)

The subtitle is accurate; 100 projects in varied service areas set out in step-by-step form. Based on specific successful examples.

*Coover, Virginia, Ellen Deacon, Charles Esser, and Christopher Moore. *Resource Manual for a Living Revolution.* Philadelphia: New Society Press [Movement for a New Society], 1977. (B, P)

Covers a lot of ground: the theoretical basis for change, personal growth, working in groups, running workshops, support communities, organizing for institutional change. Contains many individual and group awareness-building exercises.

Freundlich, Paul, Chris Collins, and Mikki Wenig. *A Guide to Cooperative Alternatives.* New Haven, Conn. and Louisa, Va.: Community Publications Cooperative, 1979.

Contains chapters on food, housing, economics, health, family life, energy, community organizing, communications, politics, etc., each chapter with essays and resource listings of cooperative and alternative groups nationwide.

*Trecker, Audrey R., and Harleigh B. Trecker. *Handbook of Community Service Projects.* New York: Association Press, 1960. (B, H, O)

A 500-page book with examples of 850 successful club projects in 28 different content areas. An excellent idea-starter, nicely cross-indexed. Also has a good general introduction on how to organize and operate a community program. Out of print now, but worth looking for.

U.S. Department of Housing and Urban Development, Office of Neighborhoods, Voluntary Associations, and Consumer Protection. *Neighborhood Self-Help Case Studies: Abstracts of Reports on Revitalization Projects Funded by the Office of Neighborhood Self-Help Development.* Washington, D.C.: Author, 1980. (F, P)

Fifty-four summaries of neighborhood projects, mostly in housing rehabilitation and economic development. Up to three full-length case studies may be obtained free on request. Also lists well-established neighborhood organizations in appendix.

*U.S. Office of Consumer Affairs, Consumer Information Division. *People Power: What Communities Are Doing to Counter Inflation.* Washington, D.C.: Author, 1980. (Order from Consumer Information Center, under "Organizations.") (B, F, P)

Four long sections on food, housing, energy, and health. A great many program examples and places to write for further information. Well-illustrated and fully referenced. An outstanding publication.

Washington Consulting Group, Inc. *Uplift: What People Themselves Can Do.* Salt Lake City: Olympus Publishing Co., 1974.

One hundred case histories of varied self-help projects undertaken mostly by the urban poor.

*"Women's Magazines" (*McCall's, Ms., Women's Day*)

Draw your own conclusions from the fact that a primary (the best?) source of regularly appearing information on community support ideas comes from "women's magazines." *McCall's* "Survival in the Suburbs" column (not just for suburbanites) stands out. The *"Ms. Gazette"* ("Making Change") in *Ms.* and "Neighbors" feature in *Women's Day* are also both valuable and current.

GROUPS AND GROUP DYNAMICS

*Auvine, Brian, Betsy Densmore, Mary Extrom, Scott Poole, and Michel Shanklin. *A Manual for Group Facilitators.* Madison, Wisc.: Center for Conflict Resolution, 1977. (B, P)

A comprehensive manual dealing with virtually all aspects of group process. Consensus-oriented. Includes special group techniques, material on evaluation of meetings, and a trouble-shooting guide.

Fulcher, Claire, and Mary Grefe. *Techniques for Organizational Effectiveness.* Washington, D.C.: American Association of University Women, 1978. (P)

Establishes group dynamics principles by presentation of more than two dozen exercises. Also good on workshop planning models.

Hereford, Carl F. *Organizing Group Discussions.* Austin, Tex.: Hogg Foundation for Mental Health, 1961. (F, P)

A short pamphlet summarizing basic points on organizing and facilitating. Emphasizes discussions centered around educational programs.

Meacham, William. *Human Development Training Manual.* Austin, Tex.:
    Human Development Training, 1980. (P)
A mimeographed booklet on communications, meeting skills, decision-
making, leadership. Highly concentrated and to-the-point.

LEADERSHIP

Cheavens, Frank. *Leading Group Discussions.* Austin, Tex.: Hogg Founda-
    tion for Mental Health, 1958. (F, P)
Discusses starting, stopping, silent or overtalkative members, lulls in the
action, side conversations, maximizing participation. A good beginning
pamphlet.

*Lawson, John, Leslie Griffin, and Franklyn Donant. *Leadership Is Every-
    body's Business: A Practical Guide for Volunteer Membership Groups.* San
    Luis Obispo, Calif.: Impact Publishers, 1976.
An excellent starting point for community-group leaders and members
too. Much emphasis on structure – agenda-setting, conducting the meeting,
delegating to committees, building participation between meetings. Well-
designed and pleasant to read.

National Committee for Citizens in Education. *Developing Leadership for
    Parent/Citizen Groups.* Columbia, Md.: Author, no date. (P)
A short handbook with a school-related orientation.

Schul, Bill D. *How to Be an Effective Group Leader.* Chicago: Nelson-Hall,
    1975.
A straightforward, nontechnical discussion for the inexperienced leader.
Lots of examples and problem-solving strategies.

MANAGEMENT

Brandow, Karen, Jim McDonnell, and Vocations for Social Change. *No
    Bosses Here: A Manual on Working Collectively and Cooperatively.* 2d ed.
    Boston: Vocations for Social Change, 1981. (P)
An honest treatment of consensual decision-making, hirings, firings,
salaries, and other issues in collective work situations. Also discusses relationships between collectives and social change. Appendices contain basic
bookkeeping, pricing, and legal information.

Caplow, Theodore. *How to Run Any Organization: A Manual of Practical
    Sociology.* New York: Holt, Rinehart and Winston, 1977.
Tough-minded advice on authority, communication, productivity,
morale, and change, for paid or unpaid managers, from an academic
sociologist.

Connors, Tracy Daniel, ed. *The Nonprofit Organization Handbook.* New
    York: McGraw-Hill, 1980. (H)
A reference book for the agency administrator or advanced reader. Ency-

clopedic in scope. Includes sections on tax exemption, fiscal management, revenue, resources, public relations, planning, leadership, daily operations.

Hummel, Joan. *Starting and Running a Nonprofit Organization.* Minneapolis: University of Minnesota Press, 1980. (B)

Covers many of the same topics as Connors and Wolfe, in this section. About midway between them in complexity. Good sections on bylaws, boards of directors, legal aspects.

Lakein, Alan. *How to Get Control of Your Time and Your Life.* New York: New American Library, 1974.

Management of personal time, with hints on planning, scheduling, list-making, and especially prioritizing into "A," "B," and "C" tasks. Possibly heavy-handed for some, but definitely useful. One of many popular books in its field.

Mathiasen, Karl III. *The Board of Directors of Nonprofit Organizations.* Washington, D.C.: Planning and Management Assistance Project, 1977. (B, F, P)

A short booklet of use to current and prospective board members.

Phillips, Michael, and Salli Rasberry. *Honest Business: A Superior Strategy for Starting and Managing Your Own Business.* San Francisco: Clear Glass Publishing Co., and New York: Random House, 1981.

Small community businesses, say the authors, should provide community service in the broad sense of the term; by doing so, they will be in the self-interest both of the community and the individual entrepreneur.

Sperry, Len, Douglas J. Mickelson, and Phillip L. Hunsaker. *You Can Make It Happen: A Guide to Self-Actualization and Organizational Change.* Reading, Mass.: Addison-Wesley, 1977.

Lists a variety of strategies for both personal and institutional change. An unusual mix. Emphasizes organization development principles, and focuses on the individual within the institutional (largely business) system.

Wolfe, Joan. *Making Things Happen: The Guide for Members of Volunteer Organizations.* Andover, Mass.: Brick House Publishing Co., 1981.

A basic discussion of management principles applied to volunteer groups.

MISCELLANEOUS

Muggeridge, Malcolm. *Something Beautiful for God: Mother Teresa of Calcutta.* New York: Ballantine Books, 1973.

A sketch of and interview with the former winner of the Nobel Peace Prize for her work with the Indian poor. Especially instructive in describing the interplay of faith and action: if we fail to work for God's sake, "we may become only social workers."

Simple Living Collective (American Friends Service Committee, San Francisco). *Taking Charge: Achieving Personal and Political Change through*

Simple Living. New York: Bantam Books, 1977. (Order from American Friends Service Committee, under "Organizations.") (B, P)
A definition of and convincing argument for simple living, with practical applications to consuming, personal growth, community, children, clothing, health care, energy, food, and economics.

Slater, Philip E. *The Pursuit of Loneliness: American Culture at the Breaking Point.* rev. ed. Boston: Beacon Press, 1976.
A diagnosis of current malaise. In Slater's view, excessive individualism and competitive motivation lead to loneliness, a loss of community, and other negative social consequences.

Smith, David Horton, Jacqueline Macaulay, and Associates. *Participation in Social and Political Activities: A Comprehensive Analysis of Political Involvement, Expressive Leisure Time, and Helping Behavior.* San Francisco: Jossey-Bass, 1980. (B, H)
A highly detailed sourcebook on the title topics. Reviews copious amounts of technical literature. Includes a 103-page (!) bibliography.

Social psychology and/or community psychology textbook.
No specific recommendations here, but a reading or review of one of many solid texts in each field will build upon existing factual knowledge.

NEEDS ASSESSMENT

Hertzberg, Joe. *Doing a Community Survey with Volunteer Help.* Portland, Ore.: Northwest District Association, 1979. (Order from Institute for Local Self-Reliance, under "Organizations.") (P)
A medium-length booklet emphasizing written questionnaires. Roughly keyed to the level of this book. Rigorous and thorough without being too technical. Many sample questions.

Orlich, Donald C. *Designing Sensible Surveys.* Pleasantville, N.Y.: Redgrave Publishing Co., 1978.
More sophisticated and more detailed than may be necessary for many community groups, but contains numerous borrowable examples.

Warheit, George J., Roger A. Bell, and John J. Schwab. *Needs Assessment Approaches: Concepts and Methods.* Rockville, Md.: National Institute of Mental Health, 1977. (F, P)
A relatively short, moderately technical manual which is very thorough on formal assessment methods for large target groups. Includes samples, and discussion of pre- and postassessment phases.

NEIGHBORHOODS/COMMUNITIES

Cassidy, Robert. *Livable Cities: A Grass-Roots Guide to Rebuilding Urban America.* New York: Holt, Rinehart and Winston, 1980. (B)
Focuses on neighborhood revitalization in central cities. Optimistic in

terms of what an individual or community group can do. Gives case studies. Has a particularly good bibliography.

Fischer, Claude S. *The Urban Experience*. New York: Harcourt Brace Jovanovich, 1976. (B)

A scholarly review of the social and psychological consequences of city life by a noted urban sociologist. Deemphasizes the role of neighborhoods, arguing that many people don't need them and do well without them.

Jacobs, Jane. *The Death and Life of Great American Cities*. New York: Vintage, 1961.

Jacobs was among the first to write about the support-building character of street life. Her insights and ideas on city planning are as cogent now as they were almost a generation ago.

Lingeman, Richard. *Small Town America: A Narrative History 1620–the Present*. New York: G. P. Putnam's Sons, 1981.

A rich source of the rise, decline, and rebirth (?) of small-town life, deftly illustrating the pros and cons of small-community living in the process.

*Morris, David, and Karl Hess. *Neighborhood Power: The New Localism*. Boston: Beacon Press, 1975. (B)

Political-economic emphasis. A more general precursor to Hess's *Community Technology*, listed further on.

National Commission on Neighborhoods. *People, Building Neighborhoods: Final Report to the President and the Congress of the United States*. Washington, D.C.: U.S. Government Printing Office, 1979. (P)

A presidential commission report. Stresses economic development, but has one long chapter on human services. Full of specific recommendations (38 pages of them in introduction alone). Also, two separate volumes of appendices.

Neighborhood Development and Conservation Center. *Neighborhood Notebook*. Oklahoma City, Okla.: Author, 1978. (P)

Newsletter-format, with a variety of neighborhood ideas.

Packard, Vance. *A Nation of Strangers*. New York: Simon and Schuster, 1974.

Commercial but well-researched sociology, with original data. Studies American mobility and transiency, and shows how they lead to uprootedness, disconnectedness, and fragmentation.

Shull, Jane. *On Your Own: A Guide to Neighborhood Self-Development*. Philadelphia: Institute for the Study of Civic Values, 1977. (P)

A manual focusing on community housing and economic development.

Social Policy magazine.

Has "Neighborhood Action" feature pages in recent bimonthly issues. Note also: Vol. 10, no. 2 (1979) is a special issue on organizing neighborhoods.

U.S. Department of Housing and Urban Development, Office of Neighborhoods, Voluntary Associations, and Consumer Protection. *Neighborhoods: A Self-Help Sampler.* Washington, D.C.: Author, 1980. (Order from U.S. Government Printing Office, under "Organizations.") (B, P) Case studies plus general organizational information. Stresses economic and housing development. Appendices list many relevant governmental and nonprofit organizations.

Zablocki, Benjamin D. *The Joyful Community: An Account of the Bruderhof, a Communal Movement Now in Its Third Generation.* Chicago: University of Chicago Press, 1980. An account of a religiously influenced communal society, founded in 1920, now based in America. Describes in depth how the community functions in daily practice, with materials on problem solving and decision making.

PLANNING

Larsen, Judith K. *Planning for Change.* Palo Alto, Calif.: American Institutes for Research, 1973. (P) A short pamphlet describing a change model including Ability, Values, Information, Circumstances, Timing, Obligation, Resistances, Yield–"A Victory."

Lauffer, Armand. *Social Planning at the Community Level.* Englewood Cliffs, N.J.: Prentice-Hall, 1978. (B, H) A comprehensive text, written from an agency point of view. See especially material on cost-benefit analysis. Also has much material on services for the elderly.

Rothman, Jack, John L. Erlich, and Joseph G. Teresa. *Promoting Innovation and Change in Organizations and Communities: A Planning Manual.* New York: John Wiley & Sons, 1976. (H) Offers specific research-based "action guidelines" for planning. Stresses formation of "bite-sized" plans and the use of planning logs. Much logbook material is presented here.

*Urban Systems Research & Engineering, Inc. *Neighborhood Planning Primer.* Washington, D.C.: U.S. Department of Housing and Urban Development, Office of Neighborhoods, Voluntary Associations and Consumer Protection, 1980. (B, P) Teaches how to assess needs and how to create and use a plan. Attractively designed. Includes several case studies.

Wheeler, Daniel D., and Irving L. Janis. *A Practical Guide for Making Decisions.* New York: Free Press, 1980. (H) Lots of itemized advice, drawn from combined experimental and social-psychological knowledge. Written at an intermediate level. Uses a Franklin-style balance sheet. Many case histories. Includes material on overcoming setbacks.

PRINTING/GRAPHICS

*Brigham, Nancy. *How to Do Leaflets, Newsletters and Newspapers.* Somerville, Mass.: New England Free Press, 1976. (Order from Urban Planning Aid, under "Organizations.") (P)

Describes different methods for reproducing copy. Also covers paste-up, layout, how to interview, write, and edit. Well-illustrated. A top-notch booklet.

Burke, Clifford. *Printing It: A Guide to Graphic Techniques for the Impecunious.* Berkeley, Calif.: Wingbow Press, 1972. (Order from Book People, 2940 7th St., Berkeley, Calif. 94710.) (P)

A thorough summary, stressing low-cost methods. Written so that a beginner could follow the presentation and move from helplessness to competence.

Pawlak, Vic. *How to Publish Community Information on an Impossibly Tight Budget.* Phoenix: Do It Now Foundation, 1976. (P)

An inexpensive, densely written pamphlet with a good overview of self-printing basics.

Urban Planning Aid. *Slide-Shows for Community Action.* Boston: Author, no date. (P)

A short how-to pamphlet, preceded by a rationale. Assumes only a very basic knowledge of photography.

PUBLICITY/MARKETING

Applebaum, Judith, and Nancy Evans. *How to Get Happily Published: A Complete and Candid Guide.* New York: Harper & Row, 1978. (B, H)

Written mostly for book and magazine writers (and excellent on those terms), but recommended here primarily for its section on self-publishing and for its long annotated bibliography on printing and publishing topics.

Cauble, Michelle. *Effective Promotion: A Guide to Low Cost Use of Media for Community Organizations.* Phoenix: Do It Now Foundation, 1977. (P)

A companion piece to Pawlak's pamphlet (see under "Printing"), this one focusing on mass media.

Klein, Ted, and Fred Danzig. *How to Be Heard: Making the Media Work for You.* New York: Macmillan, 1974. (H)

A basic, thorough, easy to read text.

Kotler, Philip. *Marketing for Nonprofit Organizations.* Englewood Cliffs, N.J.: Prentice-Hall, 1975. (H)

A serious text, at the top of its field, outlining the fundamentals of nonprofit marketing with many case examples.

National Committee Against Discrimination In Housing. *Media Action Handbook.* Washington, D.C.: Author, 1975. (P)

An intermediate-level booklet, geared more to TV and radio than print media.

Simon, Julian L. *How to Start and Operate a Mail-Order Business.* 3rd ed. New York: McGraw-Hill, 1981. (B, H)

Profit- and product-oriented, but very good on design of a direct mail piece, display ads, figuring out mailing costs. Emphasizes testing your techniques, and shows you how to do it.

Weaver, Ralph. *Media Access Guide.* Boston: Boston Community Media Council, Inc., no date. (Order from Urban Planning Aid, under "Organizations.") (P)

An inexpensive, basic, beginning-level guide to gaining access to newspapers and broadcasting.

RESEARCH METHODS/STATISTICS

Campbell, Donald T., and Julian C. Stanley. *Experimental and Quasi-Experimental Designs for Research.* Chicago: Rand McNally, 1966.

Probably the best short summary in its field. Highly technical, and not for the casual or beginning reader, but almost guaranteed to improve evaluation of programs if the main points are grasped.

Horwitz, Lucy, and Lou Ferleger. *Statistics for Social Change.* Boston: South End Press, 1980.

A beginning statistics text, distinguished by its exercises, examples, and interpretations drawn from real-life social change attempts.

Selltiz, Claire, Lawrence S. Wrightsman, and Stuart W. Cook. *Research Methods in Social Relations.* 3rd ed. New York: Holt, Rinehart and Winston, 1976.

One of many good texts on research methods, including detailed material on research design, questionnaires, interview techniques, and field observation procedures.

SELF-HELP

Evans, Glen. *The Family Circle Guide to Self-Help.* New York: Ballantine Books, 1979.

An overview written for the general audience. Includes self-help group case histories. Has comprehensive listings of national self-help organizations, and information on how to start a group of one's own.

Gartner, Alan, and Frank Riessman. *Help: A Working Guide to Self-Help Groups.* New York: New Viewpoints, 1979.

Discusses (a) how self-help groups can work more effectively; (b) the relationship betwen professionals and self-help groups; and (c) different types of self-help groups, with detailed listings. See also Gartner and Riessman's *Self-Help in the Human Services* (San Francisco: Jossey-Bass, 1977), geared more to agency staff.

Humm, Andy. *How to Organize a Self-Help Group*. New York: New York City Self-Help Clearinghouse, 1979. (Order from National Self-Help Clearinghouse, under "Organizations.") (B, P)
   A beginning organizational manual.

Kennedy, Eugene. *On Becoming a Counselor: A Basic Guide for Non-Professional Counselors*. New York: Continuum Publishing Corp., 1980.
   Written largely for professionals in other fields, but accessible to non-professionals as well. One of many similar books. Discusses types of emotional problems, emphasizes understanding, and gives both general and specific advice on helping.

SERIES

Adult Education Association of the United States of America. Leadership Pamphlet Series. Washington, D.C.: Author, various dates. (P)
   Sixteen short beginning-level pamphlets on leading discussions, training, role playing, supervision, volunteers, group dynamics, and related topics.

*Citizen Involvement Training Project. Project Manuals. Amherst, Mass.: University of Massachusetts [Citizen Involvement Training Project], 1978. (B, P)
   *Biagi, Bob. *Working Together: A Manual to Help Groups Work More Effectively*.
   *Dale, Duane. *How to Make Citizen Involvement Work: Strategies for Developing Clout*.
   *Dale, Duane, David Magnani, and Robin Miller. *Beyond Experts: A Guide for Citizen Group Training*.
   *Dale, Duane, and Nancy Mitiguy. *Planning for a Change: A Citizen's Guide to Creative Planning and Program Development*.
   *Gordon, Robbie. *We Interrupt This Program...: A Citizen's Guide to Using the Media for Social Change*.
   *Mitiguy, Nancy. *The Rich Get Richer and the Poor Write Proposals*.
   *Speeter, Greg. *Playing Their Game Our Way: Using the Political Process to Meet Community Needs*.
   *Speeter, Greg. *Power: A Repossession Manual: Organizing Strategies for Citizens*.
   Eight manuals of uniformly high quality—all written for the general reader, all well-designed and illustrated, all insightful and easy to follow. The best series of its kind I've seen.

*The Grantsmanship Center. Grantsmanship Center Reprints. Los Angeles: Author, various dates. (P)
   More than 40 in all, by different authors, averaging about 10-20 pages

each. Many dealing with grant writing and fund raising, but also including public relations, marketing, program evaluation, personnel management, etc. Norton Kiritz's "Program Planning and Proposal Writing" (expanded version) is especially recommended.

SPECIALIZED PROGRAMS

Allen, Patricia R. *Youthbook: Models and Resources for Neighborhood Use.* New York: The Citizens Committee for New York City, Inc., 1980. (B, P)
A superlative, labor-of-love compilation of 245 program models for youth in New York City. Definitely exportable. An especially thorough bibliography, and thoughtful introductory material.

Citizen Volunteer Skillsbank Project. *The Volunteer Skillsbank: An Innovative Way to Connect Individual Talents to Community Needs.* Washington, D.C.: Volunteer: The National Training Center for Citizen Involvement, 1980. (P)
A system for identifying and utilizing individuals for short-term volunteer assignments.

*Hess, Karl. *Community Technology.* New York: Harper & Row, 1979.
Growing vegetables on rooftops, food fish in basement tanks. Visions of community machine shops, warehouses, and junkyards. Argues that people can and must learn about the basic technology of daily life. Much accompanying rhetoric, but an eye-opener.

Purcell, Arthur H. *The Waste Watchers: A Citizen's Handbook for Conserving Energy Resources.* Garden City, N.Y.: Anchor Press/Doubleday, 1980.
Outlines energy-conservation projects for both individuals and community groups.

Raimy, Eric. *Shared Houses, Shared Lives: The New Extended Families and How They Work.* New York: St. Martin's Press, 1979.
Not so much a "program" as an increasingly common lifestyle. Deals with group houses (of unrelated people), and gives ideas for reducing frictions and increasing satisfaction in group living.

Trapp, Jack. *How to Barter and Trade.* New York: Simon and Schuster, 1981.
A short beginning book, one of many in the field. Lists items and services one can barter and trade and tells how to do it. Also has information on how to start your own barter organization.

U.S. Department of Housing and Urban Development, Office of Public Affairs. *The Urban Fair: How Cities Celebrate Themselves.* Washington, D.C.: Author, no date. (Order from U.S. Department of Housing and Urban Development, Community Service, Room 9243, 451 7th St., S.W., Washington, D.C. 20410.) (F, P)
Profiles of ten successful urban fairs and an additional section on urban fair planning and management.

Vellela. Tony. *Food Co-ops for Small Groups.* New York: Workman, 1975.
A simple explanation of how food co-ops (pre-order, not storefront) can
work. Describes alternative systems, and includes sample flow charts and
forms. Very appropriate for neighborhood groups.

SUPPORT SYSTEMS

Kleiman, Carol. Women's Networks: *The Complete Guide to Getting a Better
Job, Advancing Your Career, and Feeling Great as a Woman Through
Networking.* New York: Lippincott & Crowell, 1980.
A general introduction to networks in business, the professions, health,
sports, art, etc. Includes listings of national, state, and local networks, and a
chapter on how to set up your own.

Lynch, James J. *The Broken Heart: The Medical Consequences of Loneliness.*
New York: Basic Books, 1979.
Biological and medical data showing that loneliness and isolation hasten
death. Shows how human contact can relieve physical symptoms.
Scholarly – lots of statistics – but accessible.

Sarason, Seymour B., Charles Carroll, Kenneth Maton, Saul Cohen, and
Elizabeth Lorentz. *Human Services and Resource Networks: Rationale,
Possibilities, and Public Policy.* San Francisco: Jossey-Bass, 1977. (H)
A textbook describing a resource exchange network (basically, extending
limited service resources through barter), providing a rationale, and giving
a detailed account of one such network in Connecticut. See also Sarason
and Lorentz's follow-up book, *The Challenges of the Resource Exchange
Network: From Concept to Action* (San Francisco: Jossey-Bass, 1980).

*Sidel, Ruth. *Families of Fengsheng: Urban Life in China.* Baltimore: Penguin
Books, 1974.
"The organization of life in China's neighborhoods can perhaps best be
viewed as a total community support system. . . " This book provides the
details. Sidel describes the deprofessionalization, the intimacy, and the
control in China's neighborhoods, and considers implications for Western
service systems.

TEACHING/TRAINING

Davis, Larry N. *Planning, Conducting, and Evaluating Workshops.* Austin,
Tex.: Learning Concepts, 1974.
"Planning" fills 2/3 of this book, though it's good on conducting and evaluating, too. Strong on objective setting and logistics. A structured book, with
many worksheets.

Havelock, Ronald G., and Mary C. Havelock. *Training for Change Agents: A
Guide to the Design of Training Programs in Education and Other Fields.*
Ann Arbor, Mich.: Institute for Social Research, 1973. (H)

A fairly technical handbook, written largely for professional trainers. Well organized, with alternative training models and case examples.

Highet, Gilbert. *The Art of Teaching.* New York: Vintage, 1950. A chestnut; a lyrical essay. Highet is decidedly against a scientific approach to teaching, but is incisive on the qualities of a good teacher, teaching methods, great teachers in history, and teaching in everyday life.

Ingalls, John D. *A Trainer's Guide to Andragogy: Its Concepts, Experience and Application.* rev. ed. Washington, D.C.: Social and Rehabilitation Service, U.S. Department of Health, Education, and Welfare, 1973. (Order from U.S. Government Printing Office, under "Organizations.") (B, P)

Andragogy = adult learning. A long manual, with many exercises and worksheets.

*Mager, Robert F. *Preparing Instructional Objectives.* 2d ed. Belmont, Calif.: Pitman Learning, Inc., 1975.

A short book with a programmed-text format. Stresses the establishment of measurable criteria. An excellent book for preparing objectives for anything. See also other books by the same author.

ORGANIZATIONS

Additional resources for the community worker are national organizations in the field. The following organizations are among those concerned with social change at the community and neighborhood levels; some stressing local economic, educational, or political change are also included, as are organizational sources for printed materials listed in the bibliography. Many of these organizations have newsletters or journals of their own, and/or useful publications not specifically cited above. Times change: but all of them at this writing will supply details on request.

Adult Education Association of the United States of America, 810 18th St., N.W., Washington, D.C. 20006.

American Association of University Women, 2401 Virginia Ave., N.W., Washington, D.C. 20037.

American Friends Service Committee, Peace Literature Service, 1501 Cherry St., Philadelphia, Penna. 19102. Emphasis on nonviolent political action. Also has regional offices.

American Institutes for Research, P.O. Box 1113, Palo Alto, Calif. 94302.

Association of Community Organizations for Reform Now (ACORN), 1605 Connecticut Ave., N.W., Washington, D.C. 20009. A grass-roots membership organization of low and moderate income people.

Center for Community Change, 1000 Wisconsin Ave., N.W., Washington, D.C. 20007. Community development oriented.

Center for Community Economic Development, Inc., 1320 19th St., N.W., Mezzanine Level, Washington, D.C. 20036.

Center for Conflict Resolution, 731 State St., Madison, Wisc. 53703.

Center for Neighborhood Technology, 570 W. Randolph St., Chicago, Ill. 60606. Journal, *The Neighborhood Works*, acts as a clearinghouse for technological information.

Citizen Involvement Training Project, Cooperative Extension Service, 138 Hasbrouck, University of Massachusetts, Amherst, Mass. 01003.

The Citizens Committee for New York City, Inc., 3 W. 29th St., 6th Floor, New York, NY 10001.

Civic Action Institute, 1010 16th St., N.W., Washington, D.C. 20036.

Communities, Box 426, Louisa, Va. 23093. Journal, *Communities*, is recommended.

Community Service, Inc., P.O. Box 243, Yellow Springs, Ohio, 45387. Promotes the small community as a basic social institution.

Conference on Alternative State and Local Policies, 2000 Florida Ave., N.W., Room 420, Washington, D.C. 20009.

Consumer Education Resource Network (CERN), 1555 Wilson Blvd., Suite 600, Rosslyn, Va. 22209 (toll-free phone, 800-336-0223). Resource lists and reference searches.

Consumer Information Center, Pueblo, Colo. 81009. Free and low-cost consumer publications.

Cooperative League of the USA (CLUSA), 1828 L St., N.W., Washington, D.C. 20036. Cooperatives of different types.

Do It Now Foundation, P.O. Box 5115, Phoenix, Ariz. 85010.

The Foundation Center, 888 7th Ave., New York, N.Y. 10106 (toll-free phone, 800-424-9836). Has affiliated organizations in many states. Some free pamphlets on criteria for good proposals. Also has computerized search service for foundations in a given subject area.

The Grantsmanship Center, 1031 S. Grand Ave., Los Angeles, Calif. 90015. Reprints previously cited, plus an excellent magazine (*The Grantsmanship Center News*) and national training programs.

Hogg Foundation for Mental Health, Publications Division, P.O. Box 7998, University of Texas Station, Austin, Tex. 78712. Free publications on mental health.

Human Development Training, c/o William Meacham, 1004 Elm St., Austin, Tex. 78703.

Institute for Community Economics, 151 Montague City Rd., Greenfield, Mass. 01301. Specializes in community land trusts.

Institute for Information Studies, 200 Little Falls St., Suite 104, Falls Church, Va., 22046. Information and publications on human service systems.

The Institute for Local Self-Reliance, 1717 18th St., N.W., Washington, D.C. 20009. Emphasis on local economic development.

Institute for the Study of Civic Values, 401 N. Broad St., Room 810, Philadelphia, Penna. 19108.

League of Women Voters of the United States, 1730 M St., N.W., Washington, D.C. 20036. Politically-oriented publications. Also has a series of inexpensive booklets on public relations and a simplified guide to parliamentary procedure.

The Learning Exchange, P.O. Box 920, Evanston, Ill. 60204. Publishes a manual by the same name on setting up an information and referral network for adult education.

Midwest Academy, 600 W. Fullerton Ave., Chicago, Ill. 60614. A training organization.

Movement for a New Society, 4722 Baltimore Ave., Philadelphia, Penna. 19143.

National Center for Appropriate Technology, P.O. Box 3838, Butte, Mont. 59701.

National Center for Urban Ethnic Affairs (NCUEA), 1521 16th St., N.W., Washington, D.C. 20036.

The National Citizen Participation Council, 1620 Eye St., N.W., Suite 609, Washington, D.C. 20006.

National Committee Against Discrimination in Housing (NCDH), 1425 H St., N.W., Room 410, Washington, D.C. 20005.

National Committee for Citizens in Education, Suite 410, Wilde Lake Village Green, Columbia, Md. 21044 (toll-free phone, 800-638-9675).

National Community Education Association, 1030 15th St., N.W., Suite 516, Washington, D.C. 20005. Free publications and referral service.

National Congress of Neighborhood Women, 11-29 Catherine St., Brooklyn, N.Y. 11211.

National Institute of Mental Health, Mental Health Education Branch, 5600 Fishers Lane, Rockville, Md. 20857. Free pamphlets on mental health ideas, especially concerning children.

National Institute of Mental Health, National Clearinghouse for Mental Health Information, Public Inquiries Section, Room 11A-21, 5600 Fishers Lane, Rockville, Md. 20857. Has bibliographic services and a variety of free publications.

National Neighbors, 815 15th St., N.W., Washington, D.C. 20005. Multiracial emphasis.

National Self-Help Clearinghouse, Graduate School and University Center/ CUNY, 33 W. 42nd St., Room 1227, New York, N.Y. 10036. Publishes *Self-Help Reporter*, a superior bimonthly newsletter.

National Training and Information Center, 1123 W. Washington Blvd., Chicago, Ill. 60607. Another training organization, geared toward neighborhoods.

National Trust for Historic Preservation, 1785 Massachusetts Ave., N.W., Washington, D.C. 20036. Its newsletter, *Conserve Neighborhoods*, is highly recommended. Also has a good bibliography for neighborhood leaders, and an organizing guide, single copies free.

Neighborhood Development and Conservation Center, 525 NW 13th St., Oklahoma City, Okla., 73103.

The New School for Democratic Management, 589 Howard St., San Francisco, Calif. 94105. Oriented toward small business management.

Organize Training Center, 1208 Market St., San Francisco, Calif. 94102.

Planning and Management Assistance Project, 1705 DeSales St., N.W., Suite 401, Washington, D.C. 20036.

Public Relations Society of America, Inc., 845 3rd Ave., New York, N.Y., 10022. Mostly for professionals, but has some publications for general audiences.

Rural America, 1346 Connecticut Ave., N.W., Washington, D.C. 20036. "A voice for small town and rural people."

The Self-Help Center, 1600 Dodge Avenue, Suite S-122, Evanston, Ill. 60201.

The Sperry and Hutchinson Company, Consumer Services, 2900 W. Seminary Drive, Fort Worth, Tex. 76133. The promoters of green stamps also publish inexpensive booklets on publicity, public affairs, membership, and fund raising.

Stimulating the Neighborhood Action Process (SNAP), 1017 Avon St., Flint, Mich. 48503. Free search service and information on neighborhood resources.

Urban Planning Aid, Inc., 120 Boylston St., Room 523, Boston, Mass. 02116.

U.S. Department of Housing and Urban Development, Office of Neighborhoods, Voluntary Associations, and Consumer Protection, 451 7th St., S.W., Washington, D.C. 20410.

U.S. Government Printing Office (Superintendent of Documents), Washington, D.C. 20402. Central source of government publications.

Vocations for Social Change, P.O. Box 211, Essex Station, Boston, Mass. 02112. Workplace-oriented publications.

Volunteer: The National Center for Citizen Involvement, 1111 N. 19th St., Suite 500, Arlington, Va. 22209. (Order publications from Volunteer, P.O. Box 4179, Boulder, Colo. 80306.)

The Youth Project, 1555 Connecticut Ave., N.W., Washington D.C. 20036.

Acknowledgments

I thank Abhay, Lauren Flewelling, Tony Giulino, Richard Hammerschlag, Madelon Hope, Laurie Manny, Howard Marantz, and Barbara Wolff for reading and commenting on various chapter drafts; their comments were useful and supportive. I appreciate too the help of Judy Bellizia, Tana Onanian, Joan Lewis, and Betty Woodhouse in manuscript typing. Sara Arrand, my editor, saw to my reeducation in the English language; she and other staff at Schenkman were always gracious and helpful.

Much of what I know about community work comes from experiences in the Greater Lowell community. I'm thankful to past colleagues and associates there for teaching me. I'm especially grateful to Anne Kaplan, former Executive Director of the Mental Health Association of Greater Lowell, for showing me the meaning of dedication, and to Drs. J. Sanbourne Bockoven and Kenneth Bryant, past Superintendents of Solomon Mental Health Center in Lowell, for giving me the freedom to learn and grow.

Index